I0445887

Transpacific Crossings

Transpacific Crossings:
Art, Trade, and the Manila Galleon

Edited by Jorge F. Rivas Pérez, Karina H. Corrigan,
and Kathryn Santner

MAYER CENTER FOR ANCIENT AND LATIN AMERICAN ART
AT THE DENVER ART MUSEUM, DENVER, CO

A free online edition of this publication is available at mayer2024.denartmus.org. A free PDF of the publication is also available to download.

Published by the Mayer Center for Ancient and Latin American Art at the Denver Art Museum.
100 W. 14th Ave. Pkwy
Denver, CO 80204
mayercenter.denverartmuseum.org
www.denverartmuseum.org

Publication text and design © 2026 Denver Art Museum

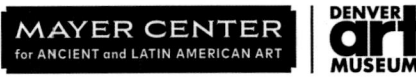

The Denver Art Museum is located on the homeland of the Arapaho, Cheyenne, and Ute people, along with many people from other Indigenous nations that call this place home. Learn more about our commitments to better represent, elevate, and support Indigenous cultures and people, past and present, on our website.

All rights reserved. This book may not be reproduced, in whole or in part, including illustrations, in any form (beyond that copying is permitted by Sections 107 and 108 of the US Copyright Law and except by reviews for the public press), or by any means, electronic or mechanical, including photocopy, recording, or other information storage and retrieval system, without prior written permission from the publisher. For questions, email publicationsdept@denverartmuseum.org with the subject line "Publication Permission."

The images in this publication are published with the permission of the rights holders whenever possible. In instances where the Denver Art Museum could not reach the rights holders, notwithstanding good-faith efforts, we request that any contact information concerning such rights holders be submitted via imagerights@denverartmuseum.org so that they may be contacted for future publications.

Reasonable measures will be taken by the Denver Art Museum to avoid this volume being used as input for Artificial Intelligence or by any other technology that does not respect author and creator rights.

The manufacturer's authorized representative in the EU for product safety is Mare Nostrum Group B.V., Mauritskade 21D, 1091 GC Amsterdam, The Netherlands, email: gpsr@mare-nostrum.co.uk

This publication was created using Quire™, a multiplatform publishing tool created by the J. Paul Getty Trust and customized by the Denver Art Museum.

978-1-945483-21-9 (PDF)
978-1-945483-20-2 (Print)

Library of Congress Control Number: 2025945180

Managing Editor: Valerie Hellstein
Editor and Project Manager: Leslie Murrell
Curatorial Assistants: Lisbet Barrientos
Developer: Matt Popke
Design: Tasso Stathopulos

Cover image: Attributed to José de Alcíbar, *De Espanol y Negra, Mulato, Mexico*, ca. 1760 (detail). Oil on canvas, 30⅝ × 38¾ in. (77.79 × 98.43 cm). Denver Art Museum: Gift of the Collection of Frederick and Jan Mayer, 2014.217.

CONTENTS

Director's Foreword

Christoph Heinrich, Frederick and Jan Mayer Director,
Denver Art Museum

The Denver Art Museum boasts the largest and most comprehensive collection of colonial Latin American art in the United States and since 1968 has presented numerous exhibitions, catalogs, and symposia that have deepened the knowledge and broadened the scholarship in this area. However, no art is made in a vacuum, and styles, techniques, and materials from around the world influence local practices. For instance, our broader collection includes Puebla pottery that imitates Chinese blue-and-white porcelain, Mexican paintings glinting with the iridescence of inlaid nacre that were inspired by Asian lacquerware, and Asian ivories that depict the wounded Saint Sebastian and curly-haired Christ Child.

For centuries, oceans provided the most significant means of transmitting art and ideas around the globe. The establishment of the Manila Galleon trade between New Spain and the Philippines in the sixteenth century provided an annual passage of art and ideas between the Americas and Asia. With objects from China, Japan, and India readily accessible to consumers in the viceroyalties and in Spain, local artists in Manila, Mexico, Lima, and elsewhere began to imitate and incorporate aspects of the new Asian luxury goods into their own practices.

Despite the profound impact of Asia on colonial Latin America, the subject has received relatively less attention than comparable cross-cultural narratives. The Denver Art Museum has pioneered this research and brought it to the fore on numerous occasions as the field has expanded to include the impact of the galleon trade on cultures at both ends of the route. Through the efforts of the Mayer Center for Ancient and Latin American Art, we are delighted to do so once again, bringing together scholars to interrogate this vital moment of cultural crosspollination. In November 2024, scholars from the United States, Mexico, and Singapore converged for two days to examine how the exchanges of materials, techniques, and ideas across the Pacific Ocean impacted the trajectory of art in both

Latin America and Asia. The papers here result from the engaging conversations held at the Denver Art Museum in the midst of an early November snowstorm.

I wish to express my gratitude to Karina H. Corrigan, Deputy Chief Curator and the H. A. Crosby Forbes Curator of Asian Export Art at the Peabody Essex Museum, and to Jorge Rivas Pérez, former Frederick and Jan Mayer Curator of Latin American Art at the Denver Art Museum and current Emily Rauh Pulitzer Deputy Director and Chief Curator at the Saint Louis Art Museum, for their dedication to organizing the 2024 symposium. My thanks also go to Kathryn Santner, Assistant Curator of Latin American Art at the Denver Art Museum, who tirelessly led the editorial efforts for these proceedings. And I gratefully acknowledge Jan Mayer, whose ongoing support for the museum and the Mayer Center, along with that of her late husband, Frederick Mayer, has been so crucial to the advancement of the study of the arts of ancient and colonial Latin America.

Introduction

Kathryn Santner, Karina H. Corrigan, and Jorge F. Rivas Pérez

In 1662, the Franciscan friar Bartolomé de Letona wrote of Manila, "All things necessary to human life [are found there] and even articles of superfluity, ostentation, pomp, and luxury. . . . The diversity of the peoples . . . who are seen in Manila and its environs is the greatest in the world."[1]

Letona's wonder was echoed by other early modern chroniclers who remarked on the cosmopolitanism of the city, its multiethnic populace, and the quantity of finished goods, spices, gems, and other global curiosities that could be found there. The Italian adventurer Giovanni Francesco Gemelli Careri, writing in *Giro del Mondo* (1699), was even more fulsome in his description:

> *For here are found the Silver of* New Spain *and* Peru, *and for the East, the Diamonds of* Golconda, *the Rubies, Topazes, Sapphires, and precious Cinnamon of* Ceilon; *the Pepper of* Sumatra *and* Java; *the Cloves and Nutmegs of the* Molucos, *the Pearls and rich Carpets of* Persia; *the fine Silks and Stuffs of* Bengala; *the Camphir of* Borneo, *the Benjamin and Ivory of* Camboia; *the Musk of* Lequios; *the Silks, Muslins, Callicoes, and Quilts, with the curious Purcellane, and other Rarities of* China. *When there was a Trade with* Japan, *there came from thence every Year two or three Ships, and brought pure Silver, Amber, Silks, Chests, Boxes, and Boards of precious Wood, delicately varnish'd; in exchange for Hides, Wax, and the Fruit of the Country.*[2]

From Manila's Parián market—the Philippine clearinghouse for exports from across Asia—these riches were transshipped to the Americas. Having survived the treacherous journey on a galleon across the Pacific, these novel and sumptuous goods were unloaded in Acapulco and transported to the capital of New Spain and across the viceregal territories and beyond. For over two hundred fifty years, this trade, both licit and clandestine, connected vast distances, goods, and peoples.

Compelled by the ambition and precarity of the venture and the great wealth and human suffering that it embodied, historians have long been drawn to the saga of the galleon trade. Art historians, in particular, have been inspired by the complex objects created within this global network of exchange—from Asian porcelains, lacquer objects, and silk to *biombos, talavera poblana*, and *enconchados* (figs. 1–3). As curators, these glittering wares inspire us for many of the same reasons that they fascinated the merchants of Manila and Mexico City and their eager clients in the Parián markets. Art history as a discipline may be reconsidering the notion of hybridity, but the plurality of these objects in motion remains a central component of their nature and enduring appeal.[3]

This is the third time that the Mayer Center symposium has addressed the theme of Asian and Latin American exchange. The first symposium—*Asia and Spanish America: Trans-Pacific Artistic and Cultural Exchange, 1500–1850*—was organized in 2006 by Donna Pierce and Ronald Otsuka. Its focus was largely unidirectional, exploring the influence of Asian goods on the furniture, decorative arts, textiles, and painting of Mexico. This groundbreaking symposium was a watershed for this emerging field. The second symposium, in 2010, *At the Crossroads: The Arts of Spanish America and Early Global Trade, 1492–1850*, was also organized by Pierce and Otsuka. Here, they revisited many of the themes explored in the first convening, but expanded the timeframe and markets for

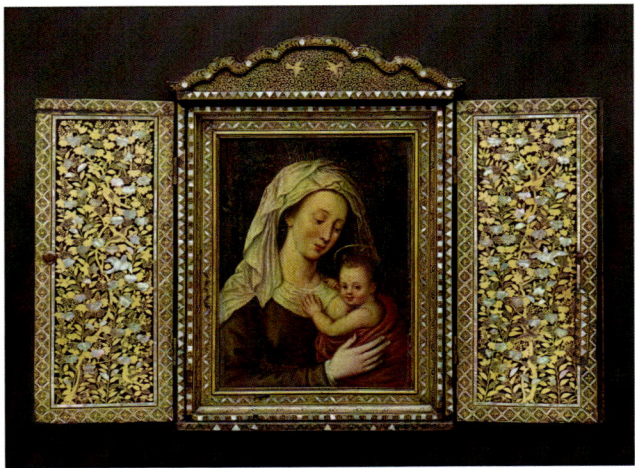

Fig. 1 Attributed to the School of Giovanni Niccolò and the Jesuit Seminary workshop, Kyushu, Japan, with lacquer case by artists in Japan, probably Kyushu, Portable shrine, about 1597. Oil on wood panel, in a lacquered wood case with mother-of-pearl inlay. Peabody Essex Museum, Salem: Museum purchase, made possible by an anonymous donor, 2000. AE85752.

Asian goods to also include the impact of Asian export goods on colonial New England and the early American Republic.

Transpacific Engagements: Visual Culture of Global Exchange (1781–1869), a conference held in 2014 in the Philippines, marked another important step forward for the field. Centering both the conference in and its narrative on Manila, the organizers considered the impact of the galleon trade on artistic production within the Philippine *entrepôt*.[4]

When organizing the 2024 Mayer Center symposium, we similarly strove to center Manila within this global narrative and to expand our understanding of this complex node of exchange. One underrepresented component of transpacific studies, at least art historically, has been the impact of Latin America on the Philippines and its trading partners. The importation of raw materials

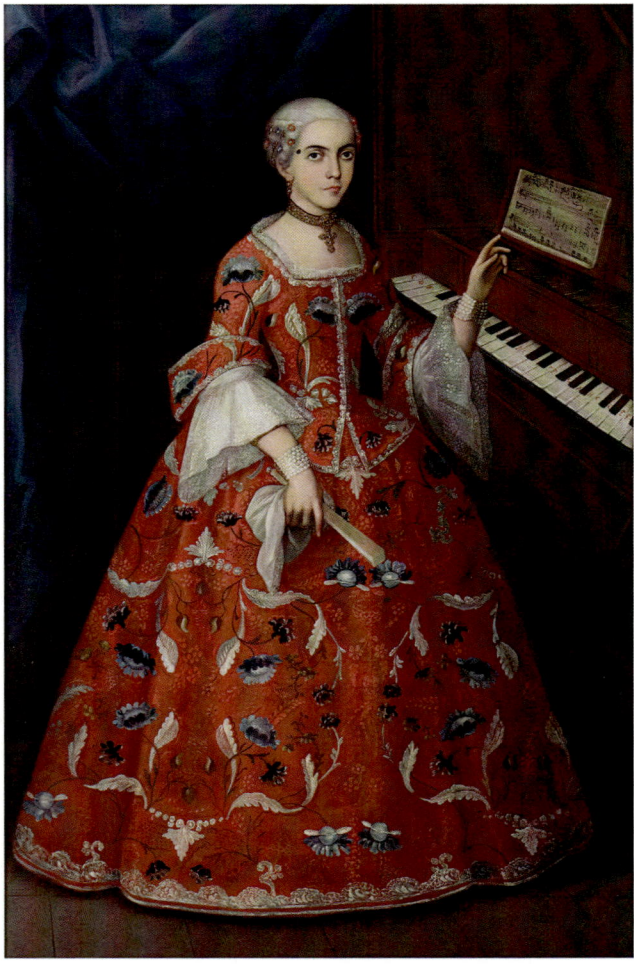

Fig. 2 Unknown artist, *Young Woman with Harpsichord*, Mexico, 1735–50. Oil on canvas, framed 72¼ × 50⅞ × 3 in. (183.5 × 129.2 × 7.6 cm). Denver Art Museum: Gift of the Collection of Frederick and Jan Mayer, 2014.209.

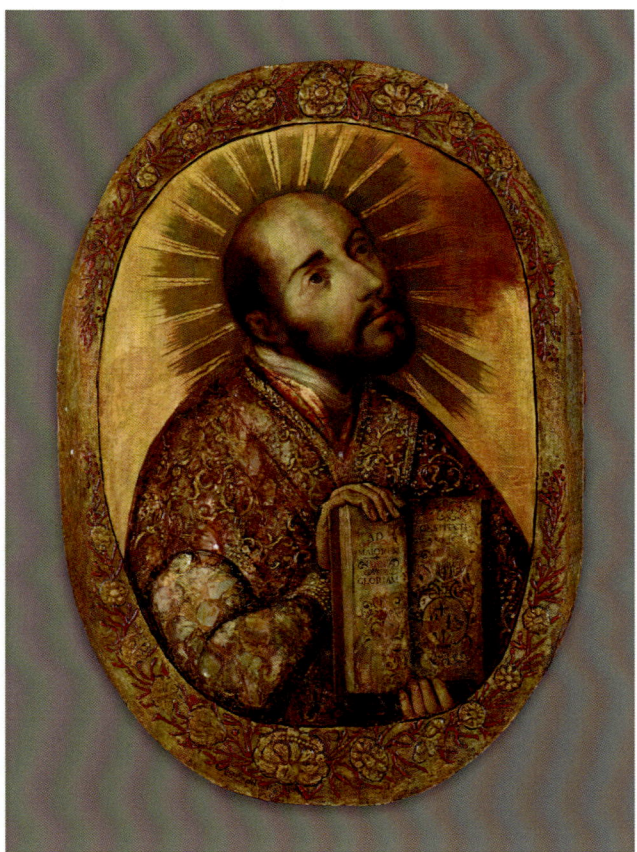

Fig. 3 Agustín del Pino, *Saint Ignatius Loyola, Mexico*, ca. 1700. Oil and shell inlay on wood panel (*enconchado* painting), framed: 43½ × 33⅛ in. (110.5 × 84.1 cm). Denver Art Museum: Gift of the Collection of Frederick and Jan Mayer, 2013.302.

from the Americas impacted local production in Asia, including the extensive use of cochineal in Chinese silks and brocades. Finished goods also flowed the other way and had a profound influence on Asian art and culture. In fact, some objects were transshipped multiple times, passing between Asian, European, and Latin American ports, finding reuse—and sometimes refashioning—in each location.

One critical advancement in the eighteen years since the first symposium is a more nuanced understanding of the vital role that China had on art and life in the Philippines during this period. Fujianese merchants and artisans living in the Philippines represented an important and sizable community; they considered Manila a central node in their expansive network of trade routes that spanned much of East and Southeast Asia.

The 2024 Mayer Center symposium brought together emerging and established scholars advancing different aspects of transpacific studies. The first two essays consider the individuals impacted by the galleon trade. Opening the volume, Diego Javier Luis's "The Manila Galleon: An Historical Primer" provides a concise overview of this complex history and forefronts the movement of people and human costs associated with the galleon trade. He argues that we cannot consider the aesthetic and cultural impact of global trade without also considering the individual stories of loss, enslavement, and displacement associated with it.

Turning to those who enjoyed the abundance of the galleon trade, Jorge F. Rivas Pérez's essay, "Inventories of Luxury and Wealth: Asian Trade and Material Culture in Spanish America," mines the posthumous inventories associated with four elites in Mexico City and Lima. He interprets this rich archive to consider how Asian objects were integrated into domestic interiors and used in the Americas during the long eighteenth century.

Multiple essays in the volume focus on objects in specific media. Two center on Asian textiles. Karina H. Corrigan explores the global circulation of Chinese silk during the early galleon trade in "'Brocades of Gold and Silver upon Silk': A Microhistory of a Set of Chinese Silk Church Vestments for the Spanish Market." Corrigan approaches this rare surviving set as a document, reading a history of an interwoven globe in the structure and pattern of these resplendent ecclesiastical textiles. Exploring a less well-known luxury textile, Abi Lua considers *piña*, the celebrated Philippine cloth made of pineapple-leaf, in "Cut from the World: Philippine *Piña* Fabric in the East India Marine Society Collection." Lua documents the journey of a nineteenth-century

fragment of piña from the island of Panay to Salem, Massachusetts. Collected by an American sailor in the decades after the Manila galleon route had collapsed, this piña fragment became an "article of curiosity" for scientific inquiry in the collection of the East India Marine Society, a predecessor institution to the Peabody Essex Museum.

Two essays explore artistic exchange in ceramics. In his contribution, Roberto Junco considers the importation of Chinese porcelain through surviving potsherds in "An Ocean of Blue and White: Archaeological Excavations at the Port of Acapulco." These fragments, which likely arrived broken after their long transpacific crossing, reveal both the shifting tastes of consumers in Mexico and the styles that influenced the enterprising potters of Puebla. Deposits of these sherds have also identified the likely locations of the old fort of San Diego and the annual Acapulco Fair that assembled to distribute goods arriving on the Manila Galleon. Margaret E. Connors McQuade considers the artisans in the colonial city of Puebla who reimagined Chinese porcelain designs on talavera in "Name that Pot! Viceregal Potters and Workshops of Puebla de los Ángeles." Many of the Puebla potters are well-documented archivally, but it has historically been difficult to link them to specific works. Connors McQuade argues for the attribution of select works based, in part, on makers' marks that potters incorporated into their works.

The remaining essays in the volume reflect the enduring impact of the galleon trade on cross-cultural works in a variety of media. In "For the Consolation of Manila: A Case Study of a New Spanish Image of Christ," Ronda Kasl considers an image of the ecce homo sent to Manila to console a city beleaguered by poverty, conflict, and natural disasters. She documents the object's creation in Mexico from cornstalk paste, its transmission on a galleon—where it gained a reputation for miraculous powers—and finally its arrival in the blighted Philippine capital, where it became an important cult image.

Kathryn Santner's contribution, "The Other Silver Flow: Liturgical Objects in the Philippines," discusses the production of silver by *sangley* and Indigenous silversmiths in Manila to satisfy the needs of the archipelago's churches. While Chinese artisans in Manila have mostly been appraised for their work as ivory carvers, immigrants from Fujian and Guangdong were also master silversmiths and made up the bulk of the artisans in the city. These craftsmen furnished churches in the Philippines with the liturgical objects that mediated the profound sacramental relationships between parishioners and the divine.

Turning to the understudied topic of furniture in "A Cabinet of Many Cultures," Clement Onn discusses a seventeenth-century narra wood cabinet featuring Mexican imagery of the founding of Tenochtitlan: an eagle atop a cactus flanked by the figures of a Mexica ruler (*tlatoani*)

and a noblewoman. Onn argues convincingly for the cabinet's production in the Philippines and, drawing on influences from European and Chinese furniture, traces the visual and tangible history of a truly global object.

In "'Graceful, Rich, and Pleasing to the Eye': Seamless Facture Across the Pacific," Samuel Frédéric Luterbacher examines lacquer objects at the intersection of Japanese and Iberian aesthetics. He explores seamlessness, a flawless surface quality that resonated across cultures and obscured the labor of an object's creation. That such facture was associated with miraculous creation and luxury goods speaks to the increasing emphasis on commodification during this time period.

Closing the volume, "*Biombos* in Modern Mexican Interiors," by Aldo Solano Rojas, discusses the afterlives of *biombos* (folding screens) in twentieth-century domestic interiors in Mexico. Initially imported from Japan to the Americas, screens quickly became such a part of local visual culture that they came to be an emblem of Mexicanness. Modernist furniture designers and architects abstracted the form, utilizing biombos in the homes, cinemas, and hotels they designed. Their contemporary appropriation of this quintessential form attests to the enduring legacy of the galleon trade over a century after its cessation.

The 2024 Mayer Center symposium brought together scholars with diverse areas of expertise to advance transpacific material culture studies. It also sought to lay the groundwork for future exhibitions exploring this complex and fascinating narrative. In the last twenty-five years, several important exhibitions have explored the themes connected to the galleon trade.[5] Most recently, *Across the Pacific: Art and the Manila Galleons*, organized by Clement Onn for the Asian Civilisations Museum in Singapore, offered an expansive view of the artistic cross-pollination fostered by the galleon trade. But, despite the captivating nature of objects produced over three centuries of contact between Asia, the Americas, and Europe, this subject remains unfamiliar to many American audiences. Our hope is that these proceedings will inspire new scholarship and exhibitions that will continue to mine the complex and expansive narratives of the world's first global network.

Notes

1. Emma Helen Blair and James Alexander Robertson, *The Philippine Islands, 1493–1898*, 55 vols. (The Arthur H. Clark Company, 1905), 36:202, 205.

2. John Francis [Giovanni Francesco] Gemelli Careri, "A Voyage Around the World," in *A Collection of Voyages and Travels: Some now first Printed from Original Manuscripts . . .*, vol. 4 (H. C. for Awnsham and John Churchill, 1704), 444.

3. See Carolyn Dean and Dana Leibsohn, "Hybridity and Its Discontents: Considering Visual Culture in Colonial Spanish America," *Colonial Latin American Review* 12, no. 1 (2003): 5–35.

4. Florina H. Capistrano-Baker and Meha Priyadarshini, *Transpacific Engagements: Trade, Translation, and Visual Culture of Entangled Empires (1565–1898)* (Ayala Foundation; Getty Research Institute; Kunsthistorisches Institut in Florenz, 2020).

5. Important exhibitions that have previously explored these themes include *El Galeón de Manila* (Hospital de los Venerables, Sevilla, Museo Franz Mayer, Museo Histórico de Acapulco, Fuerte de San Diego, 2000), *Made in the Americas: The New World Discovers Asia* (Museum of Fine Arts, Boston, Winterthur Museum, 2015–16), *Tornaviaje. La nao de China y el barroco en México (1565-1815)* (Museo Franz Mayer, 2016), and *El Galeón de Manila: La ruta española que unió 3 continentes en 1565* (Museo Naval, 2016–17).

The Manila Galleon: An Historical Primer

Diego Javier Luis, Rohrbaugh Family Assistant
Professor, Department of History, Johns Hopkins
University

The early modern Spanish domain was an empire that, on paper, stretched across half the globe. The Treaty of Tordesillas in 1494 had infamously divided most of the world in two and established the vertical meridian that separated Portuguese claims from those of the Spanish. At the moment of the treaty's signing, Spanish overseas ambitions were oriented toward reaching Asia via the Atlantic Ocean. Of course, the American continents would prove a significant hindrance to this mission, and due to their relative proximity to the Iberian Peninsula, they would receive considerably more European contact than later colonies in Asia. Consequently, most scholars studying Spain's empire have prioritized the American hemisphere. However, as Elizabeth Horodowich and Alexander Nagel have argued, the Americas and Asia were rarely imagined as separate entities, even late into the sixteenth century.[1] The Spanish domain—extending

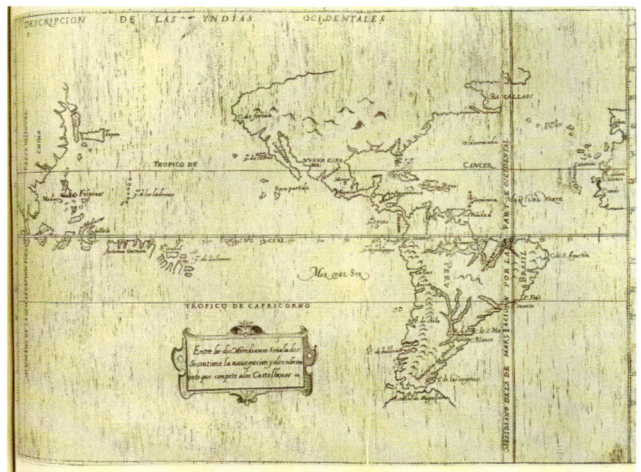

Fig. 1 Antonio de Herrera y Tordesillas (died 1626), The official, imperial representation of the "West Indies," which stretched from the Atlantic to Asia. "Descripcion de las Yndias Ocidentales," 1601. Fold-out engraved map, 11 × 14⅝ in. (28 × 37 cm). *Descripcion de las Indias Ocidentales* (En la Emprenta Real, 1601). Courtesy of the John Carter Brown Library.

all the way to Asia's eastern shores—was considered contiguous (fig. 1). As such, the study of Spanish empire in the Americas cannot be conducted in isolation of the empire's extension across the Pacific.

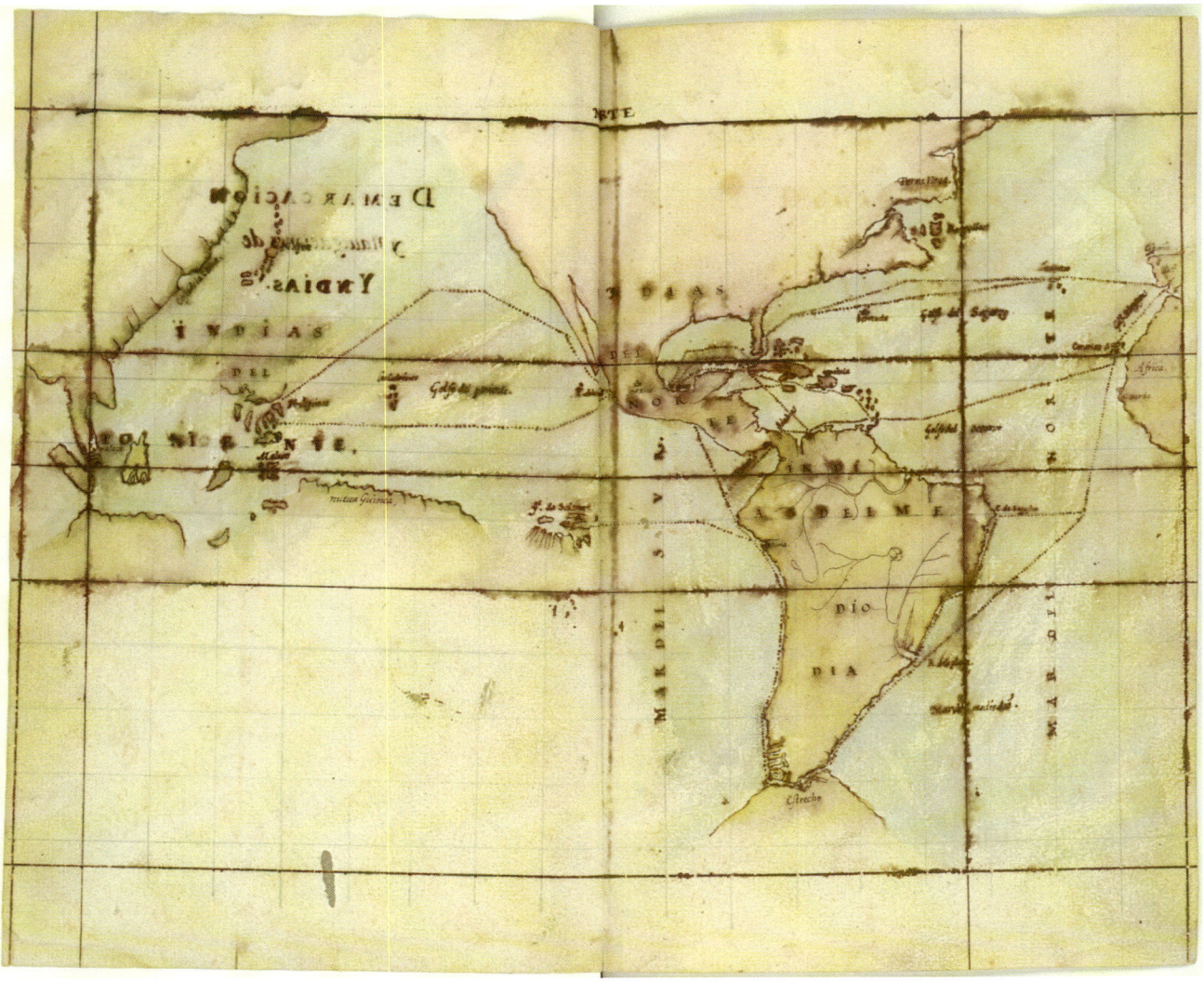

Fig. 2   Juan López de Velasco (died 1598), Manuscript map of the Spanish empire including routes of Spanish expeditions. "Demarcacion y nauegaciones de Yndias," 1575. Manuscript map, 8¼ × 12¾ in. (20.8 × 32.5 cm). "Demarcacion y diuision de las Yndias." Courtesy of the John Carter Brown Library.

In the years immediately following the fall of the Mexica capital of Tenochtitlan in 1521, numerous expeditions sailed into the Pacific Ocean from the Americas in search of the route to Asia.[2] It would take more than forty years for Spanish ships to successfully sail back from Asia to the Americas. The first was a small vessel called the *San Pedro* with an Afro-Portuguese navigator named Lope Martín at the helm.[3] That crossing from the Philippine archipelago to Mexico via the North Pacific in 1565 was a watershed

historical moment. It made possible the establishment of a regular trade route across the Pacific between Asia and the Americas and, through this link, the founding of long-term Spanish colonies in the Philippines. As scholars of the Spanish Pacific have made abundantly clear, these developments would have enormous economic, demographic, and cultural repercussions for both sides of the ocean.[4]

The Spanish ships that sailed this transpacific trade route from Cavite,

Philippines, to Acapulco, Mexico, are called the Manila galleons, and they operated from 1571 to 1815 (fig. 2).[5] Since the publication of William Schurz's landmark book, *The Manila Galleon*, in 1939, scholarship on these ships has developed mainly in two directions.[6] First, there is the trade itself, the material circulation at the heart of transpacific colonialism and the principal reason Spaniards in Mexico invested so heavily in colonial ventures in the Philippines. Silver mined by coerced and often enslaved Indigenous, African, and Afro-descended laborers in the Americas flowed across the Pacific. Through predominantly Fujianese merchants in Manila's Parián (Chinese quarter), that silver ended up not only on the Chinese mainland but throughout the region.[7] In return, merchants, sailors, and elites brought back precious porcelainware, refined and unrefined silk, textiles, furniture, devotional images, and much more for consumers in the Americas and western Europe. This trade fueled the emergence and coherence of a truly global economy that regularly connected all oceans in both directions for the first time in world history.[8]

Second, the ships conveying trade goods simultaneously facilitated the movement of European, Indigenous, African, Afro-descended, Asian, Pacific Islander, and multiracial people in both directions across the Pacific. Some of these populations were transient, while others settled permanently far from their homelands. In my previous work, I have studied the movement of over twenty thousand free and enslaved Asians to the Americas, which long predated the conventional nineteenth-century origins of Asian migration to the Western Hemisphere.[9] Much work remains to be done to follow the mobility of Indigenous and Black people from the Americas into the Pacific.

Traditionally, the themes of global trade and human mobility have been siloed as separate fields with limited overlap. One either studies objects or people, not both. In part, this bifurcation is not just a problem of disciplinary boundaries but one of archives. The very sources documenting the crates upon crates of Asian wares entering Acapulco silence or, at best, vastly minimize the presence, activities, and subjectivities of marginalized colonial subjects. Yet, these subjects were there, always just out of frame. On the galleons and even after disembarkation, the histories of goods and the people who handled them were, indeed, deeply entangled. In the case of the enslaved, humans *were* the commercial products. People were bought and sold alongside precious porcelain. From the late sixteenth to late seventeenth centuries, Déborah Oropeza estimates that anywhere between 3,776 and 10,000 enslaved Asians arrived in Mexico on the galleons.[10] These numbers do not include the transpacific trafficking in Africans and Afro-descendants that persisted into the eighteenth century after the abolition of *chino* (Asian) enslavement in 1672.[11] That the Manila galleons were slave ships should add a wrinkle to grandiose narratives that unflinchingly celebrate the arrival of luxurious Asian goods in the Americas.

More broadly, the commercial value of transpacific trade had an immeasurable impact on the experiences of people crossing the world's largest ocean. On the galleons, everyone from the ship's commander and navigator down to the poorest sailors carried goods from the Philippines to be sold in Acapulco or anywhere from Mexico to Peru. In fact, the opportunity to sell a trunk of Asian wares after disembarking was a major incentive for sailors to risk their lives crossing the Pacific. The route left so many dead that such a policy was necessary to keep the ships fully staffed.[12]

The voyage from the Philippines to Mexico typically lasted an excruciating five to six months, sometimes more, sometimes less. The ships navigated from Cavite and through the Visayas before exiting the Philippine archipelago through the Embocadero and rising to the latitude of Japan to cross the tumultuous North Pacific eastward. Then, after spotting Cape Mendocino in California, they dropped south past Baja California—careful to avoid the rocky coast—until hitting Mazatlán to the east and continuing south. Finally, the ships sailed into the protected Bay of Acapulco and anchored under the guns of the Fort of San Diego (fig. 3).

Free and enslaved Asian sailors were almost always the majority on Spanish ships sailing this route. Most served as *grumetes* (cabin boys); that is to say, they were the lowest-ranking crew members who received the lowest pay and rations. While most grumetes were from Luzon in

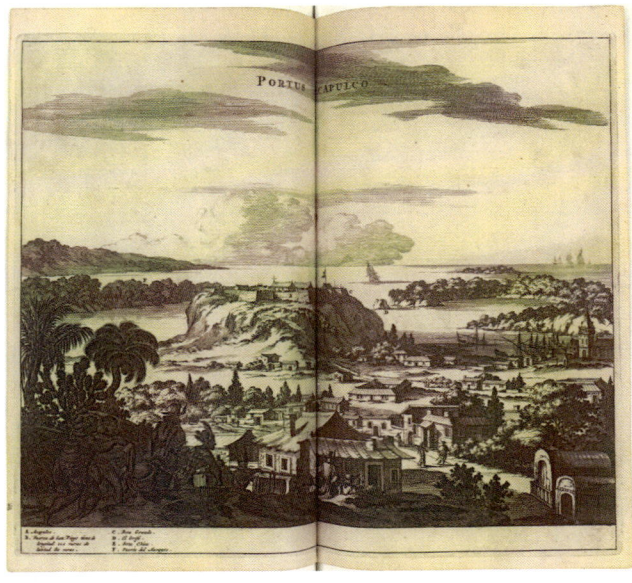

Fig. 3 Arnoldus Montanus (died 1683), View of Acapulco, including the port, the town, the fort, and the galleons. "Portus Acapulco," 1671. Engraving, 11¼ × 13⅞ in. (28.7 × 35.1 cm). *De Nieuwe en onbekende Weereld: of Beschryving van America* (Jacob Meurs Boek-verkooper en Plaet-snyder, 1671).

the Philippines, a handful originated from elsewhere in coastal Asia. Meanwhile, most of the enslaved—who also performed sailing duties onboard—were either from South Asia or elsewhere in the Philippines. The survival of all and the maintenance of transpacific trade depended on the labor of these grumetes and the enslaved.[13]

The experience of sailing on a transpacific galleon was unlike that of any other early modern Spanish trade route, precisely because of the high valuation of galleon cargos. In 1605, Hernando de los Ríos Coronel wrote that galleon commanders would overload their ships with trade goods to maximize the profit of each voyage despite royal orders capping the value of the cargo. Consequently, there was very little room below the deck to accommodate people. Only a privileged few could afford to rent a cabin. The rest, including the grumetes and the enslaved, slept exposed to the elements, either partially under one of the galleons' two superstructures or simply uncovered on the deck itself. Many froze in the North Pacific.[14]

Full cargos meant that galleons often sailed with low stocks of food as well. According to Coronel, galleon officials often stored what food there was topside, where storms often swept it away. Sailors and officers were expected to supplement shipboard rations with their own supplies. The wealthier brought aboard live animals. The rest subsisted on a little fresh food during the first month of the voyage and then maggoty rice and hardtack during the rest. Malnourished sailors also fished on calm days and snared unfortunate birds resting their wings on the ship. Inevitably, crew members without access to live animals developed scurvy, dysentery, and beriberi by the end of the voyage.[15] People were considered expendable; valuable goods were not.

The problem of lading space was so severe that cannons were similarly an afterthought. Galleons beset by privateers lacked the means to fight back. The most extreme example of this reality was the fate of the *San Diego*, a fully loaded galleon that brought aboard cannons to fight off the Dutch Oliver van Noort's attack on Manila in 1600. Under the command of the chronicler Antonio de Morga, the vessel sailed in pursuit of the *Mauritius*, the Dutch flagship. The weight of merchandise, cannons, and three hundred to four

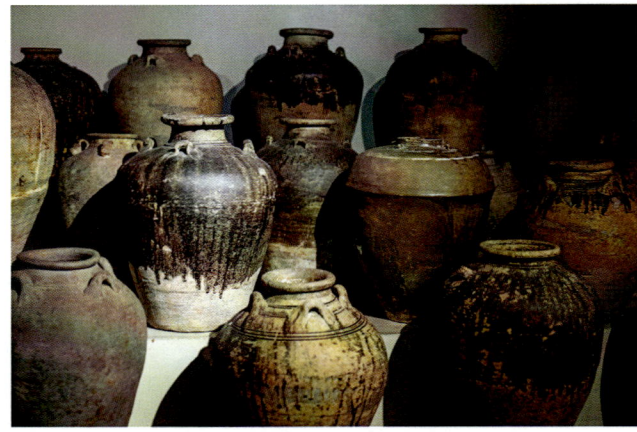

Fig. 4 Earthenware jars that stored water and were used as ballast, recovered from the *San Diego* and displayed in the National Museum of Anthropology in Manila. Earthenware. Photograph courtesy the author.

hundred soldiers and sailors contributed to the *San Diego*'s sudden sinking during combat despite successfully boarding the enemy vessel. Interestingly enough, merchandise recovered from the wreck of the *San Diego* during the 1990s remains one of the best sources to visualize the vast scope of the cargo on the Manila galleons (figs. 4 and 5).[16]

All of these factors contributed to the immense loss of life that became a defining reality of the transpacific crossing. It was not unusual for a "successful voyage" to lose 30 percent or more of its crew. When Pedro Cubero Sebastián made the crossing toward the end of the seventeenth century, only 192 of the original 400 onboard survived. Similarly, in 1616, 150 out of the ship's 200 crew members died, primarily due to a lack of provisions.[17] Survivors were often hospitalized for months in Acapulco, and some failed to return to health and perished on land. In total, thousands died, though no reliable estimates of casualties exist. This was the

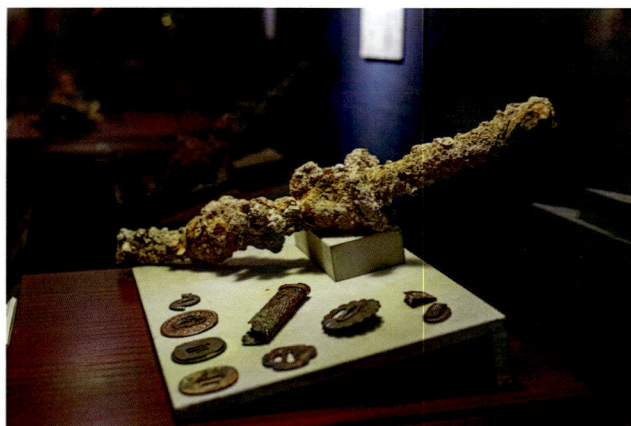

Fig. 5 Katana and tsuba (a circular guard for a katana), recovered from the wreck of the *San Diego*. Courtesy the author.

true cost of the transpacific trade. People were made to give their lives for every Asian product unloaded in Mexico.

After disembarkation at Acapulco, following the confluence of objects and people leads us to other unexpected histories beyond formal sites of exchange at trade fairs and urban plazas. In fact, much of the cargo changed hands through informal means. Outside of the marketplace, non-elites gained access to Asian products. Middling merchants led mule trains through the central Mexican highlands, up the coast to Zihuatanejo, and further north to Guadalajara. On the way, they passed through smaller *pueblos de indios* (Indigenous towns) and peddled their wares to buyers with access to silver coins, cacao beans, and other goods for barter. One of these many merchants was Domingo de Villalobos, a thirty-one-year-old Kapampangan man from the Philippines. He lived on the Colima–Guadalajara trade corridor in Tzapotlan (also Zapotlán). From his will in 1618, we can approximate the inventory

that these informal traders brought to small towns and scattered populations outside of urban centers in central Mexico:

Inventory

- 9 mules
- 56 *sinabafas* (a type of linen fabric) with a sack
- 49 *lanquines* (cloth or silk textiles or clothing, associated with the Chinese city of "Lanquin" [Nanjing]) with a sack[18]
- 8 pieces of taffeta from *china* (Asia) with a piece of damask
- 32 pairs of cotton socks from china
- a blue-patterned silk pincushion pillow
- 16 cotton laces from china
- a dark coat with tawny and purple decoration
- 24 breeches
- a doublet
- a cloak decorated with green trimming and with a fabric jerkin
- 7 *varas* (yard-lengths) of wool-blend fabric
- 1½ varas of taffeta of the land (from Mexico)
- 3 varas of material to make footware
- 4 ounces of purple and tawny trimmings with buttons and silk

- some silk-cloth breeches with a chamois leather jerkin
- a sword and dagger with belt and bullets
- 2 pairs of socks from Castille (1 tawny pair and 1 white pair)
- 2 high-quality garters, 1 colorful and 1 from Japan
- a Japanese sash embroidered with silk
- a worn outer garment
- 2 hats with their fastenings
- a stuffed mattress with wool covering and pillow with 2 pairs of blankets (1 still being made)
- 4 pairs of shirts (2 still being made), 6 of coarse woolen cloth
- a harquebus with a powder flask and a smaller flask with a small pistol with its flask
- a katana
- 2 tanned deerskin pouches with iron fittings
- 5 bundles of feathers for a girl
- several colorful cotton petticoats from Pampanga
- silk breeches from china with several green silk socks from Castille
- 2 pieces of fine linen cloth from china with their tail and cord
- 5 scarves of sinabafa
- 180 pesos in *reales* (100 of which are in the possession of Alonso Gutiérrez; 8 reales equaled 1 peso)
- 40 bushels of salt bought from Alonso Gutiérrez
- a shipment of cacao in the possession of Nicolas Rodríguez from Maquili
- owed debt to Gaspar Sánchez (1 peso, 1 tomín)
- 10 bushels of corn
- a hairband with 43 gold brooches
- 13 sacks (11 new, 2 old)
- a new tent from Lanquin
- an armored riding seat with saddle strap and iron stirrups
- a woolen covering with a deerskin decoration
- a horse headstall with its bit
- a pillion with its breast strap
- a silver Agnus Dei figure
- a rosary
- a little coarse cloth
- 2 new ropes with 10 knots
- 7 worn ropes with their knots
- a 6-handspan large box with a padlock in Acapulco in the house of Agustín Pampango chino
- 3 collars with hoods made of thick wool
- 5 big nets
- 4 pounds of cinnamon

- 10 pounds and 4 ounces of white wax from china in loaves
- debts owed by Pedro Pablo (13 pesos for 6 varas of velvet), Alonso Garrucho (2 shipments of cacao), Pedro Moreno, Francisco Luis chino (owed clothing), Gaspar Necio (25 pesos), the heirs of Andrés García from Colima (17 pesos, 4 *tomines* [worth ⅛ peso each]), Chavos indio (4 pesos, 2 tomines), Jorge Carrillo (12 pesos for cotton cloth), Alonso mulato (3 pesos for a hat), Nicolas Malanquiz chino (10 pesos for salt), Pedro Timban (3 pesos for a bushel of salt), Sebastián (2 pesos, 4 tomines), María Vázquez (3 pesos, 1 tomín for cotton cloth and 10 tomines for a silver knife), Juan Triana chino (2 pesos, 4 tomines for clothing), Juan Botete (3 pesos for clothing), Agustín Solampao (1 peso, 6 tomines in reales for cacao), Alonso Ramos (5 pesos), and Francisco Mathias chino (4 pesos, 4 tomines), don Francisco (12 bushels of salt), Andrés Malate chino (10 pesos), Andrés *alcalde* (magistrate) (2 bushels of salt), Juan Simentro (2½ bushels of salt), Catalina Tuxpaneca (2½ bushels of salt and 10 tomines in cacao), Francisco de Atecosahuic (3 pesos), Madalena Cecilia (1 peso), Pedro Timban (4 pesos of earrings), Pedro de Atlacosahuic (1½ pesos), and Miguel Capisayo (1 bushel of salt) [19]

The inventory makes clear that Villalobos was a socially mobile, even fashionable, chino merchant operating in rural zones of Nueva Galicia to the northwest of Mexico City. He owed his commercial success to trade in both local commodities and Asian products. For example, he had large quantities of salt either in his possession, in that of intermediaries, or owed to him. Salt flowed from the Pacific coasts to Indigenous consumers in the highlands, and Villalobos was clearly an agent of this trade.[20]

However, of particular interest here are his dealings in Asian goods, which were primarily fabrics and clothing, including Chinese cotton, silks, and taffeta. Acapulco was the source of these products, where Villalobos had a contact, a fellow Kapampangan man named Agustín. Villalobos likely traveled with his nine mules and a horse to the port when galleons were anchored in the bay to make purchases for rural consumers desiring to craft their own clothing using Chinese silks and wool.

Villalobos seems to have kept the best items for himself, though. He must have struck quite an image rolling into town with a purple-trimmed cloak, leather jerkin, silk breeches, Japanese garters, a silk-embroidered Japanese sash, Chinese-cotton socks, hat, and a katana on his sword belt.

Then again, other merchants with access to Acapulco had finery of this quality as well.

From his homeland, Villalobos kept only several petticoats that he described as "colorful" and made of "cotton." These items clearly had sentimental value. When Villalobos fell sick, he stayed in the house of his close business associate (and likely friend), a fellow Kapampangan man named Alonso Gutiérrez. Gutiérrez's wife, an Indigenous woman named *doña* Mariana, nursed Villalobos back to health. When he recovered, Villalobos publicly gifted one of these petticoats to doña Mariana.[21] Sadly, Villalobos relapsed into illness and returned to Gutiérrez's home, where he was bedridden for seven months before passing away.[22]

As exceptional as a character like Villalobos might initially seem, his will makes abundantly clear that there were many other Kapampangan and Asian merchants operating in pueblos de indios in colonial Mexico. Like other mule train drivers connected to Acapulco, they facilitated the wide dispersion of Asian products to communities otherwise unlikely to buy the finest wares at the main plaza in Mexico City. In this case, diasporic Philippine networks made such exchanges possible.[23]

The entanglement of the movement of goods and people extended across the Atlantic to Spain as well. In 1623, a prominent Spanish judge in Mexico hired a Japanese man named Juan Antonio to accompany a Japanese bed being shipped as a gift to the recently crowned Spanish king, Philip IV.[24] His predecessors, Philip II

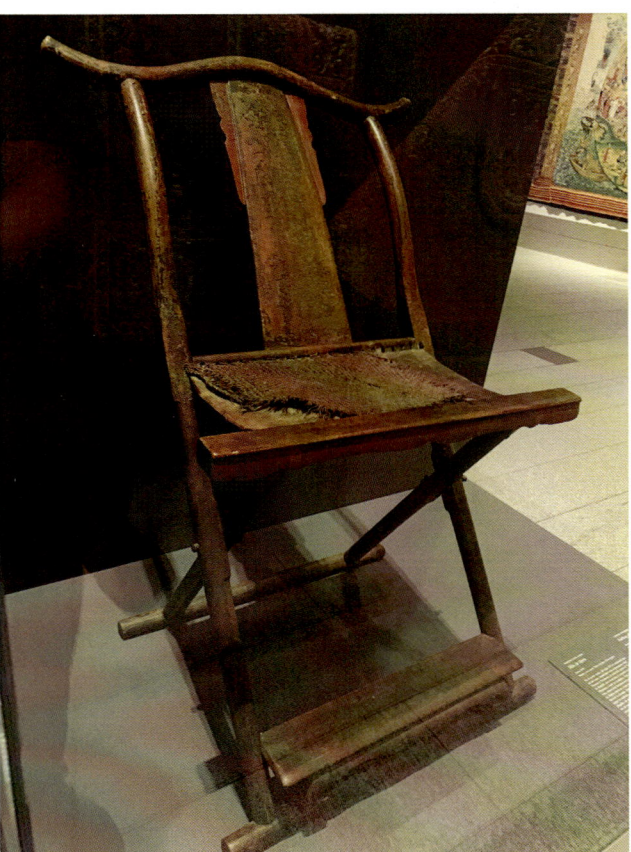

Fig. 6 Unknown artist, Ming dynasty (1368–1644) Chinese chair gifted to Felipe II, on display in the Hapsburg apartments of El Escorial. Spain's royal palaces are filled with Asian products. Courtesy the author.

and Philip III, had already hosted impressive Japanese embassies traveling to Rome and received lavish gifts that can still be seen in the Real Armería (Royal Armory) in Madrid today. Upon arrival at the royal court, Juan Antonio presented the king with a letter from the judge stating that this man could repair the bed if it had arrived damaged. He could also fix *biombos* (Japanese screen panels) or any other Japanese product. In the king's presence, Juan Antonio assembled the bed (fig. 6).

However, the rest of his stay in Spain would be nothing so glamorous. Like many Asian subjects who arrived at the seat of the empire, Juan Antonio soon found himself stranded with no means of returning overseas. He was merely a disposable accessory to the judge's gift. Subsequently, Juan Antonio submitted multiple petitions to the Crown begging for employment as a soldier, an interpreter, and eventually, as a sailor so that he could earn enough money to return to Mexico.[25] For him, there was no separating material fascination with Asian products from his long-distance displacement. His entire existence had been reduced to the service of a gift.

The disciplinary boundaries that often silo the study of objects and people have obscured the extent to which both were historically inseparable. Searching for their many intersections brings us to understudied histories, like the harrowing nature of the Pacific passage, the mule trains crisscrossing colonial Mexican hinterlands, and the rare case of a Japanese man accompanying a bed sent to the king of Spain. These examples merely scratch the surface, but in their brevity, they also prove that the texture of history—the lived experience of it—constantly and triumphantly resists the fragile categories we are trained to harness it with. I find it more liberating to surrender to the innumerable ways the messiness of history challenges the way we think, with its fantastical idiosyncrasies. To study the storied galleons and the ways in which the transpacific trade remade the early modern world is to embark on an inward journey—alongside that of our historical subjects—because the value of doing history is not simply in reassembling the past into new configurations but, rather, in how it forces us to constantly reform the tools we deploy to perceive our world and its past.

Notes

1. Elizabeth Horodowich and Alexander Nagel, *Amerasia* (Zone Books, 2023), 14.

2. Guillaume Gaudin, "On the Legal Grounds of the Conquest of the Philippines (1568)," in *The Spanish Pacific, 1521–1815, Volume 2: A Reader of Primary Sources*, ed. Christina H. Lee and Ricardo Padrón (Amsterdam University Press, 2024), 97–99.

3. Andrés Reséndez, *Conquering the Pacific: An Unknown Mariner and the Final Great Voyage of the Age of Discovery* (Houghton Mifflin Harcourt, 2021).

4. For a summary, see Ryan Dominic Crewe, "Connecting the Indies: The Hispano-Asian Pacific World in Early Modern Global History," *Estudios Históricos* 30, no. 60 (2017): 17–34; Lee and Padrón, "Introduction," in *The Spanish Pacific, 1521–1815*, 9–20.

5. In Spanish, the vessels were called *naos de china* (Asia ships). On "Manila galleons" as a misnomer, see Diego Javier Luis, *The First Asians in the Americas: A Transpacific History* (Harvard University Press, 2024), 8.

6. William Lytle Schurz, *The Manila Galleon: Illustrated with Maps* (E. P. Dutton, 1939).

7. For the most complete study of Manila's Chinese community and their economic activities, see Juan Gil, *Los chinos en Manila: Siglos XVI y XVII* (Centro Científico e Cultural de Macau, 2011).

8. Arturo Giráldez, *The Age of Trade: The Manila Galleons and the Dawn of the Global Economy* (Rowman & Littlefield, 2015), 2–3.

9. For an analysis of numbers regarding early modern Asian mobility to the Americas, see Luis, *The First Asians in the Americas*, 15.

10. Déborah Oropeza, *La migración asiática en el virreinato de la Nueva España: Un proceso de globalización (1565-1815)* (El Colegio de México, 2020), 151; Luis, *The First Asians in the Americas*, 15.

11. Pablo Miguel Sierra Silva, *Mexico, Slavery, Freedom: A Bilingual Documentary History, 1520–1829* (Hackett Publishing Company, Inc., 2024), 92, 104–7.

12. Luis, *The First Asians in the Americas*, 92–93.

13. Ibid., 76.

14. Ibid., 68, 79–80.

15. Ibid., 78.

16. Jose M. Buhain, "The Recovery of the *San Diego*," *Philippine Studies* 42, no. 4 (1994): 543–48.

17. Luis, *The First Asians in the Americas*, 78.

18. Andreia Martins Torres, "Quimonos chinos y quimones criollos. La moda novohispana en el cruce entre Oriente y Occidente," in *La nao de China, 1565-1815: Navegación, comercio e intercambios culturales*, ed. Salvador Bernabéu Albert (Universidad de Sevilla, Secretariado de Publicaciones, 2013), 261–62.

19. "Bienes de difuntos: Domingo de Villalobos," 1621, Archivo General de Indias (AGI), Contratación, 520, N.2, R.14, ff. 31r–46r.

20. Jonathan D. Amith, *The Möbius Strip: A Spatial History of Colonial Society in Guerrero, Mexico* (Stanford University Press, 2005), 65–66.

21. "Bienes de difuntos: Domingo de Villalobos," 1621, Archivo General de Indias (AGI), Contratación, 520, N.2, R.14, f. 130v.

22. Luis, *The First Asians in the Americas*, 129–32.

23. Ibid., 17.

24. "Decreto enviando petición del japonés Juan Antonio," 1624, Archivo General de Indias (AGI), Filipinas, 39, N.21.

25. "Petición del japonés Juan Antonio de que se le nombre intérprete," 1624, Archivo General de Indias (AGI), Filipinas, 39, N.23; "Petición del japonés Juan Antonio de licencia para ir a Nueva España," 1624, Archivo General de Indias (AGI), Filipinas, 39, N.24; Ibid., 195–96.

Inventories of Luxury and Wealth: Asian Trade and Material Culture in Spanish America

Jorge F. Rivas Pérez, Emily Rauh Pulitzer Deputy Director and Chief Curator, Saint Louis Art Museum

Beginning in the early 1570s, with the regular annual Pacific crossing, the Spanish viceroyalties of New Spain and Peru became key nodes in a vast global trade network that connected major cities in Asia, the Americas, and Europe. The Manila Galleon (known then as *nao de China*) trade transported immense quantities of Asian goods—textiles, porcelain, furniture, lacquerware, jewelry, ivories, and other finely crafted luxury goods—across the Pacific Ocean to the Americas in exchange for silver and other raw materials such as indigo and cochineal. These exotic items found eager markets in the thriving new cities across Spanish America, in particular in metropolises such as Mexico City and Lima, where they significantly and visibly influenced local visual and material culture.

The influx of these Asian imports ignited the imaginations of both consumers and artisans in the Americas. Sumptuous textiles, fine porcelain, lacquer furniture, ivory sculptures, and other lavish objects became symbols of status and wealth and inspired local craftspeople to incorporate Asian motifs and techniques into their creations (fig. 1). This blending of Asian and local styles led to a unique cross-cultural synthesis, visible in everything from architecture and decoration to clothing and everyday objects (fig. 2).

Although much has been written about colonial society, we still know relatively little about customs regarding material culture and everyday life, particularly the role of objects in these societies. Published documents—in particular inventories—from the colonial period remain limited,

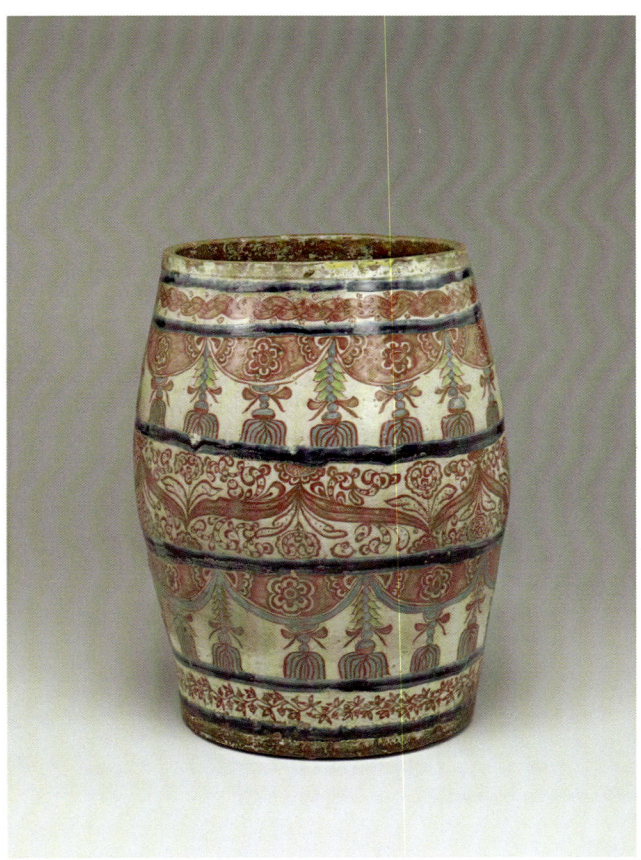

Fig. 1 Unknown artist, Barrel-Shaped *Jardiniere*, Puebla, Mexico, 1700s. Tin-glazed ceramic, 28 × 18 in. dia. (71.1 × 45.7 cm). Denver Art Museum: Funds from the Carl Patterson bequest, 2021.112.

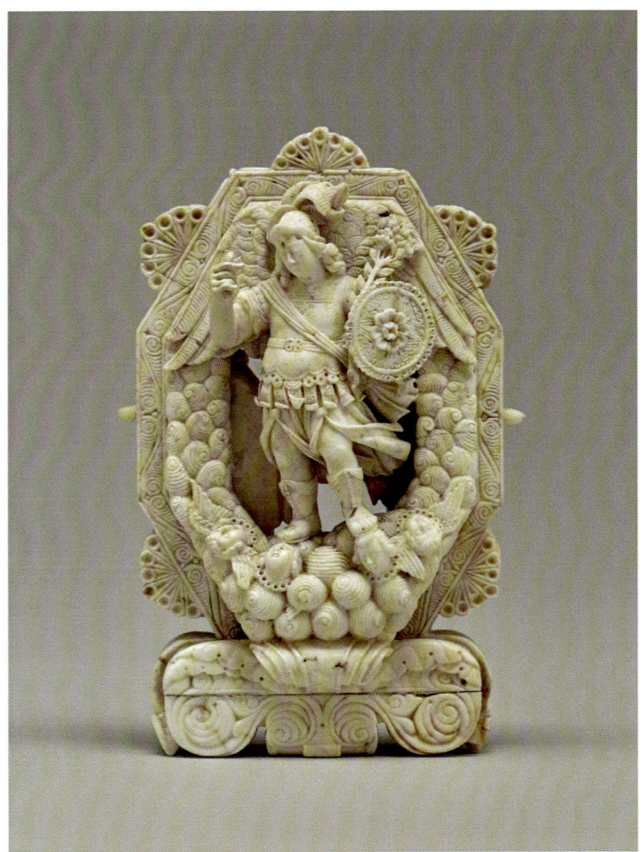

Fig. 2 Diego de Reinoso, Double-Sided Carving of Saint Michael and the Virgin and Child with Saints Dominic and John the Baptist, Mexico, ca. 1696. Alabaster, 3¼ × 2¼ × ⅞ in. (8.3 × 5.7 × 2.2 cm). Denver Art Museum: Gift of Robert J. Stroessner, 1991.1150.

and accessing original sources in Latin America often presents bureaucratic challenges and numerous other difficulties.

This is precisely why I have undertaken this opportunity to explore the context in which luxurious Asian goods for the home were used during the viceregal era. In Spanish America, Asian imports appear listed almost everywhere, from ship manifests to dowry contracts, wills, inventories, and appraisals of every possible type. However, records tend to be succinct and merely name the items without providing additional information. Yet, some inventories offer more detailed information on the specifics of the objects, generally

indicating quality or appearance, and more importantly, some documents include information on how they were used and displayed. The latter is a crucial aspect as most scholarship on Asian export goods tends to focus more on the type of items and their quantity rather than on their role in daily life.

Documents of wealthier households typically list a substantial number of Asian items of the finest kind. Yet, the variety and abundance of imported goods across Spanish America allowed even the less affluent strata of viceregal societies to access them, even if of lower quality.

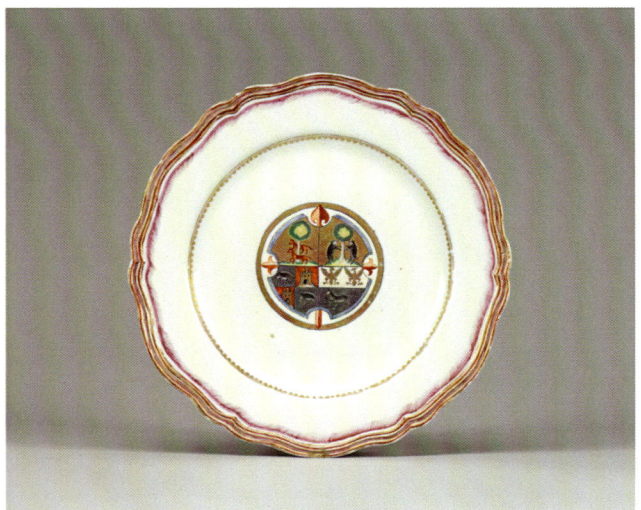

Fig. 3 Unknown artist, Plate with the Coat of Arms of Don Domingo Ignacio de Lardizábal y Arza, 1785. China, Qing dynasty (1644–1911). Porcelain, 9½ in. dia. (24.1 cm). Denver Art Museum: Funds from the Carl Patterson bequest, 2021.113.

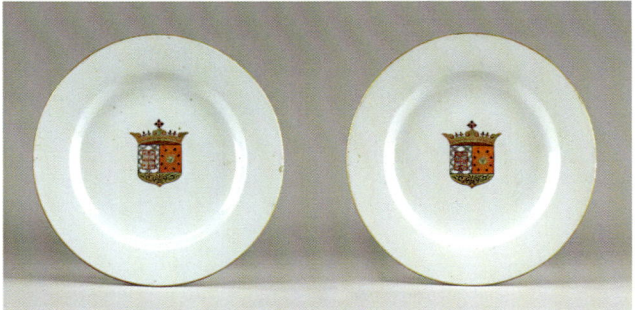

Fig. 4 Unknown artist, Pair of Plates with the Arms of Francisco José de Ovando y Solís, 1st Marquis of Ovando, 1752. China, Qing dynasty (1644–1911). Porcelain, 11½ in. dia. (29.2 cm). Denver Art Museum: Funds from Ethel Sayre Berger by exchange, 2020.563.1-2.

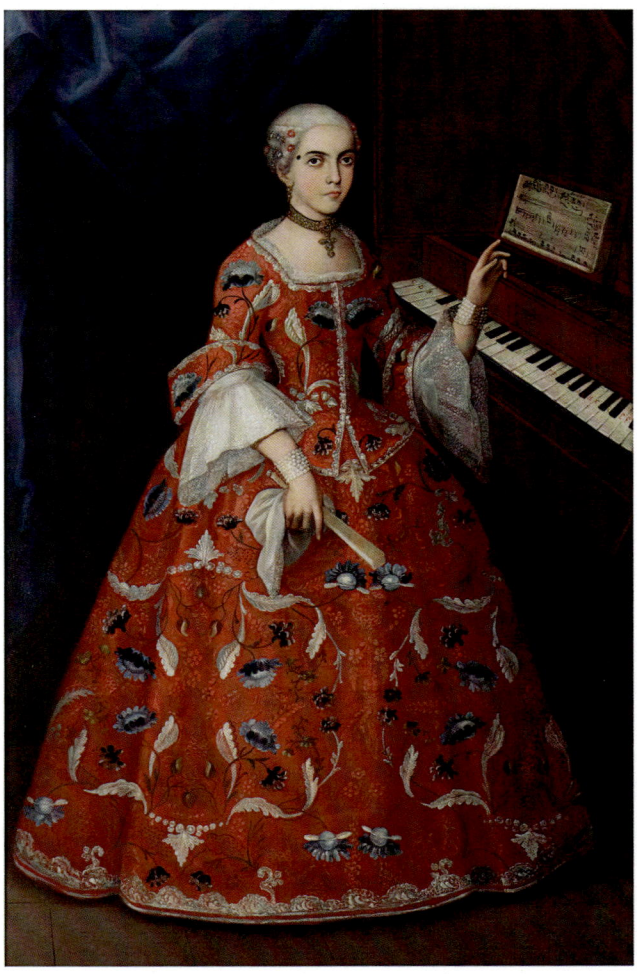

Fig. 5 Unknown artist, *Young Woman with a Harpsichord*, Mexico, 1735–50. Oil on canvas, framed: 72¼ × 50⅞ × 3 in. (183.5 × 129.2 × 7.6 cm). Denver Art Museum: Gift of the Collection of Frederick and Jan Mayer, 2014.209.

Whether it was an aristocrat or a wealthy merchant displaying a costly service of armorial porcelain made to order in China (figs. 3 and 4) or a rich lady wearing a lavish dress made from Chinese silk (fig. 5) or an individual of the middle class wearing a more affordable printed cotton garment (fig. 6) or the use of a simple porcelain bowl in the kitchen (fig. 7), imported goods were present across all social classes. It is important to note that the so-called Parián market in Mexico City was a key retail hub for global imports, while in Lima, through the port of Callao, local merchants retailed a wide range of imported products, chiefly coming from Portobello (Panama), to supply Peru's interior provinces.

Few Asian artifacts from this era have survived to the present, and nearly all are detached from their original historical context, complicating their study. Additionally, there have been limited

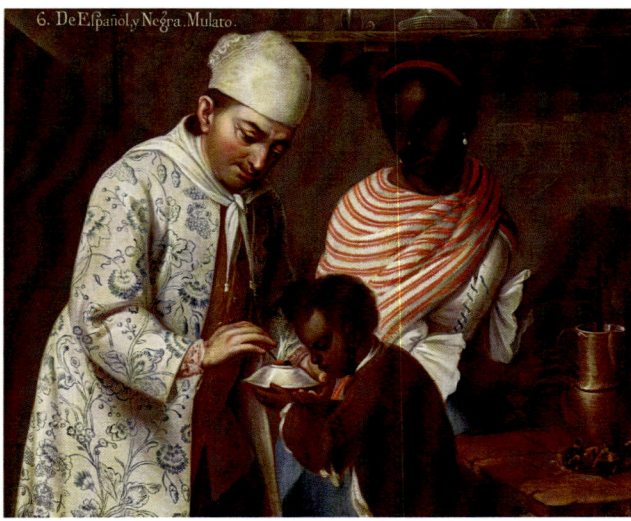

Fig. 6 Attributed to José de Alcíbar, *De Espanol y Negra, Mulato*, Mexico, ca. 1760. Oil on canvas, 30⅝ × 38¾ in. (77.8 × 98.4 cm). Denver Art Museum: Gift of the Collection of Frederick and Jan Mayer, 2014.217.

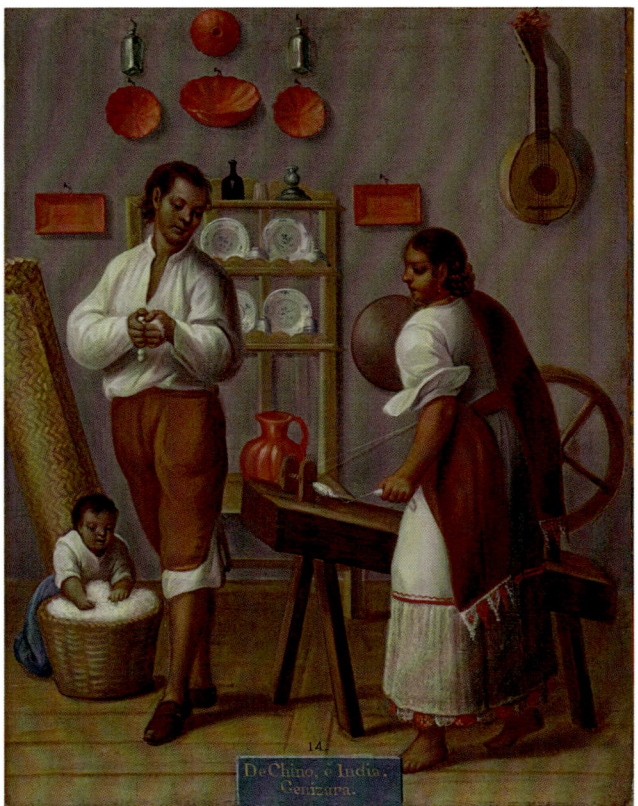

Fig. 7 Francisco Clapera, *De Chino, e India, Genizara*, Mexico, ca. 1775. Oil on canvas, 20⅛ × 15⅝ in. (51.1 × 39.7 cm). Denver Art Museum: Gift of the Collection of Frederick and Jan Mayer, 2011.428.14.

archaeological investigations into this topic, with most focusing on porcelain fragments preserved in landfills, which, by their nature, remain in relatively good condition and close to their original location. However, documents showcase the depth and durability of the transpacific connections between Asia and the Americas that emerged in the late sixteenth century, revealing a vibrant and enduring cultural exchange.

The present study focuses on four elite individuals: two viceroys—Manuel de Oms y Santa Pau (1651–1710), Marquess of Castelldosrius, Viceroy of Peru from 1707 to 1710; and Antonio María de Bucareli y Ursúa (1717–1779), Viceroy of New Spain from 1771 until his death in 1779—and two noblewomen—*doña* Teresa Francisca María de Guadalupe Retes Paz y Vera (1673–1695), Marchioness of San Jorge from Mexico City; and *doña* Rosa Juliana Sánchez de Tagle e

Hidalgo (1687–1761), Marchioness of Torre Tagle from Lima.

By no means exhaustive, the study aims to provide an analysis based on four sets of documents: two from New Spain, published and annotated by the late Mexican scholar Gustavo Curiel,[1] and two from Peru, which I have examined extensively in my previous research.[2]

The selection of these particular documents is intentional. They contain sufficient detail to provide insight into how specific objects for the home were used in colonial society while offering a perspective that spans nearly a century, from the late seventeenth century to the late eighteenth century.

Through these sources, we can begin to reconstruct the role that luxury material goods imported from Asia played in shaping the daily lives and identities of the colonial elite during this era. As is often the case with this type of documentary sources, details about the pieces are sometimes incomplete. Information such as the total number of items, techniques used, themes depicted, dimensions, authorship, or origin may be missing, making it challenging to fully understand the collections. Jewels, clothing, and textiles of Asian origin intended for personal use appear frequently in the inventories studied. However, as they constitute a distinct category, they have been excluded from this brief text, which focuses primarily on household goods.

Members of the Spanish high nobility, the viceroys, served as the monarch's direct representatives, holding the highest civic and military authority in Spanish America. They oversaw the treasury, justice system, and secular aspects of ecclesiastical governance. In Mexico City and Lima, the viceroys lived and administered affairs from grand viceregal palaces in each city's main square (fig. 8). Each viceroy furnished these official residences to their taste, so the palaces' appearances shifted with each new appointment.

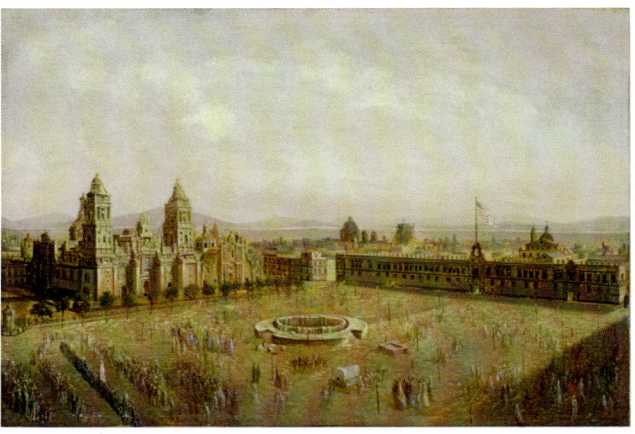

Fig. 8 Pedro Antonio Gualdi, *Zócalo of Mexico City*, Mexico, 1847. Oil and gouache on paper on canvas, 9½ × 14½ in. (24.1 × 36.8 cm). Denver Art Museum: Gift of Mrs. Frederic H. Douglas, 1956.72.

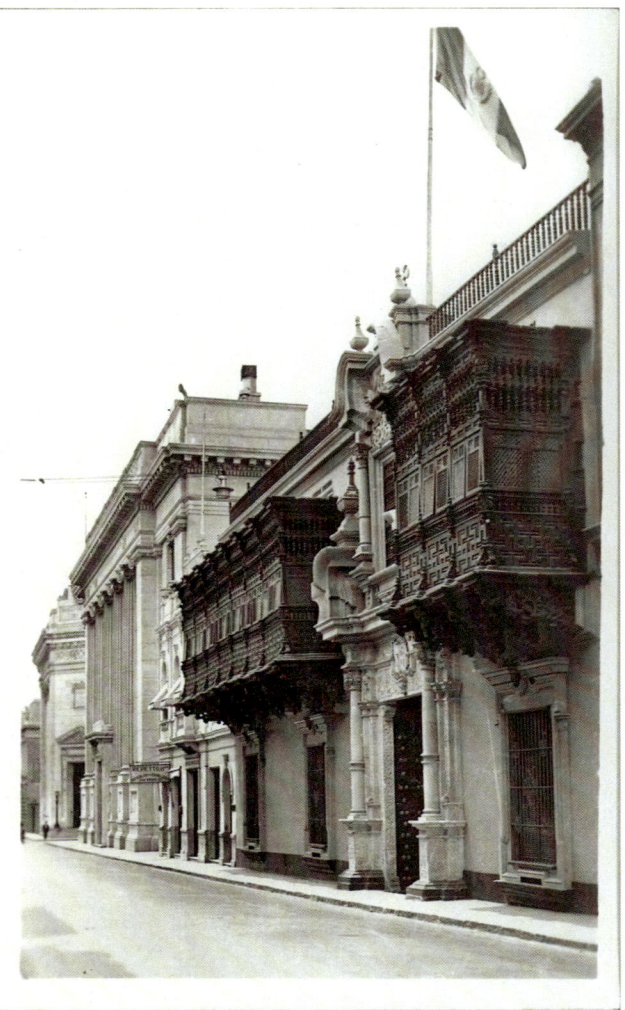

Fig. 9 Facade of Torre Tagle Palace, Lima, Peru, built ca. 1738. Postcard, 1920s. Courtesy the author.

The titled nobility in Spanish America primarily consisted of the *criollo* elite—descendants of Spanish immigrants, predominantly merchants or Crown administrators. This class modeled itself after the Spanish nobility, adopting its structure, privileges, and customs. Over time, they supplanted the earlier elite of conquistadors and their descendants. As landowners and merchants with economic resources, social prestige, and political influence, this new nobility consolidated wealth and power through strategic marriages of convenience, often incorporating members of the remaining conquistador families who still held land and wealth. The titled nobility typically lived in large houses or palaces in the city center. One example is the well-preserved palace of the marquises of Torre Tagle in Lima, which now serves as the seat of the Peruvian chancellery (fig. 9).

The analysis of the referenced documents reveals that Asian artifacts were primarily displayed in spaces designed for social representation—areas intended to showcase wealth and status. Within these spaces, four main areas stand out: table settings, reception rooms, the *estrado* (a woman's sitting area often used for formal gatherings), and bedrooms. Each of these spaces served as a stage for presenting valuable objects, demonstrating the owner's affluence and taste for exotic, expensive items. The presence of Asian artifacts in these rooms not only reflected the wealth of the household but also underscored a cultural appreciation for imported, high-quality craftsmanship.

Viceroy Manuel de Oms y Santa Pau, Lima (1710)

Born in 1651 in Barcelona, Manuel de Oms y Santa Pau, first Marquis of Castelldosrius, was appointed viceroy of Peru in 1704, in the midst of the War of the Spanish Succession. His arrival in Lima in 1707 was not without controversy, largely due to the enormous costs of his move to Peru. During his administration, he faced a series of complex problems, including economic instability, tensions between *peninsulares* and creoles, and constant threats from pirates and corsairs. Despite these difficulties, Oms y Santa Pau, a cultured and educated man, tried to modernize the colonial administration and strengthen royal power. However, his tenure was marked by strife and accusations of corruption until his death in office in 1710.[3]

Undoubtedly, the years he lived as Spanish ambassador to the French court marked his taste for the customs, styles, and pomp of the Bourbons at Versailles, as evidenced by the inventory of his possessions.[4] Among other things, the viceroy had a luxurious *casina*, or leisure pavilion, built in the middle of the garden of the viceregal palace, an ideal place for his literary evenings. Asian furniture and objects held a prominent place in the reception rooms at this time. Though its architectural features are unknown, this opulent space was adorned with ten gilt-framed mirrors and twenty gilt consoles displaying Chinese cups and figurines, among other valuable objects.[5] The seating, including chairs and canapés, featured gilded legs and crimson damask upholstery with gold *sevillaneta* trim, creating a setting of undeniable splendor. The centrality of Asian objects in this room, the most splendid of the palace and one used for entertaining diplomats and the *limeño* nobility, indicates the importance that society conferred on these exotic imported goods.

The inventory of the marquis reveals numerous entries of precious silks and other luxurious textiles. Although their origins are not explicitly specified, it is reasonable to assume that many of these items were imported from Asia. For instance, in the audience room, the marquis had three curtains of mother-of-pearl color damask and matching valances with their gold trimmings, a hanging of red damask with silk and gold trimmings and its valance of the same, and a crimson velvet canopy adorned with gold embroidery, accompanied by a matching chair and carpet, all complemented by crimson damask wall hangings.[6] While the exact provenance of these opulent textiles remains unknown, their quality suggests a connection to the trade networks of the time during which Asia had a central role. Another instance in which rich textiles played a key role is the bed. A grand, elaborately dressed bed was a staple of stately homes and palaces, inspired by the opulence of royal residences. Such beds could serve as parade beds, reserved for social and ceremonial functions, or as everyday furnishings for the owners. In either case, these extravagant pieces symbolized wealth and refined taste. The marquis of Castelldosrius owned several

beds, though their geographic origins are unspecified. Notably, the viceroy owned a cot of *granadillo* wood featuring Solomonic columns, bronze ornaments, a crimson damask skirt, two mattresses of the same material, and a mosquito net,[7] a protection from the abundant insects common in the Americas.[8] At the time of its appraisal, this last bed was undressed—likely due to the common practice of disposing of bedding after a death to prevent the spread of disease, as the marquis may have passed away in it. Nonetheless, the inventory also included crimson damask bed hangings and a crimson brocade canopy with a yellow base, luxurious textiles that might have originated in Asia, as Chinese damask would likely have been less expensive than Spanish or Italian silks.[9]

The marquis also owned inlaid furniture of possible Asian origin, among which stand out two writing desks inlaid in tortoiseshell, ivory, and mother-of-pearl and two smaller of the same type with their matching tables.[10] Attentive to the tastes and needs of their new clientele, Asian craftsmen swiftly adapted European furniture models, embellishing them with traditional Asian techniques. They often incorporated mother-of-pearl, bone, and ivory inlays, along with the lustrous lacquer finishes highly prized in Spain and its overseas territories.

Among all the inventories studied, that of the marquis is undoubtedly the least informative regarding the geographical origins of the inventoried objects. However, it is particularly revealing in its detailed mention of the geographical provenance of items within the garden pavilion, specifically noting the Chinese origin of the porcelain. This detail is especially significant, as the pavilion was the most luxurious space in the viceregal palace, underscoring the centrality of Asian objects as symbols of wealth and refined taste in early eighteenth-century Lima.

Viceroy Antonio María de Bucareli y Ursúa, Mexico City (1779)

Born in Seville, Spain, in 1717, Antonio María de Bucareli y Ursúa served as the forty-sixth viceroy of New Spain from 1771 until his death in office in 1779. The son of the second Marquis of Vallehermoso and a member of a wealthy and influential Sevillian family of Florentine origin, Bucareli was a man of refined tastes and significant wealth.[11]

As viceroy, Bucareli was celebrated for his effective governance, extensive infrastructure improvements, and dedication to implementing the Bourbon Reforms, aimed at modernizing and strengthening Spain's colonial administration. His tenure was marked by efforts to enhance economic conditions, promote public works, and expand trade. He played a pivotal role in constructing roads, aqueducts, and other essential infrastructure, significantly contributing to New Spain's economic development.[12]

The comprehensive inventory of Bucareli's belongings, also published and annotated by Curiel, offers a vivid depiction of the splendor of the viceregal court in the late eighteenth century. It also underscores the vast circulation of imported Asian goods in New Spain, highlighting the region's integration into global trade networks during that era.

Intended for hosting formal events and celebrations, the reception and audience rooms were typically the largest and most public areas in viceregal palaces, serving as ideal showcases for the viceroy's wealth, taste, and power. Inventories of these rooms often list only a few permanent furniture pieces, as items were usually brought in from other rooms and arranged according to the occasion. However, reception rooms always featured an abundance of seating—chairs, stools, benches, and settees—usually lined along the walls.

In viceregal palaces and grand homes, multiple reception rooms were standard, sometimes preceded by antechambers. As previously mentioned in the case of Viceroy Oms y Santa Pau, at the viceregal palace in Lima, a canopy room was always present, distinguished by a rich armchair set upon a dais under an opulent canopy, with portraits of the monarchs displayed as a mark of reverence for the king during audiences and official ceremonies. Viceroy Bucareli's canopy room was decorated with crimson damask from Valencia. Spanish silks, though more difficult to obtain in Mexico and costly to import, were closely associated with the royal court in Madrid. Their exclusivity made them particularly fitting for the canopy room, where the authority and prestige of the monarch were symbolically represented, which contrasts with the extensive use of Chinese textiles and a rich assortment of Asian objects present in the rest of the palace.[13] For example, in a cabinet adjacent to the oratory, there were two Chinese lidded vases in various colors with wooden bases,[14] another multicolored vase with gilded accents,[15] a Chinese *aporcelanado* (porcelain-like) armchair,[16] and a set of seating that included nineteen stools and a settee, all upholstered in straw-colored damask.[17] Elsewhere in the viceregal palace, the inventory lists four Chinese landscape paintings under glass framed in wood,[18] twelve black lacquer wooden side chairs of Chinese origin, and numerous curtains and wall hangings made from Chinese damask.[19]

Among the furnishings, Viceroy Bucareli's bed is remarkable for its extraordinary luxury; it had "a Chinese cabinet hanging, of yellow satin, painted with stories and figures of Chinese, on one side, and a bed hanging of the same color, embroidered with colored silk on both sides, whose two hangings are contained in two chests."[20] The set was valued at the extravagant sum of 1,400 pesos, and the viceroy had left instructions that it be sent to his beloved niece, the Countess of Xerena.[21] In addition, the bedding included several "Peking" bedspreads in various colors.

The service for the table was one of the areas with the greatest variety of Asian goods in Bucareli's inventory. It reflects the shift in tastes typical of the late eighteenth century, favoring Chinese porcelain over silver. His inventory lists an impressive 1,161 pieces of Chinese porcelain,[22] some bearing his coat of arms.[23] Among these are a 154-piece coffee set known as *de la cabrita* (the little goat), a 104-piece set with the viceroy's arms, a 67-piece set *con cenefita* (with a small fringe), a 136-piece set *del elefante* (of the elephant),[24] along with sets of plain white chinaware and another 144-piece set of the same.[25] The porcelain pieces are richly varied in shape and style, some featuring animal shapes like fish, rabbits, deer, dogs, ducks, and lions,[26] as well as human figures such as a pair of *chinos* (Chinese men)[27] and six *muñecos* (dolls) used as candlesticks.[28] The collection includes a wide array of plates, bowls of various sizes, chocolate cups, *mancerinas* (a type of wide saucer with a cup holder in the center), and serving dishes like tureens, salvers, trays, sauce boats, and salt cellars.[29] Some items are plain white porcelain, while others are decorated in blue or colors in different patterns with gilded edges.[30] Additionally, the inventory lists jars of various sizes and types of decoration, with or without lids—some with iron lids and latches for storing valuable spices—alongside different types of vases and basins.[31]

The most remarkable pieces in Viceroy Bucareli's Chinese tableware collection are undoubtedly the gilded *copella* silver (silver and lead alloy) items embellished with enamel, which the viceroy specifically set aside for his niece, the Countess of Xerena. Born of Chinese entrepreneurship, ingenuity, exceptional craftsmanship, and cultural cosmopolitanism, silver objects crafted for export were among the most coveted luxury goods, seamlessly blending precious metals with sophisticated decorative techniques. These exquisite pieces include two filigree pelicans that served as salt cellars, adorned with gilded branches: a duck and a heron, whose backs could be used to hold salt, each perched on a rock and resting on small tables crafted from white and gilded copella silver with enamel accents.[32] Among these Chinese treasures for the table were also two turkeys, one with its wings extended and the other tucked in, with gilded and enameled tails, separated by a small gilded and enameled tree mounted on its little table.[33] Completing this set were four delicate *ramilleteros* (ornate table centerpieces), each with screws and small plates, decorated in intricate filigree with tiny roses and gilded overlays.[34] The viceroy also had a Chinese silver toothpick holder embellished with filigree and gilding.[35] Among other Chinese metalwork, the inventory lists a brass and black enamel candlestick with its small plate, its snuffer, and a wick trimmer.[36]

As the viceroy of New Spain, the king's representative, and a symbol of the magnificence of the Spanish court, Bucareli was expected to uphold a high level of luxury and pomp in all palace events. By the late eighteenth century, French court customs—introduced to Spain with the Bourbon dynasty's ascension—were fully assimilated, further refining the etiquette, fashion, and ceremonial splendor that defined the viceroyalty's elite social life. The lavishness, abundance, and exquisite quality of Bucareli's table settings reflect both the wealth and grandeur of late eighteenth-century banquets and galas, as well as the sophistication and meticulous attention that elite society devoted to such events.

The Marchioness of San Jorge, Mexico City (1695)

Teresa Francisca María de Guadalupe Retes Paz y Vera (1673–1695), Marchioness of San Jorge, was among the wealthiest women in late-seventeenth-century Mexico City, as the sole heir of the prosperous merchant *don* José de Retes y Ortiz de Largacha. Despite her immense fortune, Teresa's life was marked by vulnerability; her intellectual disability placed her under the guardianship of her uncles, José Sáez de Retes and Dámaso de Saldívar, following her father's death. In 1688, she married her first cousin, don Domingo de Retes, in what was likely a marriage of convenience designed to preserve and manage her substantial estate. Her life, however, was tragically short, ending at the age of twenty-two.[37]

The detailed inventory and appraisal of the marchioness's estate, also studied by Curiel, offer a vivid glimpse into the wealth and sophistication of New Spain's colonial elite in the late 1600s, highlighting their affinity for luxury goods, in particular fine imports from Asia.

As previously mentioned, lavishly decorated reception rooms were standard in the houses of the titled nobility. Asian luxury furniture and objects played a central role in wealth display. For example, the marchioness of San Jorge owned a substantial number of pieces of fine Asian furniture, including four valuable Asian lacquer cabinets, appraised at an impressive 450 pesos—a significant sum for the period.[38] Beyond their exotic origin, lacquer objects and furniture held a place of honor in the world of luxury goods. Their waterproof, glossy surfaces, rich hues of red and black, and intricate ornamentation in gold, silver, or mother-of-pearl made them highly prized for their beauty and craftsmanship. In addition to the cabinets, she also had two more Chinese lacquer cabinets (*escritorios*), a small Chinese low table (*bufetillo*), a Chinese lacquer chest, a Chinese lacquer writing chest, and two cedar and narra wood boxes from China, inlaid with bone (likely of Philippine origin), and an additional wooden box made in China.[39] The inventory further lists eleven small tables inlaid with mother-of-pearl, though it does not specify these as Asian in origin.

It was common for the titled nobility to maintain a canopy room specially prepared for the hypothetical possibility of a royal visit. It also served as a symbol of allegiance to the Crown. The marchioness of San Jorge's canopy was made of crimson fabric with gold fringe; although further details are not available, it is possible that the fabric was of Asian origin.[40]

The estrado was a dedicated area within the larger reception room and, in some cases, an entire room, reserved for women to engage in social activities and display their collections of valuable objects. As the quintessential feminine space during the viceroyalty, it often served as a focal point for showcasing Asian export goods.[41] In the case of the marchioness of San Jorge, her inventory reveals a striking collection displayed inside an ebony and ivory cabinet with glass doors, functioning as a sort of treasure presentation with objects from all over the world.[42] Inside were numerous prized Asian pieces. These included two small Chinese cups embellished with silver mounts, two other silver-mounted cups with lids, four small Chinese jars (*tibores*), and over seventy small porcelain items and figurines from China.[43] Additionally, there was a pair of Chinese wooden chests embellished with silver nails.[44] Seating in this room was provided by twenty-four Chinese cushions, elaborately embroidered with gold and silver thread, arranged on top of three exquisite Chinese carpets, completing an opulent display.

The bedroom, generally adjacent to the estrado, was another important room for social functions. The marchioness owned an exquisite ebony and ivory bed with double Solomonic headboards adorned with richly embroidered silk hangings from China.[45] These hangings alone were appraised at 950 pesos, underscoring their fine quality.[46] In addition, the inventory lists several other Chinese textiles, including a gauze hanging with a matching bedspread embellished with gold flowers and fringe and another bed hanging made of colorful satin with its ceiling and skirting panels.[47] Also featured are a green silk *ormesí* bedcover from China, a door curtain, and a cotton bedcover embroidered in green, likewise imported from China.[48] The marchioness's collection included a tall, twelve-panel Chinese screen, likely used near the bed to provide privacy, as was customary in that period.[49] This screen not only served a practical function but also enhanced the room's aesthetic richness.

As in the other inventories previously mentioned, the service for the table often included Asian export goods. Following the custom of the late seventeenth century, the marchioness used an extensive collection of silver for the table service, very likely of Mexican origin, as silversmithing was highly sophisticated in Mexico by the seventeenth century.[50] However, in addition, she had a large cupboard filled with Chinese porcelain for dining, although the exact contents are not listed.[51] The inventory, however, details other items in her collection of Chinese porcelain in varying qualities—fine, semi-fine, and ordinary—including numerous cups, bowls, plates, and lidded jars.[52] Another notable Asian item in her collection, reflecting her passion for chocolate, was a set of a dozen Chinese lacquer *jícaras* (chocolate cups), each paired with a matching lacquer saucer.[53]

The Marchioness of Torre Tagle, Lima (1761)

Rosa Juliana Sánchez de Tagle e Hidalgo (1687–1761), future Marchioness of Torre Tagle, was born in San Jerónimo de Sayán, Huaura (Peru), to don Francisco Sánchez de Tagle y Castro Velarde, a Spanish nobleman and prosperous merchant, and doña María Josefa Hidalgo Sánchez y Velázquez Gómez, a wealthy heiress of Spanish descent.[54]

On November 13, 1707, Rosa Juliana married her distant cousin, don José Bernardo de Tagle Bracho, in Lima's cathedral. With Rosa Juliana's substantial dowry and her father's backing, José Bernardo rapidly amassed a fortune through commerce. His social ascent culminated in the title of Marquis of Torre Tagle, granted by King Felipe V in 1730 for his services to the Crown. This honor elevated the family's status, cementing their position among the Peruvian elite.

The detailed inventory and appraisal of the marchioness's estate provide a remarkable window into the opulence and refined lifestyle of Lima's colonial elite during the first half of the 1700s.[55] These records reveal not only the vast wealth amassed by prominent families but also their sophisticated tastes and aspirations to display power and status through material possessions. Among the most striking features of the estate are the numerous luxury goods, including fine textiles, porcelains, and other exquisite imports from Asia, acquired through the thriving transpacific trade via the Manila Galleon.

The Torre Tagle reception room followed the tradition of showcasing Asian furniture. Its inventory lists an "antique black Chinese cabinet, twin to the one in the bedroom."[56] Notably, only one of this pair remained in the reception room (the other was likely relocated to the bedroom later). Typically, such matched pairs were placed symmetrically, especially for high-value items meant to highlight the owner's wealth. This pair of black lacquer Chinese cabinets, adorned with metal plates and handles, was appraised at 500 pesos, making them the most valuable furniture in the entire house.

The estrado of the marchioness of Torre Tagle included several notable Asian furnishings and objects.[57] Among them were two small black lacquer Chinese boxes with metal hardware, each displayed on its own wood table, and atop each box rested an antique Chinese jar "painted" (enameled) in blue. Additionally, there was a small box inlaid with mother-of-pearl, tortoiseshell, and ivory, though its origin is unspecified. The *rodaestrado* (estrado hanging) of antique green damask to match the curtains that adorned the doors leading to the sleeping quarters and the reception room may also have been Chinese, but their origin is not specified.

As tradition mandated, the main estrado was followed by the bedroom.[58] While the marchioness of Torre Tagle's bed hangings were crafted from the locally produced *macana de Quito* fabric, her bedroom featured numerous Asian imports. For example, beside her bed, she had an

additional smaller, more intimate estrado area (which was customary among aristocrats) with an assortment of pieces, including an antique black lacquer Chinese tray table. In the same room, the inventory lists a flask case containing ten Chinese porcelain flasks, an antique red lacquer Chinese box embellished with metal fittings, and an antique black lacquer cabinet from China adorned with metal plates and handles—a matching piece to the one in her reception room. A small antique Chinese porcelain jar sat atop this desk, completing a richly layered display highlighting her appreciation for Asian artistry.

The marchioness of Torre Tagle stored and displayed her porcelain table service, crystal, and other luxury goods in a luxurious cedar cabinet of "antique workmanship," adorned with silver hardware and plaques.[59] This cabinet, along with three substantial mahogany chests, was situated in an antechamber (*antecuadra*) adjacent to the master bedroom, emphasizing both the aesthetic and functional importance of her tableware collection.

Inside the cabinet, a considerable array of blue-and-white Chinese porcelain was presented. This collection included a variety of saucers, platters in different sizes and shapes, chocolate cups, salt cellars, lidded cups, gravy boats, and figurines of dogs and lions. This porcelain table service was further complemented by an extensive set of locally crafted silver tableware stored in one of the large mahogany chests.

Among the other Asian "treasures" displayed in the luxurious cabinet alongside the Chinese porcelain listed above was an ivory image of the Virgin Mary, two small ivory candlesticks, a black wooden tray from China, and another small round one of enameled metal.

As a Coda

This limited sample offers a revealing glimpse into the prominence of imported Asian goods within viceregal material culture. While it does not constitute an exhaustive study—such an undertaking would require a far broader selection—this focused analysis, spanning approximately a century, sheds light on the luxury objects present in the homes of the viceregal elite and their specific functions. Moreover, it underscores a notable contrast between New Spain and Peru: Households in New Spain contained significantly more Asian items than their Peruvian counterparts. This disparity is further corroborated by numerous other inventories examined over years of research. The most plausible explanation lies in New Spain's privileged access to Asian markets via the Manila–Acapulco Galleon trade, which facilitated a steady influx of Asian goods at a lower cost and with greater convenience compared to other parts of Spanish America.

In any case, the widespread presence of imported Asian objects in the residences of the colonial elite attests to their integral role in viceregal material culture. Beyond their practical uses, these objects functioned as markers of luxury, economic power, and refined taste, reinforcing social status and cultural aspirations. Their enduring appeal over more than a century of daily life in Latin America speaks to the deep entanglement of global trade networks with local expressions of wealth and prestige, shaping the visual and material landscapes of the Spanish American viceroyalties.

Notes

1. Gustavo Curiel, "El efímero caudal de una joven noble. Inventario y aprecio de los bienes de la marquesa Doña Teresa Francisca María de Guadalupe Retes Paz Vera (Ciudad de México, 1695)," in *Anales del Museo de América* 8 (2000): 65–101; and Gustavo Curiel, *Inventario y aprecio de los bienes de la testamentaria de don Antonio María Bucareli, Virrey de la Nueva España (1779): El ajuar de palacio y su librería* (Universidad Nacional Autónoma de México, Instituto de Investigaciones Estéticas, 2020).

2. On the marchioness of Torre Tagle, see Jorge F. Rivas Pérez, "A Stage for Wealth and Power in Eighteenth-Century Lima: The *Estrado* of Doña Rosa Juliana Sánchez de Tagle, First Marchioness of Torre Tagle," in *Intimate Interiors: Sex, Politics, and Material Culture in the Eighteenth-Century Bedroom and Boudoir*, ed. Tara Zanardi and Christopher M. S. Johns (Bloomsbury Visual Arts, 2023), 99–121; and Jorge F. Rivas Pérez, "Muebles que cuentan cosas. El ajuar doméstico de doña Rosa Juliana de Tagle, primera marquesa de Torre Tagle (Lima, 1762)," in *Casa y espacio doméstico en España y América (siglos XVI-XIX)*, ed. Margarita María Birriel Salcedo and Francisco García

González (Iberoamericana Editorial Vervuert, 2022), 269–97. For the original documents used for this work, see Archivo General de la Nación (hereafter AGN), Peru, Protocolos, Diego de Castro, 1689–1715, n° 309, "Inventario de bienes del Marqués de Castelldosrius," fols. 1047r–1064v; and AGN, Protocolos, Agustín Jerónimo Portalanza, 1761–1763, n° 871, "Inventario y tasación de bienes de doña Rosa Juliana Sánchez de Tagle, Marquesa de Torre Tagle," fols. 312r–343v.

3. On the marquis of Castelldosrius, see Núria Sala i Vila, "La escenificación del poder: El marqués de Castelldosrius, primer virrey Borbón del Perú (1707-1710)," in *Anuario de Estudios Americanos* 61, no. 1 (2004): 19–29.

4. AGN, Protocolos, Diego de Castro, 1689–1715, n° 309, "Inventario de bienes del Marqués de Castelldosrius," fols. 1047r–1064v.

5. Ibid., f. 1049v.

6. Ibid., f. 1047v.

7. Ibid., f. 1047r.

8. Ibid., f. 1053r.

9. Ibid.

10. Ibid., f. 1048r.

11. Curiel, *Inventario y aprecio,* 19–21.

12. Ibid., 22–36.

13. Ibid., 118.

14. Ibid., 34.

15. Ibid.

16. Ibid., 121.

17. Ibid., 130.

18. Ibid., 106.

19. Ibid., 130.

20. Ibid., 133. This and all translations are by the author. Yellow was one of the most common ground colors for Chinese embroidered bed hangings in the eighteenth century. For a closely related set of bed hangings from the 1770s, see Ebeltje Hartkamp-Jonxis, "Sleeping in Style: Chinese Embroidery and Other Bed Furnishings, 1770–1850," *Rijksmuseum Bulletin* 61, no. 2 (2013): 174.

21. Ibid.

22. Ibid., 44.

23. Ibid., 107.

24. Ibid.

25. Ibid., 108.

26. Ibid., 110.

27. Ibid.

28. Ibid.

29. Ibid., 108–12.

30. Ibid.

31. Ibid.

32. Ibid., 78.

33. Ibid.

34. Ibid. For surviving examples of related Chinese export silver filigree, see Maria Menshikova and Jet Pijzel-Dommisse, *Silver Wonders from the East: Filigree of the Tsars* (Waanders Uitgevers, 2006).

35. Ibid., 79.

36. Ibid., 113.

37. Curiel, "El efímero caudal," 65–69.

38. Ibid., 81.

39. Ibid., 84.

40. Ibid., 87.

41. For more on the estrado, see Sofía Rodríguez Bernis et al., *Mueble español, estrado y dormitorio* (MEAC, 1990); María del Pilar López Pérez, *En torno al estrado: cajas de uso cotidiano en Santafé de Bogotá, siglos XVI al XVIII; arcas, arcaces, arquillas, arquetas, arcones, baúles, cajillas, cajones, cofres, petacas, escritorios y papeleras* (Museo Nacional de Colombia, 1996); and Jorge F. Rivas Pérez, "Spanish Magnificence," in *Art and Empire: The Golden Age of Spain*, ed. Michael Brown (San Diego Museum of Art, 2019), 111–26.

42. Ibid., 81–83.

43. Ibid.

44. Ibid., 82.

45. Ibid., 90.

46. Ibid.

47. Ibid.

48. Ibid.

49. Ibid., 89.

50. Ibid., 71–72.

51. Ibid., 85.

52. Ibid., 85–86.

53. Ibid., 73.

54. For a biographical profile of the marchioness, see Rivas Pérez, "A Stage," 101–4.

55. "Inventario y tasación."

56. Ibid., f. 341r.

57. For the Torre Tagle estrado section, see ibid., 340v–341r.

58. For the bedroom inventory, see ibid., 338v–339r.

59. For the antechamber and cabinet inventories, see ibid., 338r.

"Brocades of Gold and Silver upon Silk": A Microhistory of a Set of Chinese Church Vestments for the Spanish Market

Karina H. Corrigan, Deputy Chief Curator and H. A. Crosby Forbes Curator of Asian Export Art, Peabody Essex Museum

Historians have primarily framed the global networks centered between Asia and the Americas during the early modern era as a "silk for silver" commodity exchange. For centuries, silk was one of the primary luxury goods exported from China to Manila and exchanged there for silver extracted from the astonishingly rich caches at Potosí, in what is today Bolivia. This microhistory of a large set of Catholic church vestments made from Chinese silk explores global circulation during the late sixteenth and early seventeenth centuries through an object-focused study of one component of that vast exchange (figs. 1, 2, and 10).[1] This visual, analytical, and archival exploration offers a focused way to better understand Habsburg Spain's connections to Asia and the world's first global network.

This set of vestments, composed of ten separate elements, was made from a bolt of silk woven in China at some point in the sixteenth or seventeenth centuries (likely between 1580 and 1640). The set currently includes two dalmatics (a long priest's tunic with broad, open sleeves), each with an accompanying collar, a chasuble (a priest's armless tunic), a stole (a textile band worn around the neck), two maniples (a shorter band worn on the left arm during Mass), a baldachin, and a fragment of unlined cut silk.[2] A chalice veil to cover the communion cup likely originally accompanied the other textiles, but given its small size, it is not

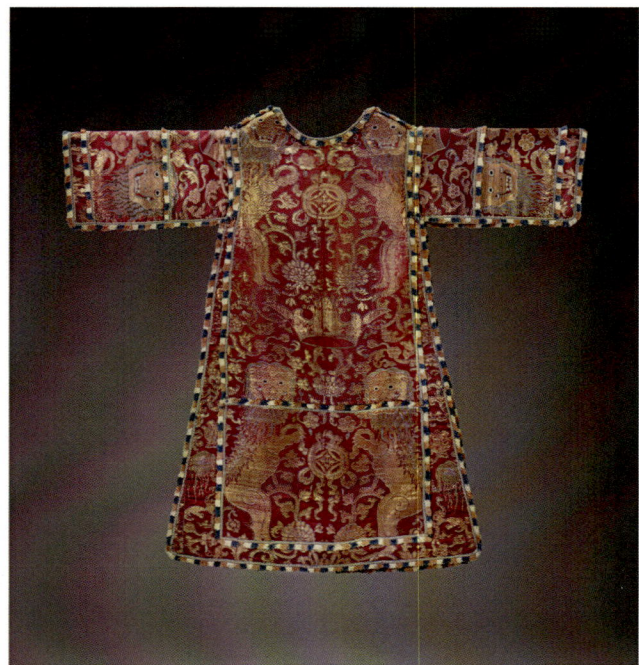

Fig. 1 Unknown artists, Dalmatic from a set of liturgical textiles, China, assembled in Spain, 1580s–1640s. Brocaded silk and cotton tape, lined with linen. Peabody Essex Museum, Salem: Museum purchase made possible in part by the Asian Export Art Visiting Committee and an anonymous donor, 2001, AE85947.3A.

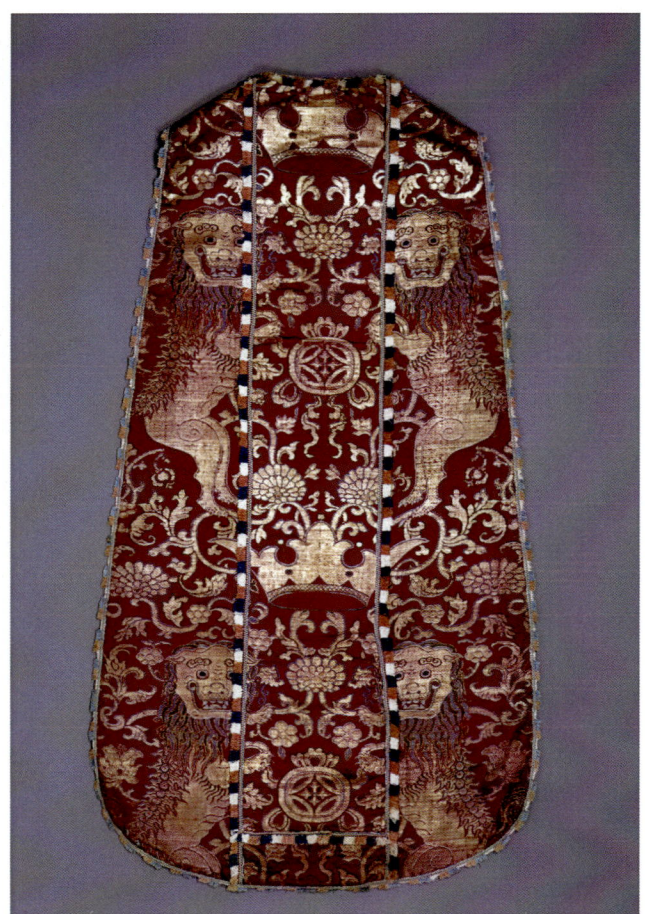

Fig. 2 Unknown artists, Chasuble from a set of liturgical textiles, China, assembled in Spain, 1580s–1640s. Brocaded silk and cotton tape, lined with linen. Peabody Essex Museum, Salem: Museum purchase made possible in part by the Asian Export Art Visiting Committee and an anonymous donor, 2001, AE85947.1.

surprising that the veil has not survived with the set. A private collector acquired the set in the 1920s from a small church in northern Spain, possibly Séron de Nágima in the province of Soria. Galerie Ruf, a textile dealer in Beckenried, Switzerland, purchased the group of vestments in the 1980s from the son of the collector and, finally, the Peabody Essex Museum (PEM) acquired the set from the gallery in 2001. This is all that we currently know about the set from the archival record, but there are other avenues to unpack the set's more than four-hundred-year history. A close analysis of the objects themselves can build an informative and interconnected narrative of the set's long journey from China to Spain and its connection to a larger global history.

Chinese silks were first introduced to the Iberian world via the land-based trade networks connecting East and West Asia. Spanish weavers began incorporating Chinese motifs in their designs as early as the 1300s.[3] But the quantities of Chinese silk that physically arrived in Europe were initially quite limited. More than one thousand patterned silks dating from the seventh to twelfth centuries are preserved in European church treasuries, but only one example is plausibly from China.[4] The initial stylistic impact of Chinese silks in Europe was likely more indirect. European weavers could have adapted their designs from imported Persian and other Central Asian textiles that had been, in turn, influenced by Chinese textiles.

Ocean-based trade dramatically changed the volume of Europeans' direct contact with Chinese silks, at least at the edges of the Spanish Crown's empire. In 1594, García Hurtado de Mendoza, fourth marquis of Cañete and viceroy of Peru, noted that in the viceroyalties, "Chinese merchandise is so cheap and Spanish goods so dear... a man can clothe his wife in Chinese silks for two hundred reales, whereas he could not provide her with clothing of Spanish silks with two hundred pesos."[5] The Spanish Crown initially banned the importation of Chinese silks to the viceroyalties in an attempt to protect the Spanish textile industries' new markets in the Americas. These edicts from the Crown were repeated (and often ignored) throughout the sixteenth, seventeenth, and eighteenth centuries. In 1718, after the latest ban was implemented, Baltasar de Zúñiga, viceroy of New Spain, refused to implement it, noting that residents in Mexico preferred the Chinese imports and their relative affordability.[6]

Silk was imported from China in a variety of forms and levels of quality—raw and floss silk, threads, dyed and undyed bolts of cloth, and woven, embroidered, and painted silks. In *Sucesos de las Islas Filipinas* (1609), Antonio de Morga, a former lieutenant governor of the Philippines, described the various kinds of Chinese silk imported into Manila:

Raw silk, in bundles, of the fineness of two strands, and other silk of inferior quality; fine untwisted silks, white and of all colours, in small skeins; quantities of smooth velvets, and velvet embroidered in all sorts of patterns, colours and fashions; and others, with the ground of gold and embroidered with the same; woven cloths and brocades of gold and silver upon silk of various colours and patterns, quantities of gold and silver thread in skeins, upon thread and upon silk, but all the spangles of gold and silver are false and upon paper; damask, satins, taffetas, and gorvarans (sic), *picotes* (sic), *and others cloths of all colours, some finer and better than others.*[7]

Elite households in the Americas utilized imported Asian silks for domestic furnishing textiles as well as for personal clothing.[8] But the Catholic Church was also a voracious consumer of imported Asian textiles for liturgical vestments and altar coverings. The earliest documented use of Chinese textiles for religious purposes in the Iberian world is in the 1521 inventory for King Manuel I of Portugal, who owned a vestment made of Chinese brocaded silk.[9] Archival records from the late sixteenth and seventeenth centuries document numerous examples of vestments constructed of Chinese silk and intended for churches in the viceroyalties and throughout Spain and Portugal. Pedro Martínez Buytrón, a priest who died in Mexico City in 1596, had a large collection of Chinese export silk vestments in his possession. Buytrón's estate inventory included a set of purple taffeta garments with a chasuble, a stole, and a maniple. Buytrón also owned a second set of vestments made of black damask silk with yellow damask borders (chasuble, stole, and maniple) as well as two blue and white taffeta silk hangings lined with blue linen and with green and red fringes.[10]

Priests in the viceroyalties seemed to have been early adopters of vestments made from Chinese silk, but the fashion extended to Spain. In 1616, *don* Diego Vásquez de Mercado, archbishop of Manila, sent his nephew don Pedro de Mercado Vásquez, a *regidor* (alderman) of Madrid, a set of Chinese silk church vestments that included dalmatics, a chasuble, and a stole.[11] Smaller Spanish villages also frequently received gifts from Asia as tribute or bequests from locals who had emigrated to the viceroyalties. Javier Pescador's microhistory of a Basque region in northern Spain outlines the sustained donations of Asian goods from expatriates throughout the seventeenth and eighteenth centuries to small parishes (and family members) in the region.[12]

The earliest documented and surviving set of Chinese export silk vestments is preserved in Portugal. The set was ordered in Macau in 1634 by a "very rich and honored Chinese mandarin esteemed for his virtue," named Francisco Carvalho Aranha, and sent to the brotherhood of Bom Jesus de São Marcos at the church of Santa Cruz (Braga).[13] The set included two chasubles, two dalmatics, and a cope (a priest's wide cape) as well as three altar frontals, a cross cover, a pulpit fall, and a baldachin. Each of the components in the set, made of cream satin silk and crimson velvet silk, was elaborately embroidered with gold and silver thread in a stylized pattern of intertwining vines. Some of the components also incorporate the symbol of the brotherhood. Likely guided by the patron, the tailors and embroiderers who assembled the set in China worked with a clear understanding of the desired forms and ornamentation of these European-style religious textiles.

Unlike Aranha's fully assembled gift to the brotherhood of Bom Jesus, the set on which this study is based was assembled in Spain using a bolt of imported Chinese silk.[14] Antonio de Morga's description of "brocades of gold and silver upon silk of various colours and patterns" best describes this long and sumptuous bolt. Woven in China in the late sixteenth or early seventeenth century, this textile has a complicated weave structure and would have been an exceptionally expensive silk when first commissioned and produced.[15]

All woven textiles are composed of warp and weft threads. Warp threads run vertically and are the fixed threads that attach to a loom during weaving. Weft threads cross over and under the warps in different configurations to create a woven textile. Compound textiles such as this example are created on large and complex drawlooms with multiple shafts manipulated by the weavers. Composed of a crimson red silk satin warp with wefts in blue, green, and white silk, the weaver has augmented the design with discontinuous

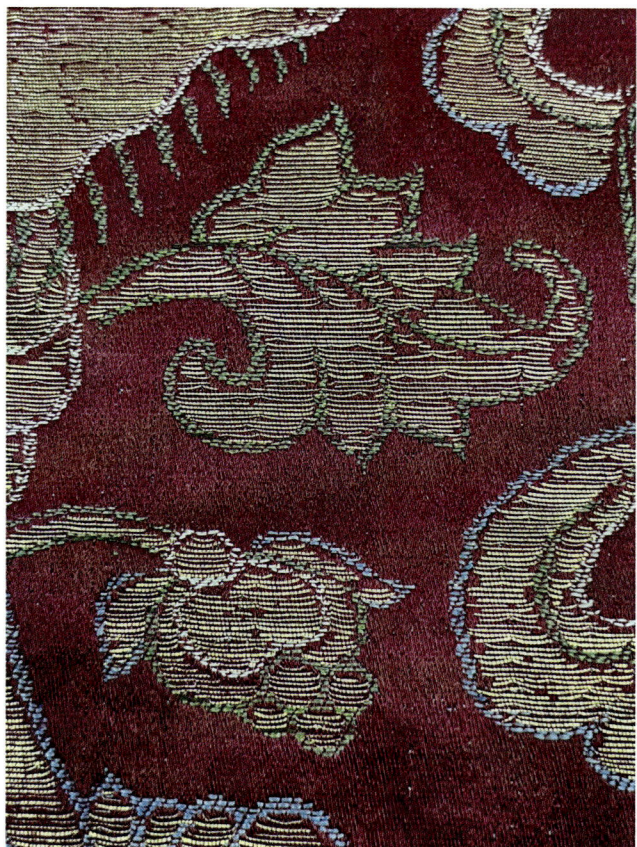

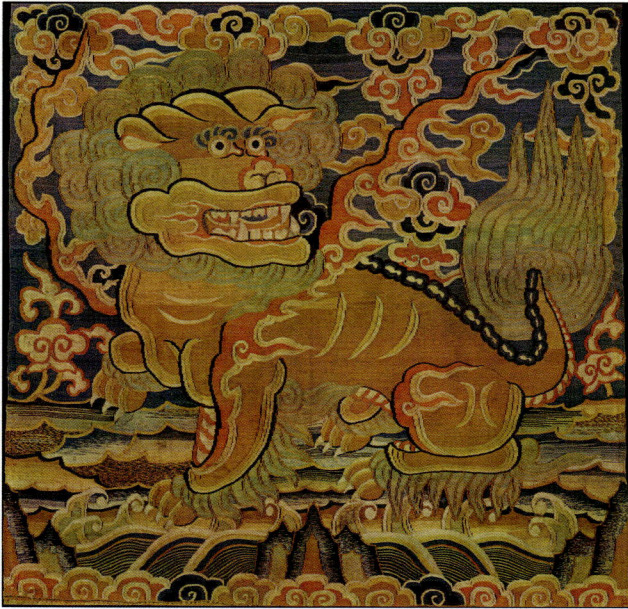

Fig. 4 Unknown artists, Rank Badge with Lion, China, 1400s. Silk and metallic-thread tapestry (*kesi*), 15½ × 14½ in. (39.4 × 36.8 cm). The Metropolitan Museum of Art, Purchase, Mr. and Mrs. C. Y. Chen and Anonymous Gifts, 1988, 1988.154.2.

Fig. 3 Unknown artists, detail of Chinese silk in fig. 1, showing the crimson satin ground and the discontinuous gilded paper floats on a length of silk used to create a set of liturgical textiles.

supplementary gilded paper wefts brocaded into the textile (fig. 3). Unlike the woven elements of the design, the black eyes of the lions dispersed throughout the design are painted onto the textile.

The creators of this Chinese brocaded silk wove a pattern with a 28½ inch repeat that features a pair of guardian or rampant lions among scrolling foliage and surmounted by a European crown. This striking combination of motifs is derived from Chinese domestic textiles and European—likely Spanish or Italian—silks imported into China. The guardian lions that dominate the design bear a close resemblance to those found on textiles

made for Chinese officials, such as a tapestry woven rank badge from the fifteenth century (fig. 4).

As early as the fourteenth century, Chinese imperial decrees outlined sumptuary laws for officials of various ranks. To identify their rank, Chinese civil and military officials wore woven or embroidered badges on the front and back of their robes. Within the elaborate hierarchies of power in late Ming imperial China, there were more than twenty different kinds of badges decorated with animals to identify an official's rank. First and second rank military officials typically wore a badge ornamented with a lion.[16] The lions in both the rank badge and the bolt of cloth feature wide eyes, open toothy grins, and bushy green tails typical of those found on Chinese textiles from the late Ming dynasty.

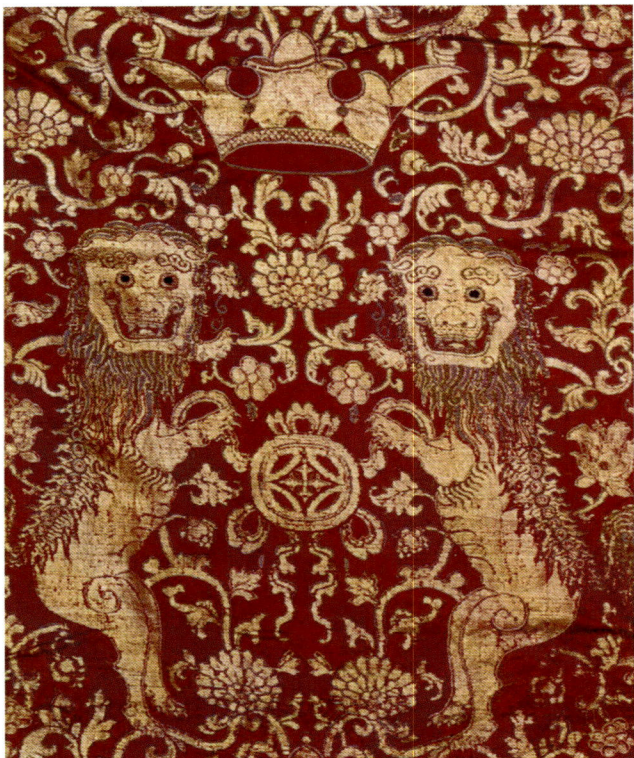

Fig. 5 Unknown artists, detail of guardian lions and crown motifs in Chinese silk on the underside of the baldachin in fig. 10.

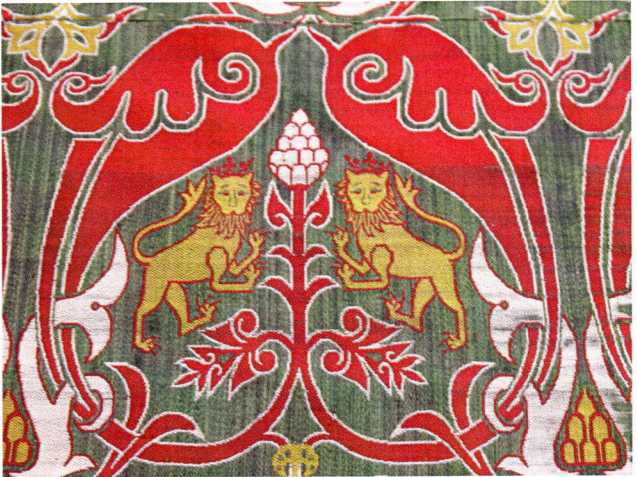

Fig. 6 Unknown artists, Fragment (detail), Granada, Spain, 1400s. Brocaded silk, 51 × 31¼ in. (129.5 × 79.4 cm). The Metropolitan Museum of Art, Rogers Fund, 1920, 20.94.1.

While the rank badge features only one lion, the silk bolt features pairs of guardian lions chasing a brocaded ball, a familiar motif in Chinese iconography that was often regarded as a symbol of happiness (fig. 5).

The charming creatures on the silk bolt are not an exclusively Chinese element—they also recall rampant lions, a symbol of nobility in European heraldry. The Chinese weavers may have used Spanish and Italian lampas silks imported to China in the sixteenth and seventeenth centuries as design sources for these rampant lions. A fifteenth-century Spanish lampas silk features a pair of crowned and confronting lions in the midst of scrolling foliage (fig. 6). The undulating plant forms and whimsical animals within this design relate to earlier

textiles produced in Spain under the Nasrid dynasty, who ruled the Iberian Peninsula prior to the Christian conquest in 1492. Fragments of silk in this design are preserved in multiple public collections, including at least one that was formerly part of a chasuble.[17] The design of a late-sixteenth- or early-seventeenth-century Italian or Spanish silk bears an even closer relationship to the Chinese silk bolt (fig. 7).[18] These fragments are examples of the kinds of European textiles that could have been sent to China to serve as design sources for the Chinese weavers.

The Chinese silk's design repeat also includes a large and distinctly European crown floating above the heads of the guardian lions. The pointed crown, primarily composed of gilded paper, has a brim with a crosshatched pattern in green, blue, and gold and is augmented with two round green jewels encircled in blue. The scrolling vines undulating throughout the background are interspersed with three

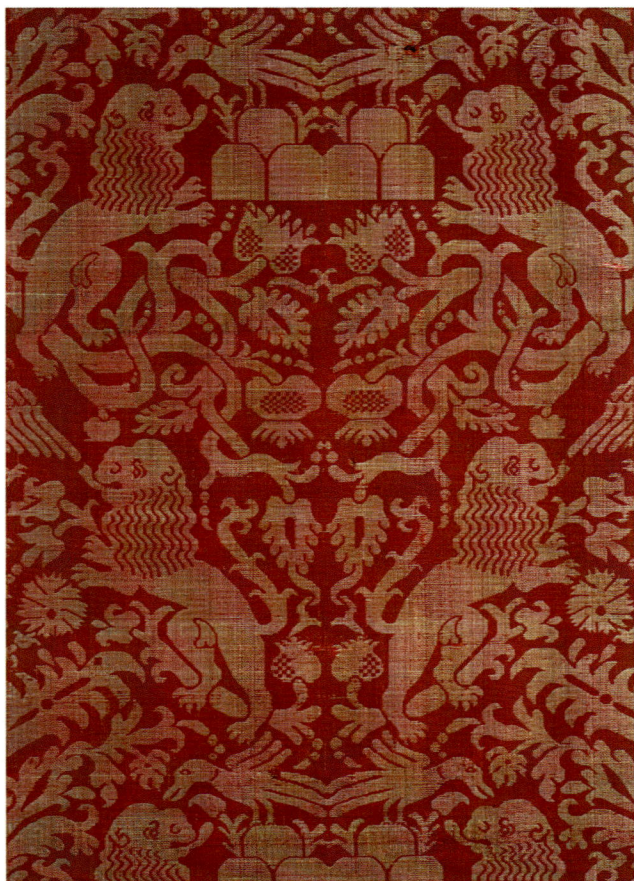

Fig. 7 Unknown artists, Fragment (detail), Italian or Spanish, late 1500s–early 1600s. Lampas silk, 30⅞ × 22¾ in. (78.4 × 57.8 cm). Art Institute of Chicago, purchased with funds provided by Mr. and Mrs. John V. Farwell III, 1973.308.

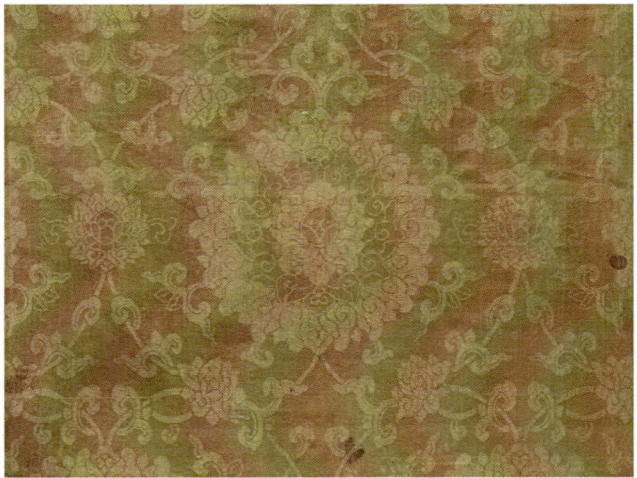

Fig. 8 Unknown artists, Fragment (detail), China, 1500s–early 1600s. Damask silk, 25¼ × 23 in. (64.1 × 58.4 cm). The Metropolitan Museum of Art, Rogers Fund, 1909, 09.50.960.

different types of flowers—one type is likely a chrysanthemum, a motif found frequently on Chinese damask silks made for the domestic market (fig. 8).[19] All of these textile designs highlight how weavers in multiple locations around the globe were part of a robust international exchange of design motifs that spanned centuries.[20]

The combination of Asian and European motifs incorporated into the pattern for the PEM silk helps identify it as Chinese, but there are other distinguishing features that support a Chinese attribution. One of the most reliable ways to identify a Chinese

textile—particularly a simple weave without a design or further embellishment—is the width of the textile. Selvage-to-selvage widths of Chinese silks are typically much wider than their European counterparts (26 to 31 inches wide vs. 19½ to 23 inches wide).[21] Many Chinese silks also have selvages woven in a contrasting color. Yet another distinguishing feature of many Chinese silks is the presence of sequential holes in the selvages. These holes are evidence of a pair of crossed rods—sometimes called temple rods—used by weavers to help maintain a symmetrical fabric width during weaving. Chinese silks also have a soft, clinging "hand" that is the result of mechanical calendering.[22] The selvage-to-selvage width of the bolt of silk used to create PEM's set of vestments is approximately 28 inches. The selvage edges—only visible now on the surviving unlined silk fragment—are white. Also visible on the fragment, just inside the selvage edge, is a thin continuous line of yellow satin weave silk. Occasionally visible at the seams of different components of the set, these yellow silk lines presumably framed the edges of the fabric and would have aided tailors in matching up seams.

Early Chinese silks incorporating European motifs have traditionally been attributed to weavers in Macau. This is likely based on the assumption that the weavers would have needed direct contact with foreign agents to produce textiles incorporating European motifs, but there is limited evidence that Macau was an early center for silk weaving in China. Export ceramic production in the sixteenth and seventeenth centuries can serve as a useful model for speculating on other plausible locations for the production of these early export silks. Potters in Jingdezhen during the late Ming dynasty successfully produced and exported customized ceramics incorporating global motifs despite being more than three hundred miles from the Chinese coastline. Using this customized porcelain production as a model, could these early export silks have been woven in one of a variety of silk production centers in southern China? Suzhou and Hangzhou produced high-quality silk for imperial and regional use during the late Ming dynasty, and Guangdong and Fujian provinces were also major silk production centers. Given that Hokkien merchants controlled the early Chinese junk trade from Fujian to Manila, perhaps the coastal cities of Fuzhou and Quanzhou could be plausible production centers for the complex silks exported to the Philippines during the sixteenth and

seventeenth centuries. Quanzhou, in particular, was known during the Ming dynasty for pattern weave silks and silks incorporating gold and silk thread.[23] We can perhaps begin to test this assumption by conducting analysis of dyestuffs and other materials used in these textiles and reviewing their weave structures.

Xian Zhang from History Echoes Analytical Services is an analytical chemist with experience in natural dyestuffs, who studied several samples from the unlined fragment in PEM's set. Her testing provides analytical information on the silk and reinforces the assertion that the textile was made in China. The crimson red silk that dominates the textile was dyed with lac, a traditional dye source used throughout Asia that is derived from the lac insect.[24] The green silk used for the bushy tails of the lions and as a border for some of the motifs was dyed with indigo (blue) and pagoda tree buds (yellow). Pagoda trees (*Styphnolobium japonicum*) are native to central and northern China and Korea. The gilded strips selectively added throughout the textile are composed of a thin sheet of gold foil attached with a mixture of animal glue, kaolin clay, and laterite to a compound paper substrate. The foil layer is composed of 70 percent gold, 17 percent silver, and other minor elements, an alloy that is consistent with Chinese gold foil samples found on ancient textiles.[25] Despite what Antonio de Morga wrote about these kinds of textiles in 1609, not "all the spangles of gold and silver are **false** and upon paper."[26]

Weavers have been incorporating paper covered in gold foil into Chinese textiles for more than two thousand years.[27] An English visitor to Hong Kong in the 1870s watched gold foil being produced while touring an alley near the street for silk embroiderers. He noted:

> *Several long, and narrow sheets of paper having been coated with a mixture of earth and glue are, in the next instance, covered either with gold, or silver leaf. In order that a bright, glossy appearance may be imparted to these sheets of paper... men rub them, heavily, from one end to the other, with pieces of crystal... [attached] to the ends of bamboo rods... the gilded, or silvered sheets of paper are [then]... cut, by means of large knives, into very thin strips.*[28]

Once woven, this sumptuous bolt of lightweight, supple, and vibrantly colored silk would have been carefully packed and shipped from southern China to Manila. Beginning in the 1570s, Hokkien merchants from Fujian dominated the Chinese junk trade in Southeast and East Asia. Junks traveled from ports along the Fujian coastline—Quanzhou and Xiamen—as well as from Guangzhou and Macao—on vessels that typically weighed 350 tons and carried a crew of between two and four hundred men. Some of the largest had crews of close to five hundred.[29] The journey from China to Manila typically took between fifteen and twenty days.

In 1589, eighty-eight Chinese junks were licensed for international maritime trade. By 1597, the licensed junks had increased to 137. Roughly half of those Chinese vessels were engaged with direct trade between Fujian and Manila.[30] Smuggling was rampant, so it is difficult to pinpoint the precise numbers of junks trading with the Philippines, but it is estimated that between twenty and forty junks visited Manila annually between the late 1570s and the early 1640s. Silk made up the bulk of their cargoes, which the Hokkien merchants sold for as much South American silver as they could acquire, annually sending as much as 150 tons of silver back to China. Jerónimo de Salazar y Salcedo reported to the king in 1599 that the profits to be made on imported Chinese silk were as high as 400 percent.[31]

Hokkien merchants also resided long-term in Manila and ran the hundreds of retail shops in the Parián market just outside the walls of the city. But unlike the many Chinese silks offered in the market, this sumptuous bolt was likely a special commission and would not have been offered for retail sale. Chinese textile merchants were particularly skilled at folding and rolling textiles to the specifications of buyers to maximize the quantities of silk that could be packed. Once loaded into the hold of a galleon for the long journey across the Pacific Ocean from Manila to Acapulco, this special commission would have been transshipped across Mexico to Veracruz for reshipment and delivery in Seville. This bolt was likely commissioned for a high-ranking priest—either as a special commission he made for himself or as a gift from a colleague or family member. When a canon was

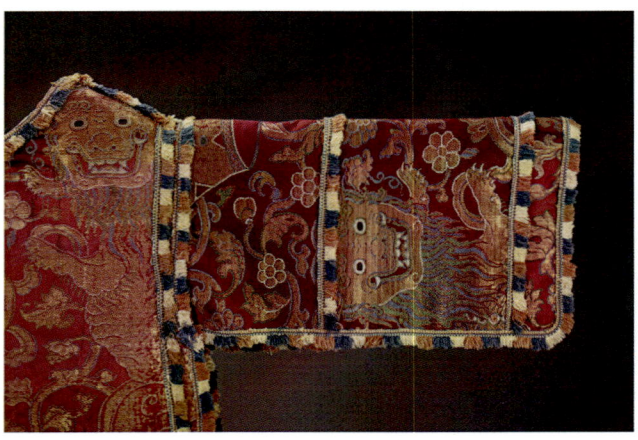

Fig. 9 Unknown artists, Dalmatic (detail) from a set of liturgical textiles, China, assembled in Spain, 1580s–1640s. Brocaded silk and cotton tape, lined with linen. Peabody Essex Museum, Salem: Museum purchase made possible in part by the Asian Export Art Visiting Committee and an anonymous donor, 2001, AE85947.3AB.

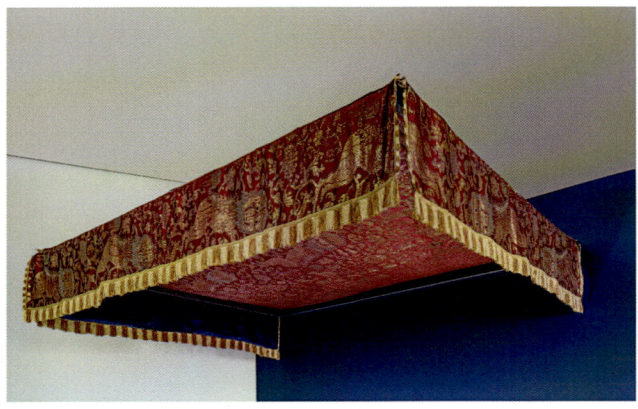

Fig. 10 Unknown artists, Baldachin from a set of liturgical textiles, China, assembled in Spain, 1580s–1640s. Brocaded silk and cotton tape, lined with linen. Peabody Essex Museum, Salem: Museum purchase made possible in part by the Asian Export Art Visiting Committee and an anonymous donor, 2001, AE85947.4.

appointed and received his prebend—the portion of the cathedral's revenue allotted to a senior member of the church—it was typical for him to order a new set of vestments. At the cathedral in Huesca, Spain, for example, it was required that a newly appointed bishop present a chasuble, tunic, tunicle, two dalmatics, and three copes to the cathedral within three years of his appointment. These vestments often reverted to a cathedral's collection upon a bishop's death, a practice that accounts for the diversity of splendid textiles preserved within Spanish church treasuries to this day.[32]

The Spanish tailors who created this set of vestments lavishly used the imported silk bolt on the most significant and visible components of the set—the underside of the baldachin and the backs of the dalmatics and chasuble. But they also ensured the maximum use of this precious textile by thriftily piecing together small fragments of the silk to create the maniples

and stole. The tailors also incorporated locally made textiles for both decorative and functional purposes when stitching the components together. Each piece is decoratively augmented with Spanish tape woven in red, white, and blue cotton (fig. 9). European tailors typically used this type of tape to reinforce and cover the seams of the narrow widths of European silks used on many church vestments. Given the wider width of Chinese silk, the tape on the PEM vestments is used more decoratively, often stitched on top of a single length of silk, rather than necessarily covering a seam.[33] Various elements of the set were also lined with European linen to provide support for the especially thin and supple Chinese silk.

The baldachin is perhaps the most unusual component of the set to survive (fig 10). Baldachins are architectural canopies that mark and enclose a space in a religious, civic, or domestic environment. As noted in Rivas's essay in this volume, textile canopies were sometimes hung above a

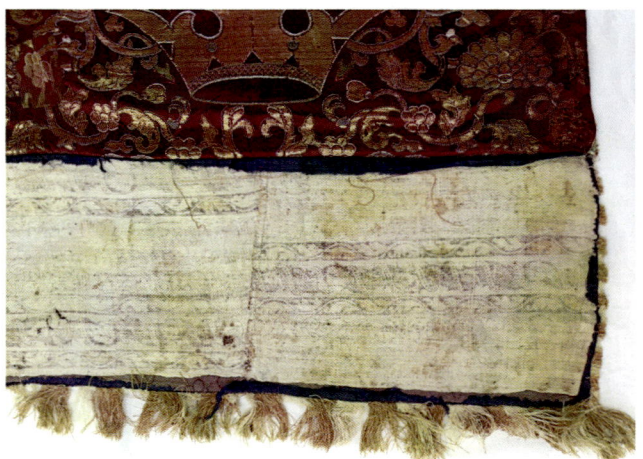

Fig. 11 Unknown artists, Inner side panel of the baldachin in fig. 10 (detail), showing fragmentary evidence of the blue silk lining and one of the European linens used to line and support the baldachin's side panels.

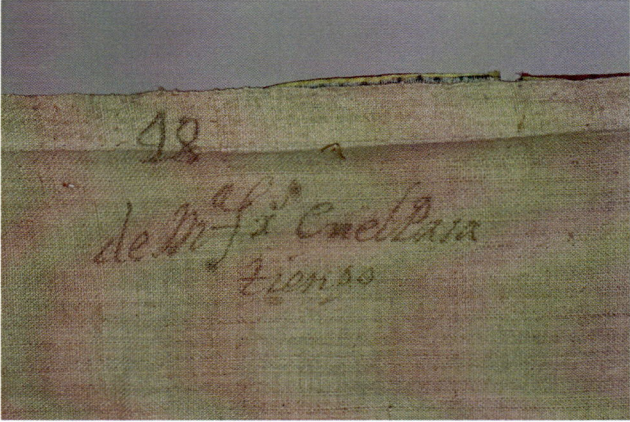

Fig. 12 Unknown artists, detail of ink inscription on linen lining of baldachin in fig. 10

throne or chair in the palaces and homes of the elite. The 1729 inventory of Carlos Bermúdez de Castro, archbishop of Manila, included a baldachin, which he used to display artworks.[34] Baldachins used religiously typically hang above an altar or devotional image, suspended from above or supported on slender columns. Encountered on its own, this baldachin could have been made for either a domestic or religious setting, but its survival with accompanying religious garments made from the same Chinese silk indicates that it was likely designed to be used religiously.

Textile panels hang from the front and sides of the canopy, but not the back, indicating that the baldachin was likely suspended over an altarpiece against a wall.[35] Iron rings stitched to the front corners of the baldachin once accommodated chains to suspend the canopy from the ceiling. Chinese silk fully lines the underside of the canopy roof so

that during prayer or a service, a viewer gazed up at the glittering lengths of the silk's beautiful design. The baldachin's sixty-inch depth is greater than two widths of the Chinese silk, so the tailors carefully stitched a narrow length of the same silk between the two full widths that run from proper left to right underneath the canopy.

The narrow panels that hang from the canopy also feature sections of silk on the exterior, but the tailors economized by using a Chinese plain weave blue silk on the inside of the hanging panels. When the Peabody Essex Museum acquired the set, this blue silk lining survived only as fragmentary evidence, revealing that the tailors had sandwiched a stabilizing linen lining between the brocaded and blue silks for greater structure (fig. 11). When the canopy was originally in use, the lining would never have been visible. An inscription in ink preserved on the lining— "48 de M^a Fr^s en el pasatienpo"—offers an enigmatic but tantalizing clue to the set's provenance (fig. 12). The "48" is possibly an inventory number for the church's collection of vestments. Since M^a is typically

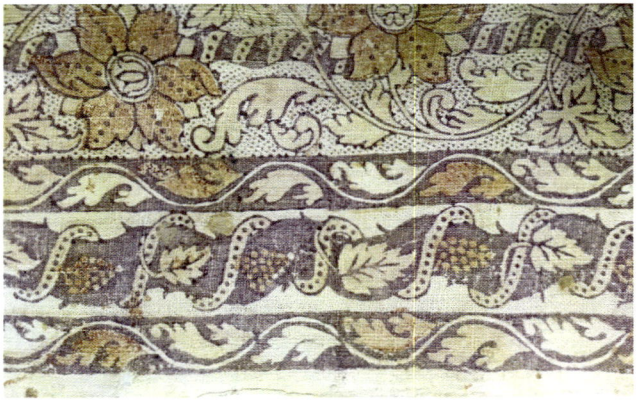

Fig. 13 Unknown artists, Fragment (detail) of European block printed linen used to line and support the sides of the baldachin in fig. 10.

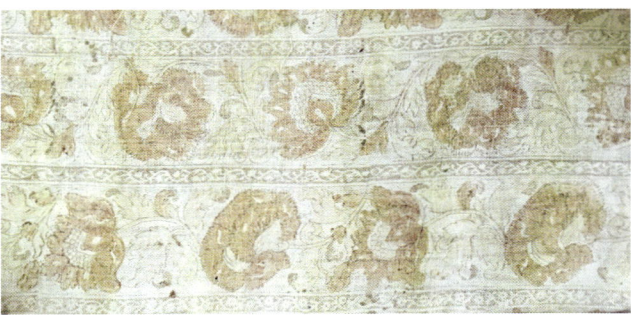

Fig. 14 Unknown artists, Fragment (detail) of European block printed linen used to line and support the sides of the baldachin in fig. 10.

shorthand for Maria, and Fr^s could be an abbreviation for Francisca, could this inscription document the participation of a female donor or seamstress in the creation of the set?[36]

The linen lining has an additional secret. While the front and proper right side panels were lined with lengths of plain linen, the tailors frugally recycled two different kinds of European block printed linen to line the proper left side panel (figs. 13 and 14).[37] Printed with a mordant dye using madder root, the simple designs on these recycled panels were inspired by more sophisticated imported Indian cottons (fig. 15).[38] Hiding in plain sight, these humble (and now rare) European linen fragments are another tangible link to the global network of exchange in textiles during this period.

Sets of vestments all made from the same fabric created a cohesive ensemble for feast days. The deep crimson red of the silk used for this set of vestments may indicate that it was used for a specific feast day or perhaps even during Holy Week, leading up to the

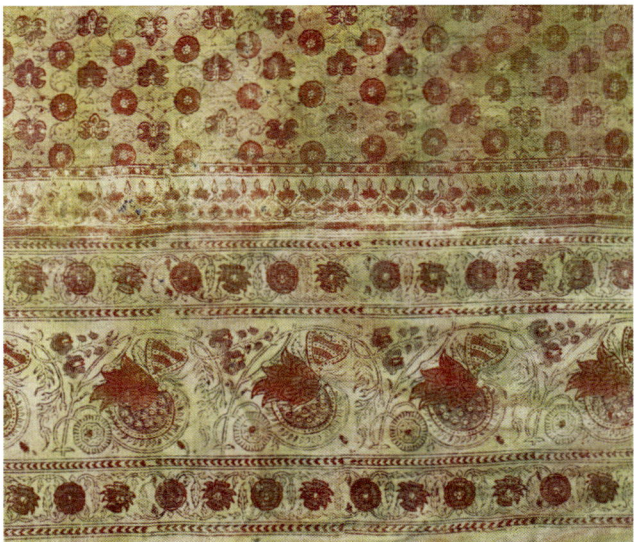

Fig. 15 Unknown artist, Fragment (detail), India, 1600s–1700s. Block-printed, mordant-dyed, and painted cotton. Victoria & Albert Museum, London, 1337-1888.

celebration of Easter. The satin weave of the silk and the gilded paper floats would have undoubtedly sparkled brilliantly by candlelight during Mass.[39] Preserved as a set for over four centuries, this rare group of liturgical textiles is a tangible link to the early global network of exchange between China, the Philippines, Mexico, and Spain and the power and wealth of the Catholic Church in this period.

The author would like to thank Lilly Barrientos, Martina D'Amato, Marta Fodor,

Deborah Kraak, Lucy Montgomery, Samuel Frédéric Luterbacher, J. David O'Ryan, Amelia Peck, Mei Mei Rado, Jorge Rivas, Kathryn Santner, Kathryn Smith, Petra Slinkard, William R. Sargent, Kathy Tarantola, Deirdre Windsor, Xian Zhang, and Zhao Feng for their assistance with this article.

Notes

1. The discipline of microhistory, first developed in the 1970s by Italian historians working with a cache of Catholic Church documents, is "based on the reduction of the scale of observation, on a microscopic analysis, and on intensive study of the documentary material." Giovanni Levi, "On Microhistory," in *New Perspectives on Historical Writing*, ed. Peter Burke (Pennsylvania State University Press, 1992), 99.

2. Not illustrated here are the collars for the dalmatics (AE85947.3B and AE85947.4B), the maniples (AE85947.5 and AE85947.6), the stole (AE85947.7), and the fragment (AE85947.8) from the set. The surviving fragment had previously been stitched and lined with plain blue silk.

3. Florence Lewis May, *Silk Textiles of Spain: Eighth to Fifteenth Century* (Hispanic Society, 1957), 119, 175–77.

4. Anna Maria Muthesius, "The Impact of the Mediterranean Silk Trade on Western Europe Before 1200 A.D.," in *Textiles in Trade: Proceedings of the Textile Society of America Biennial Symposium, September 14–16, 1990* (Textile Society of America, 1990), 129.

5. At the time, two hundred reales was worth about twenty-five pesos. Quoted in Woodrow Wilson Borah, *Early Colonial Trade and Navigation Between Mexico and Peru* (University of California Press, 1954), 122.

6. Arturo Giraldez, *The Age of Trade: The Manila Galleon and the Dawn of the Global Economy* (Rowman & Littlefield, 2015), 153.

7. Translated by and quoted in Teresa Canepa, *Silk, Porcelain and Lacquer: China and Japan and Their Trade with Western Europe and the New World, 1500–1644* (Paul Holberton Publishing, 2016), 70. A gorgoran is a type of heavy East Indian silk cloth with stripes woven in two different weave structures. Florence Montgomery, *Textiles in America 1650–1870* (W. W. Norton & Company, 1984), 247. A picot refers to a series of small loops along the edge of a piece of fabric.

8. See Rivas's essay in this volume for details on some domestic consumption. Chinese silks dominated the market in the viceroyalties, but elites also combined Castilian, Italian, and even locally produced silks into their households and wardrobes. For more on those breakdowns, see José L. Gasch-Tomás, "The Manila Galleon and the Reception of Chinese Silk in New Spain, c. 1550–1650," in *Threads of Global Desire: Silk in the Pre-Modern World*, vol. 1, ed. Dagmar Schäfer, Giorgio Riello, and Luca Molà (Pasold Studies in Textile, Dress and Fashion History, 2018), 259–60.

9. "Huũs esparamentos doratoreo de brocado da China," cited in Maria João Ferreira, "Chasuble C-4," in *Encompassing the Globe: Portugal and the World in the 16th and 17th Centuries Reference Catalogue*, vol. 2, ed. Jay Levinson (Arthur M. Sackler Gallery, 2007), 140.

10. Archivo General de las Notarías del DF, Mexico City, Notario: Andrés Moreno (374), vol. 2464, 105–6, cited in José Luis Gasch-Tomás, "Asian Silk, Porcelain and Material Culture in the Definition of Mexican and Andalusian Elites, c. 1565–1630," in *Global Goods and the Spanish Empire, 1492–1824: Circulation, Resistance and Diversity*, ed. Bethany Aram and Bartolomé Yun-Casalilla (Palgrave Macmillan, 2014), 171. See footnote 27 for a transcription of all the textiles in the priest's estate.

11. Archivo General de Indias (hereafter AGI), Seville, Contratación 1830, f. 850–52 and Contratación 1834, f. 1052–55, cited in José L. Gasch-Tomás, *The Atlantic World and the Manila Galleons: Circulation, Market, and Consumption of Asian Goods in the Spanish Empire, 1565–1650* (Brill, 2019), 29–30.

12. Javier Pescador, *The New World Inside a Basque Village: The Oiartzun Valley and Its Atlantic Emigrants, 1550–1800*, The Basque Series (University of Nevada, 2003), 37–38, 104. Thank you to Samuel Luterbacher for directing me to this fascinating study.

13. Only a portion of the set survives. Ferreira, "Chasuble," 140. See vol. 1, 284–85 for color illustrations.

14. A related set of vestments, now dispersed, was made from a similarly long bolt of Chinese export silk with gilt paper floats woven between the 1580s and the 1640s. That silk bolt's design incorporates Augustinian or Habsburg double-headed eagle motifs rendered in blue, yellow, and white silk on a red satin ground. Textile fragments from this large set survive in multiple public collections. See Royal Ontario Museum for a magnificent cope (973.422), the Rijksmuseum for a fragment of a chasuble (BK-1997-13), and the Victoria & Albert Museum for multiple fragments in the same design (T.215-1910, T.217-1910, and T.169-1929).

15. Elena Phipps, *Looking at Textiles: A Guide to Technical Terms* (J. Paul Getty Museum, 2011), 47; Florence Montgomery, *Textiles in America*, 1984, 274–75.

16. Chen Juanjuan and Huang Nengfu, "Silk Fabrics of the Ming Dynasty," in *Chinese Silks*, ed. Dieter Kuhn (Yale University Press, 2012), 418–20.

17. See also other textile fragments in variants of this pattern in the collection of The Metropolitan Museum of Art (11.23, 25.120.453, and 1981.372).

18. Fragments of this red ground silk survive in the collections of The Metropolitan Museum of Art (1971.240, 1972.66.1a, 1972.66.1b, and 1972.66.1c), Art Institute of Chicago (1973.308), Denver Art Museum (1972.131a-b) and Musée du Cinquantenaire in Brussels. A valance woven in this silk also incorporates a crowned double-headed eagle between the lions. See 1972.66.6 at The Metropolitan Museum of Art and a fragment at Cora Ginsburg LLC. For more information on the pattern's history and an illustration of a green ground version, see William DeGregorio and Michele Majer, *Cora Ginsburg Catalog 2014* (Cora Ginsburg LLC, 2014), 4–5. I thank Martina D'Amato for her insights on these textiles.

19. Canepa, *Silk, Porcelain and Lacquer*, 90.

20. For related discussions on the global exchange of Asian and European design motifs during this period, see Elena Phipps, "The Iberian Globe: Textile Traditions and

Trade in Latin America," and Maria João Pacheco Ferreira, "Chinese Textiles for Portuguese Tastes," in *Interwoven Globe: The Worldwide Textile Trade, 1500–1800*, ed. Amelia Peck (The Metropolitan Museum of Art, 2013), 28–55.

21. Leanna Lee-Whitman, "The Silk Trade: Chinese Silks and the British East India Company," *Winterthur Portfolio* 17, no. 1 (1982): 23–24.

22. Whitman, "The Silk Trade," 25. See also Aileen Ryan Earnest, "Trade and Commerce on the Pacific Coast in the Eighteenth Century: A Look at Some Chinese Silks of the Mission Period," in *Imported and Domestic Textiles in Eighteenth-Century America*, ed. Patricia Fiske (The Textile Museum, 1975), 13.

23. Chen and Huang, "Silk Fabrics of the Ming Dynasty," 374–75.

24. Xian Zhang conducted scanning electron microscopy, energy dispersive spectroscopy (SEM-EDS), and high-performance liquid chromatography with diode array detector and mass spectrometry (HPLC-DAD-MS) on the samples. The results are summarized in History Echoes Analytical Services LLC's report *25AS01*, February 3, 2025, Peabody Essex Museum object files for AE85947.8

25. For more on Chinese gold foil analysis, see J. Yang, J. Zhang and J. Jiang, "The Production Process of the Tang Dynasty Gold Thread Unearthed from the Underground Palace of Famen Temple," *Kaogu* (Archaeology) 2 (2013): 97–104; and Y. Ma, "Microstructure and Composition Analysis of the Gold Thread in the Thangka and the Plaque with the Inscription 'Long Live Emperor Kangxi' Written by Him During the Qianlong Period of the Qing Dynasty in the Palace Museum," *The*

9th Annual Conference of Chinese Conservation Society (2017): 469–78.

26. Canepa, *Silk, Porcelain and Lacquer*, 70. Emphasis added.

27. For an exploration of ancient gold foil weaving, see Zhao Feng, "Silks in the Song, Liao, Western Xia, and Jin Dynasties," in *Chinese Silks*, 282–86.

28. John Henry Gray, *Walks in the City of Canton* (De Souza & Company, 1875), 290.

29. Giraldez, *The Age of Trade*, 161.

30. James K. Chin, "The Junk Trade and Hokkien Merchant Networks in Maritime Asia, 1570–1760," in *Picturing Commerce in and from the East Asian Maritime Circuit, 1550–1800*, ed. Tamara H. Bentley (Amsterdam University Press, 2019), 82.

31. Letters from the royal fiscal to the king by Jerónimo de Salazar y Salcedo (Manila, July 21, 1599) cited in Chin, "The Junk Trade," 91.

32. May, *Silk Textiles*, 119–20.

33. Note the related tape on the chasuble in figure 2 and a seventeenth-century Portuguese chasuble incorporating Safavid and European lampas silks in the Museu Abadede Baçal, Bragança [1063A], illustrated in *Christianity in Asia: Sacred Art and Visual Splendour*, ed. Alan Chong (Asian Civilisations Museum, 2016), 23.

34. AGI Contaduría, 1283, f. 26v–r. I thank Kathryn Santner for bringing this reference to my attention.

35. The surviving fragment (AE85947.8) bears evidence of blue silk lining and stitching and

may have once hung from the back of the baldachin.

36. I thank Kathryn Santner for deciphering the inscription and offering her insights on its possible meaning.

37. Prior to the baldachin's installation in the Sean M. Healey Gallery of Asian Export Art in 2019, textile conservator Deirdre Windsor developed an innovative framework to safely suspend and display it in the gallery. During the preparatory conservation, PEM opted to replicate the original blue silk lining on the side panels, which now obscures the linen lining including the block printed European linen fragments. Unlike the recycled fragments, the plain linen and tape used to line the other sides and the top of the canopy were likely new when the baldachin was first assembled.

38. See related eighteenth-century European examples in The Metropolitan Museum's collections (26.265.72 and 26.238.8). Thank you to Amelia Peck for facilitating a study day in 2018 at the Antonio Ratti Textile Center at The Metropolitan Museum of Art to research these fragments. For more on the relationship between utilitarian Indian and European block-printed textiles, see Janet C. Blyberg, catalog entry 97, in *Asia in Amsterdam: The Culture of Luxury in the Golden Age*, ed. Karina H. Corrigan, Jan van Campen, and Femke Diercks with Janet C. Blyberg (Yale University Press, 2012), 328–30.

39. Remnants of candlewax preserved on the chasuble's linen lining presumably spilled onto the vestment from lit candles during Mass.

Cut from the World: Philippine *Piña* Fabric in the East India Marine Society Collection

Abi Lua, Assistant Curator, James A. Michener Art Museum

In 1830, Captain Joseph Jenkins Knapp Jr. (1803–1830) donated a square piece of Philippine *piña* cloth to the East India Marine Society Museum, one of the originating collections of the current Peabody Essex Museum in Salem, Massachusetts (fig. 1).[1] Piña cloth is fabric woven out of the finest fibers of pineapple leaves, creating a soft, sheer, and fine material like that of a cotton muslin. A description written directly on this fabric makes note of this material knowledge and leaves a trace of the cloth's collection history. Though now significantly faded, it reads: "4182 / Made of the fibers of the Pine Apple at Manilla [sic] by the natives" (fig. 2). Rather than an imported good brought back for consumers in the United States, this cloth was categorized under what the Society bylaws termed "articles of curiosity."[2] This language was specific to the Society's mission to build a scientific collection, in which it charged captains and supercargoes to bring back objects from their travels overseas for the Society's museum. Applied here, the cloth was designated for building scientific knowledge through early museum practice in the US.

Compared to other objects acquired by the East India Marine Society Museum, Knapp's piña cloth was unusual. Some merchants at the time did not know the original use and function of the items that they collected. For them and for the viewers who would later see these items on display, the various objects were merely viewed as representations of their respective cultures or of the exchanges that had taken place overseas.[3] However, Captain J. J. Knapp was knowledgeable about his cloth, particularly when it came to the fabric's composition. While seemingly a minute detail— especially given the ghost-like remnants of the cloth's description—Knapp's correct

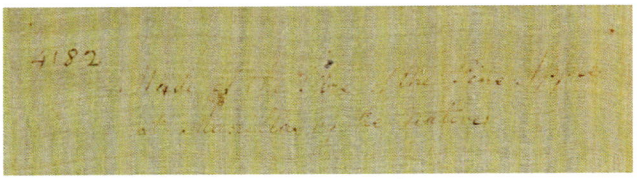

Fig. 2 Artist in Manila, Philippines, Detail of J. J. Knapp's piña cloth, Philippines, 1829. Courtesy of the Peabody Essex Museum. Photo by Patrick Doyle, 2025.

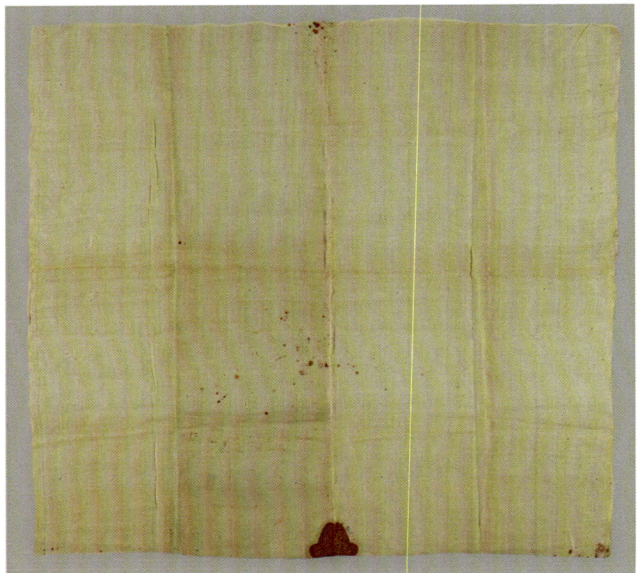

Fig. 1 Artist in Manila, Philippines, Piña cloth, Philippines, 1829. 15 × 13¾ in. (38.1 × 34.9 cm). Peabody Essex Museum, Salem: Gift of Capt. Joseph J. Knapp, 1829, E6538. Courtesy of the Peabody Essex Museum. Photo by Patrick Doyle, 2025.

identification of the fabric's pineapple leaf material is rare and exceptional. Due to its material similarity to silk, fine cotton, and linen, piña has often eluded consumers and museum practitioners both then and now.[4] Furthermore, while some items in the museum's founding collection were removed from their original ritual or spiritual environments, because piña did not have a ceremonial function in the Philippines, Knapp's cloth did not lose any sort of sacred meaning through its acquisition. For the purposes of building the growing collection at the East India Marine Society Museum, Knapp's knowledge of the cloth was accurate and sufficient.

However, as a small piece of cloth now in the United States, Knapp's piña was cut from a larger physical and cultural fabric that was left unwritten in Knapp's description, one that wove together the fabric's craft and sartorial significance in the Philippines. In the archipelago, the cloth would have moved between the hands of makers and consumers across multiple islands. The first step of production took place on the island of Panay, where artisans worked to extract, process, hand-knot, and weave pineapple leaf fibers. The woven fabric would then travel north to Manila, the present-day capital of the Philippines, and its surrounding regions, where *bordadoras* (embroiderers) and *costureras* (seamstresses) decorated and fashioned the cloth into outfits such as the men's *barong tagalog* and women's *baro't saya.* As one of the finest fabrics used in these traditional garments, piña clothed the elite echelons of Manila society. The fabric's translucence and intricate embroidery came to symbolize wealth and a cosmopolitanism that was affordable to only a few. Cut from this cultural fabric, Knapp's cloth captured both this interisland manufacture as well as the material's meaning within Philippine fashion.

Reading Knapp's description and beyond it, this essay unpacks not only the dynamic world of Philippine piña craft and fashion but also the fabric's inclusion within the founding collection of the East Indian Marine Society Museum. As a textile fragment, the cloth's very pineapple leaf material remains as an archive of its weaving methods and sartorial culture in the Philippines during the early nineteenth century. At the same time, the fragment is evidence of its significance as an object for scientific inquiry within the East India Marine Society Museum collection, a project that simultaneously projected a global citizenship for a young nation like the United States. Having arrived in the US a decade after the last galleon sailed the Manila–Acapulco trade, this example of piña at the present-day Peabody Essex Museum highlights a new facet of these transpacific crossings. While the Manila Galleon trade might have ended, transpacific exchange continued in new ways with new actors. For Salem, this exchange contributed to a cross-cultural intersection where art, trade, and scientific exploration contributed to early American museum practice at the East Indian Marine Society Museum.[5]

Nineteenth-Century Philippine Piña Craft and Fashion

Though now a plain-woven, square-cut piece of cloth, Knapp's piña fabric had once lived in the vibrant world of piña craft and fashion in the Philippines. Far from the static display at the East India Marine Society Museum, Knapp's cloth embodies a larger and more dynamic context within the textile tradition and cosmopolitan culture of the Philippines during the nineteenth century.

Yet, this dynamic context of piña fabric begins not in the Philippines but in South America. Before discussing piña craft and fashion, it is important to note that the pineapple plant itself is not native to the Philippines. The exact origin story of how the pineapple arrived in the Philippines is shrouded in myth, but most scholars believe that Ferdinand Magellan's voyages brought the fruit from South America and introduced it to Philippine soil shortly after landing in the Visayan region in 1521.[6] As pineapples proliferated in he tropical Philippine landscape, weavers adapted the techniques of creating native banana leaf fabric, or *abaca*, to producing woven cloth with this new pineapple leaf material. In particular, makers used the method of hand-knotting abaca fibers to make thread for producing piña thread as well.[7] By the early nineteenth century, Spanish friar and botanist Manuel Blanco noted this weaving tradition in his botanical text *Flora de Filipinas* (1837), which is still considered a foundational treatise for Philippine botany. In his entry on the *Bromelia ananas* species, he recorded that the Native *indios* made shirts of remarkable delicacy with the fine threads drawn from pineapple leaves.[8] Measuring the visual impact of the transpacific crossing of piña requires considering first the transpacific crossing of the pineapple. Even for a cloth closely associated with Filipino culture, Knapp's fabric must be understood as a product of not just one transpacific crossing but two: the first from South America to the Philippines and the second from the Philippines to the United States.

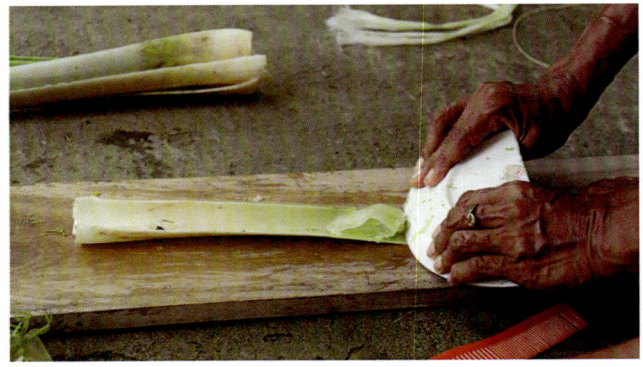

Fig. 3 Scraping the epidermis of the pineapple leaf with a porcelain plate shard, Aklan, 2022. Courtesy of the author.

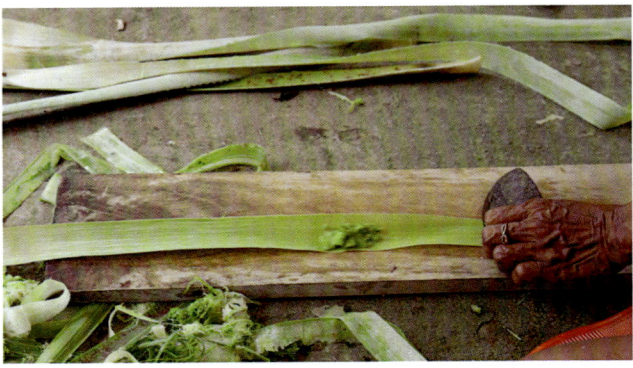

Fig. 4 Scraping for the *liniwan* fibers with a coconut shell, Aklan, 2022. Courtesy of the author.

Although Knapp had written "Manilla" on his fabric, piña production took place and continues to take place on Panay Island, located south of Manila on the western side of the Visayan region. When weavers created Knapp's cloth during the nineteenth century, centers for piña manufacture existed in Iloilo, a province located in southeast Panay.[9] Today, piña is largely woven in the northern portion of the island in the province of Aklan, where the technique remains a cottage industry traditionally practiced by women. While there have been a few technological changes in tools involved in the craft, much of scholars' and contemporary weavers' knowledge of historic processes draws from present-day practices.[10]

The first step in producing Knapp's piña cloth was harvesting pineapple leaves, which makers then scraped to extract the leaf fiber for the fabric's thread. The specific pineapple variety used for piña is the Red Spanish pineapple. According to weavers, this pineapple yields stronger fibers than other varieties. The leaves that the artisans harvested came not from the crown of the pineapple but from the bush

where the fruit grows. Each leaf measures around a meter long. Once makers gathered the amount of leaves that they planned to scrape for the day, two rounds of leaf scraping ensued to extract two kinds of piña fiber. First, using a sanded-down porcelain plate shard, the leaf-scraper would begin to scrape the epidermis of the pineapple leaf (fig. 3).[11] The scraper would remove just enough to reveal the first layer of piña fibers, called the washed-out fiber. The maker would extract these fibers by pulling them up and off the leaf by hand.

For the second round, the scraper would take a coconut shell—also sanded down—and begin scraping the leaf where she had just extracted the washed-out fiber (fig. 4). Once the leaf was thin enough, the maker would pull the second fiber from the back of the leaf, also by hand. This fiber, called *liniwan*, was the finer of the two. Today, piña textiles are often made with both the coarser washed-out fiber and the liniwan fiber. However, during the nineteenth century, all piña textiles were made only with the finer liniwan fiber.[12] Knapp's piña cloth was most likely woven with liniwan

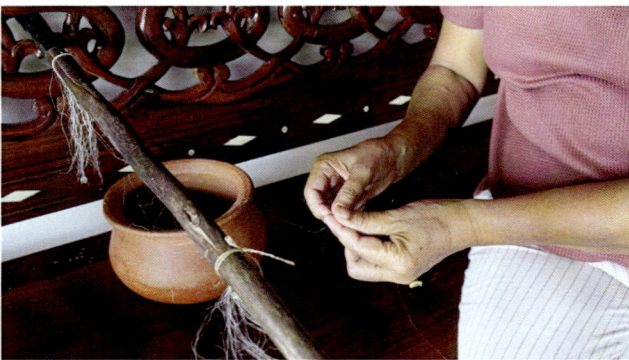

Fig. 5 Hand-knotting, or *pagpanug-ot* in Aklanon, piña fibers, Aklan, 2022. Courtesy of the author.

fiber, which is evident in the delicate and translucent materiality of its fabric.

After extracting and cleaning the piña fibers, artisans made piña thread by tying each individual fiber from end to end, resulting in one continuous filament (fig. 5). As previously discussed, piña weavers adapted this technique of hand-knotting fibers from making banana-leaf threads, which were also created by the tying of individual fibers together. Hand-knotting was not limited to preparing piña thread, however. Due to the delicate nature of the fiber, threads often broke as weavers began to prepare the warp or began to weave on the loom. To fix these breakages, the weaver would go back to the broken threads and reconnect the fibers by tying them together. Piña fabrics like Knapp's cloth display this process of hand-knotting and rehand-knotting. Under magnification, small knots appear throughout the piña fabric, bearing witness to the unique quality of piña thread and the hand-knotting technique necessary to accommodate the fine material (fig. 6). As one can imagine, the process of hand-knotting fibers, both to make and to fix

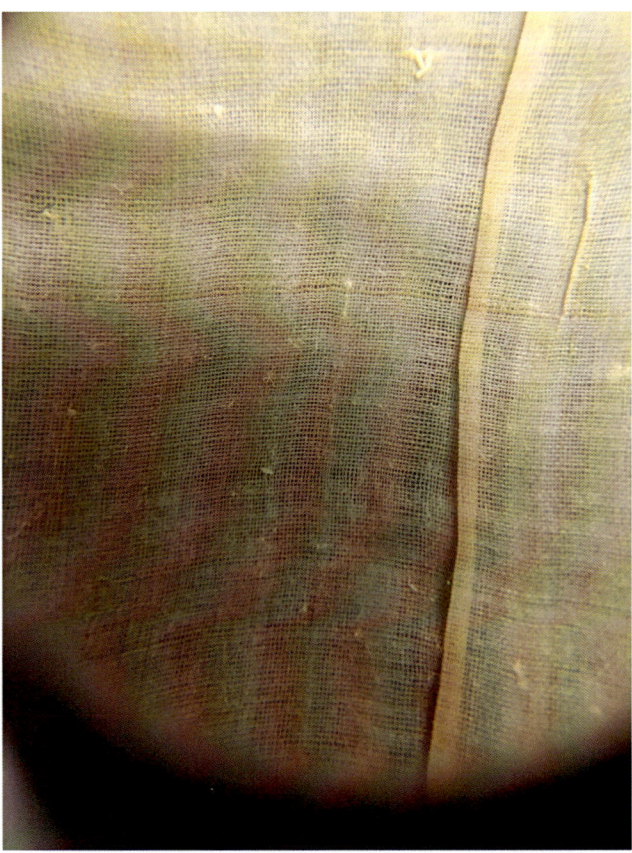

Fig. 6 Knots in Knapp's cloth under 10× magnification, Philippines, ca. 1829. Courtesy of the author.

threads, requires great patience and a deft hand.

Once hand-knotters finished creating piña thread, they supplied it to local weavers. Like most weaving traditions, weaving piña began with preparing the warp threads and weft threads. Preparing piña warp meant calculating the length of warp thread that the weaver needed for the desired length and width of the intended fabric. To calculate these measurements, the artisan would wind the hand-knotted piña thread around a cylindrical warp frame, whose wooden spokes marked different points of measurement to help the weaver keep count of the amount of warp threads she had wound (fig. 7). Preparing piña weft

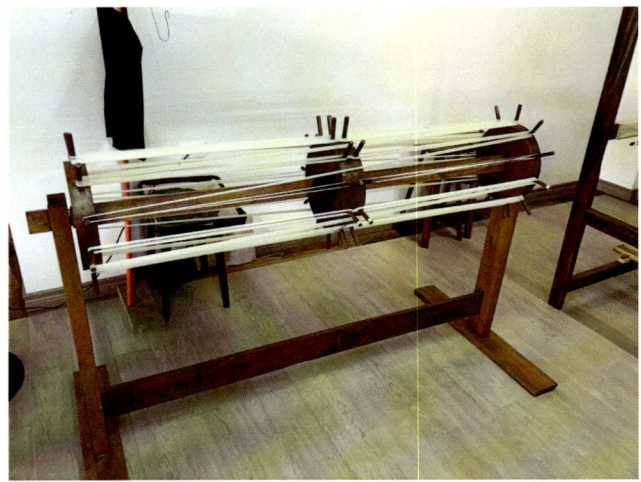

Fig. 7 Cylindrical piña warp frame, Aklan, 2022. Courtesy of the author.

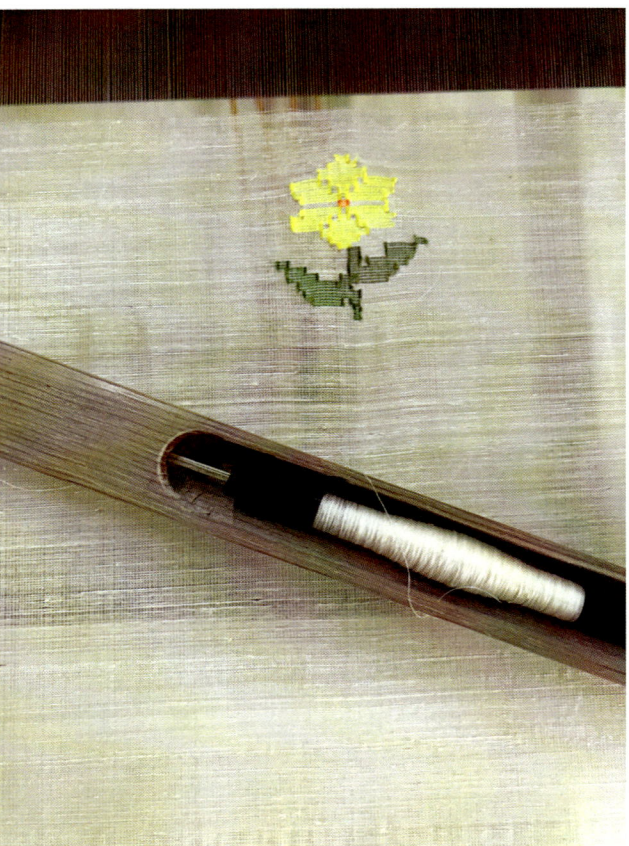

Fig. 8 Shuttle and bobbin with piña weft thread, Aklan, 2022. Courtesy of the author.

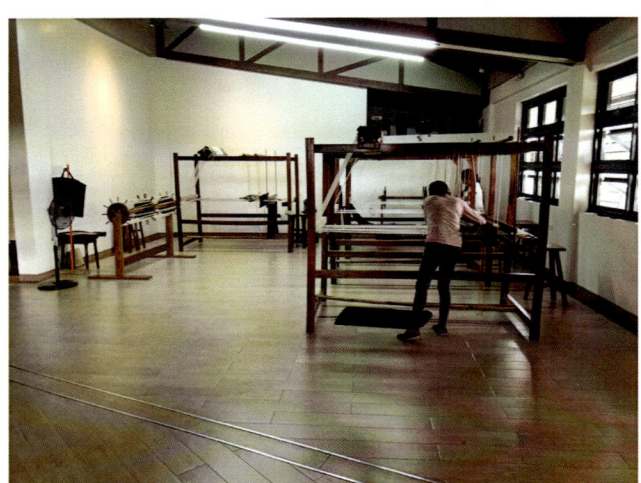

Fig. 9 Floor looms at Haboean Weaving Studio, Aklan, 2022. Courtesy of the author.

required a different process. Taking the hand-knotted piña, the weaver would use a spindle to wind thread around a bobbin. Afterward, she placed the bobbin into a shuttle, which she would then use for weaving (fig. 8). Once the weaver calculated the warp and dressed the floor loom, she began to weave (fig. 9). Most piña fabrics display a plain-weave structure or a variation of one.[13] Knapp's cloth, for instance, displays a plain-weave structure, where one weft thread is woven over one warp thread, resulting in a soft and diaphanous fabric.

The woven piña cloth could go to several textile distribution points after its completion. Within the island of Panay, vendors could sell piña along with other textiles at local, open-air marketplaces. Here, vendors ranged from the local weaver who sold her own products to the entrepreneurial *sinamayera*, or textile vendor, who sold the products of several weavers and embroiderers. Leaving Panay, ships from Manila transported these woven fabrics from the port of Iloilo back to the capital, where sinamayeras in different districts sold the piña cloth. These markets in Manila often drew in textiles from a variety of provinces, where piña was sold alongside textiles from northern provinces

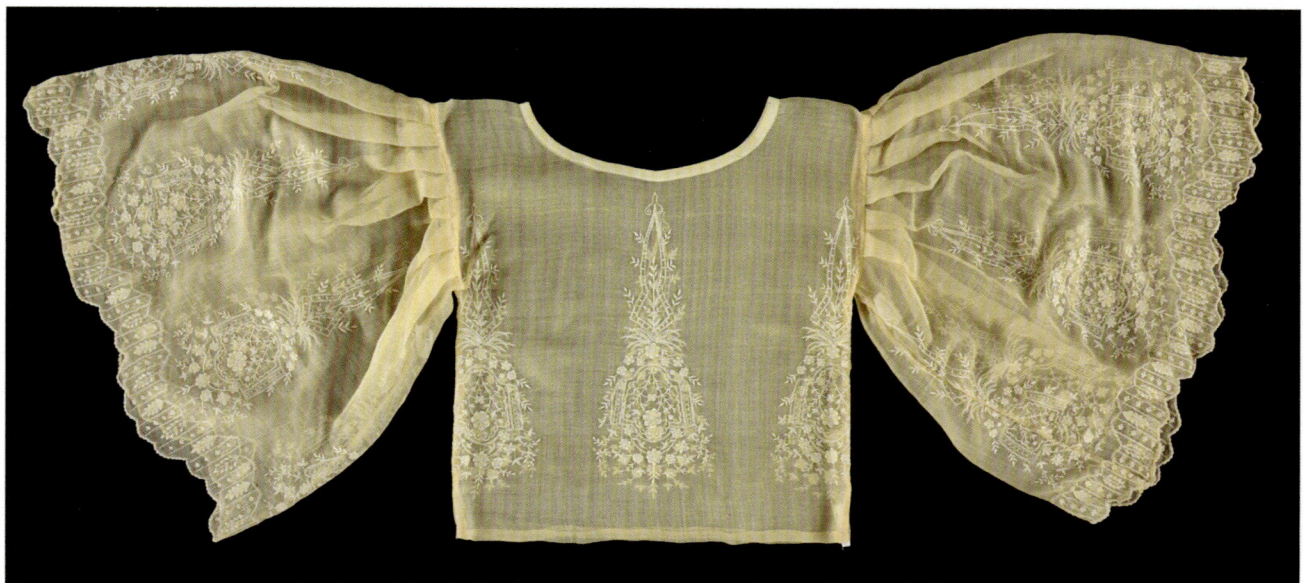

Fig. 10 Blouse, Philippines. Piña cloth, overall: 21 × 53 in. (53.3 × 134.6 cm). The Textile Museum Collection, Washington, DC, 1998.6.1A-C, Gift of Mr. and Mrs. George W. White. Photography by Breton Littlehales.

like those in the Ilocos region. Furthermore, as it had been during the height of the Manila–Acapulco trade, Manila remained as the archipelago's main *entrepôt* through which foreign merchants could access the Philippine market. Rather than describing where the cloth was woven, then, Knapp's description of "Manilla" points to the location where he, and most foreign consumers, acquired finished piña fabric.[14]

Knapp had collected his textile as an undecorated fabric, but had the cloth remained in the Philippines, a textile vendor could have taken the full piña yardage to a nearby bordadora for further embellishment. In the hands of the bordadora, plain piña fabric became a canvas for elegant florals, vines, and geometric patterns (fig. 10). Similar to piña weaving, many of the needlework techniques have remained in use since the nineteenth century.[15] During the nineteenth century, these historic

embroidery centers were located in various Manila neighborhoods, such as Ermita, Malate, Santa Ana, Tondo, and Paco.[16] First, the bordadora would directly embroider on the cloth. This technique allowed her to create the beautiful, free-flowing designs typically seen on piña. The next step was *bakbak*, or drawn threadwork, in which the bordadora pulled threads from the woven cloth to open the plain weave structure. The result is a gridlike fabric. Lastly, the bordadora would embroider other designs in these open spaces with a technique called *calado*, or open threadwork. Here, the bordadora would be able to return to decorating with organic lines and forms, and these designs are often in repeating patterns as dictated by the grid drawn by the bakbak of the previous step. Although Knapp's cloth did not feature any of these embroidered designs, piña fabrics operated within an ecosystem of craft that connected weaving and needlework across multiple islands.

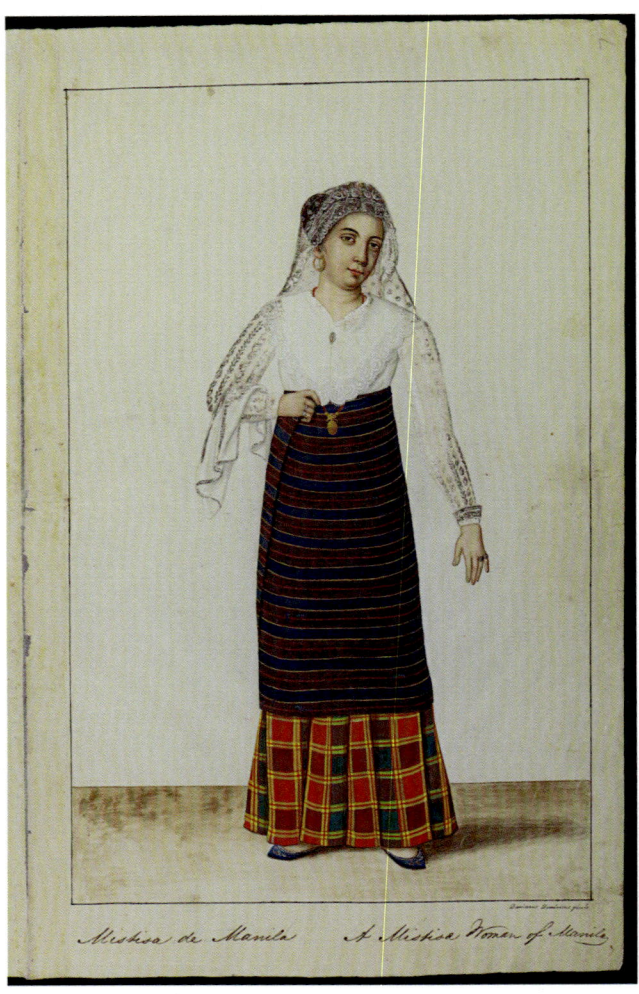

Fig. 11 Damián Domingo (1796–1834), *Mistisa de Manila (A Mistisa Woman of Manila)*, Philippines, 1827–32. Watercolor on paper, sheet: 16½ × 10⅝ in. (42 × 27 cm); image: 14⅛ × 9 in. (36 × 23 cm). Newberry Library: Edward E. Ayer Art Collection.

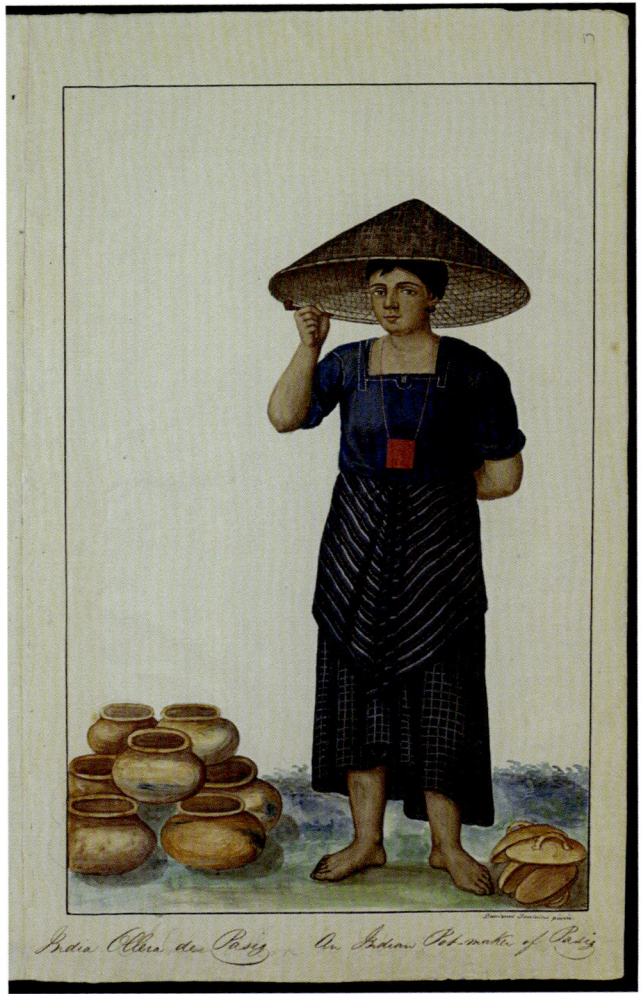

Fig. 12 Damián Domingo (1796–1834), *India Ollera de Pasig (An Indian Pot-maker of Pasig)*, Philippines, 1827–32. Watercolor on paper, sheet: 16½ × 10⅝ in. (42 × 27 cm); image: 14⅛ × 9 in. (36 × 23 cm). Newberry Library: Edward E. Ayer Art Collection.

After the cloth was embroidered—or if costumers wanted to keep their fabric undecorated—consumers would have purchased the original yardage and hired a costurera to make clothing. During the nineteenth century, the sartorial culture of the lowland Philippine region was such that the value of a garment was attributed to the material of the clothing rather than the silhouette. Due to the great labor involved in weaving piña, very few could afford to buy the fabric, and piña garments were usually reserved only for special occasions.

As a result, piña mostly clothed the elite men and women of Manila, conveying a sense of *urbanidad*, or an attitude of fashionable, urban refinement.[17]

For women's fashion, this economic hierarchy of material was especially apparent as the outfits for women were the same across every socioeconomic class. During the nineteenth century, Filipino women wore the baro't saya, which consisted of a loose, cropped blouse, called the *baro*, and a *saya*, or skirt. Sometimes,

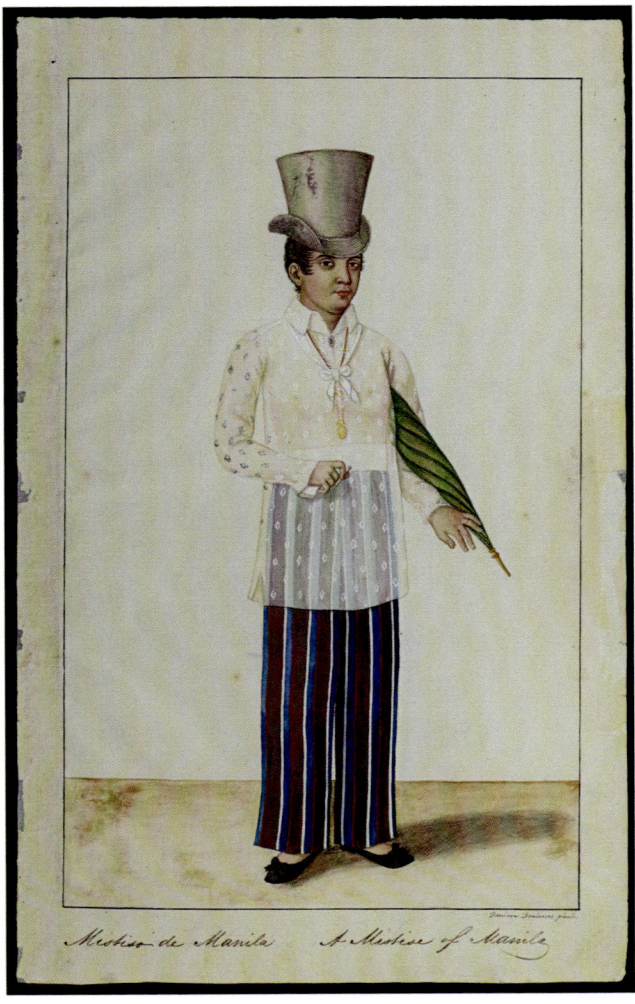

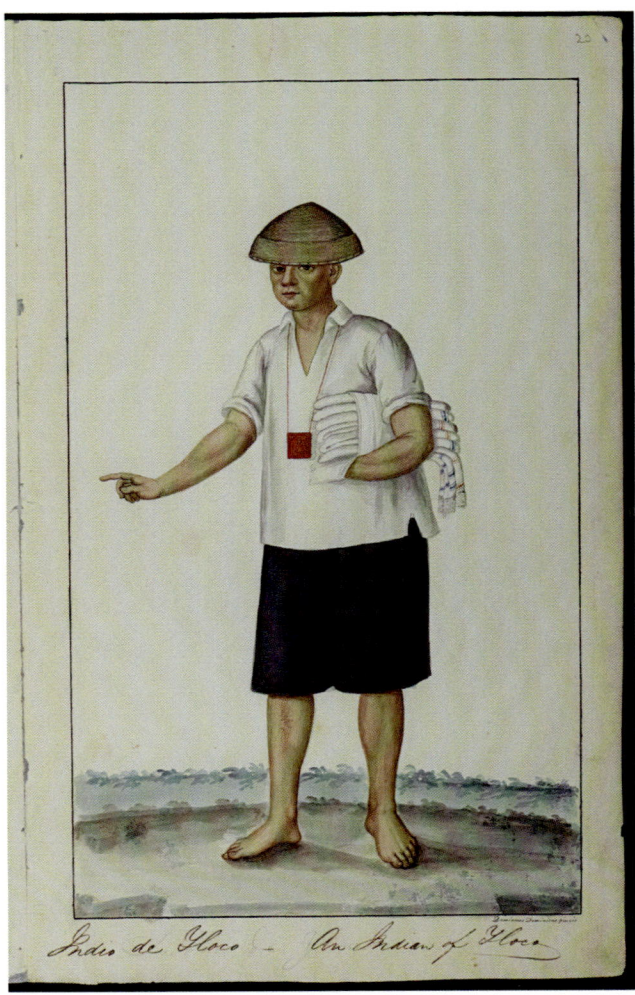

Fig. 13 Damián Domingo (1796–1834), *Mestiso de Manila (A Mestise of Manila)*, Philippines, 1827–32. Watercolor on paper, sheet: 16½ × 10⅝ in. (42 × 27 cm); image: 14⅛ × 9 in. (36 × 23 cm). Newberry Library: Edward E. Ayer Art Collection.

Fig. 14 Damián Domingo (1796–1834), *Indio de Yloco (An Indian of Yloco)*, Philippines, 1827–32. Watercolor on paper, sheet: 16½ × 10⅝ in. (42 × 27 cm); image: 14⅛ × 9 in. (36 × 23 cm). Newberry Library: Edward E. Ayer Art Collection.

women could wear a *pañuelo* (shawl) over their baro and a *tapis* (overskirt) that would be wrapped around their saya. The saya and tapis were usually made with thick, dark material, but the baro could range in materials from abaca and cotton to *jusi* and piña. Nevertheless, while the outfits' basic silhouettes were the same, the baro that was woven with piña was more expensive, which made it more luxurious than the baro woven with other materials. In the watercolor *tipos del pais*, or "country

types," paintings created by Damián Domingo (1796–1834), this shift is evident in the blue, opaque fabric of the *India Ollera de Pasig*'s baro versus the embroidered, translucent baro, pañuelo, and head covering of the *Mistisa de Manila* (figs. 11 and 12).

Men's fashion featured a greater variety of silhouettes and therefore depended less on this hierarchy of material to signify the socioeconomic status of the wearer. Among these outfits was the *barong mahaba*, a long, collared shirt that men wore untucked (fig. 13). Most men on a day-to-day basis, however, wore more simple silhouettes, such as the man featured in Domingo's *Indio de Yloco* (fig. 14). Set against this Philippine cultural context, Knapp's fragment physically and figuratively represents only a piece of this textile and fashion tradition, one whose cultural meaning pulled from botanical history, craft knowledge, and sartorial value.[18]

Piña in Salem—Mercantile and Institutional Knowledge of Piña

However, Knapp's cloth did not make it into the barong mahaba or baro't saya of a Manila man or woman. Cut from its larger fabric, Knapp's cloth instead traveled from the Philippines to Salem during a moment of economic transition. After the British invaded Manila in the 1760s, Spanish economic control over the Philippine colony weakened, resulting in the gradual cessation of the Manila Galleon trade beginning in 1810 until its last trip in 1815. Trade soon began to open to other foreign merchants outside of Spain, like merchants from the United States.[19] Within the Philippines, beginning in 1778, General-Governor José de Basco y Vargas looked to domestic agriculture to supply cash crops for export as he foresaw the end to an economy dependent on the Manila Galleon. This plan for agricultural development coincided with an upsurge in local textile production, which utilized the new crops resulting from the general-governor's

program.[20] Knapp's arrival to the Philippines and acquisition of piña was a point of convergence in the archipelago's history. The captain had set foot in Manila not only as its ports opened to merchants like him but also during a time when textiles like his piña cloth were the country's priority for economic development.

As an item categorized under "articles of curiosity," this object's classification is distinct from the return cargo that East India Marine Society members brought back as import goods. From the Philippines, Salem merchants brought back indigo, which supplied the growing New England dyeing industry, as well as sugar.[21] Abaca, or what was known as Manila hemp, later entered the market as a fiber popularly used for rope.[22] In Salem, advertisements for Manila hemp cordage appear in the *Salem Gazette* into the 1820s.[23] Although Knapp's piña cloth traveled on the same return trip as these other products, the fabric, as an article of curiosity, was separate from the items that traveled as import goods.

Instead, Knapp's piña cloth gives image to a different material culture in the United States during the 1820s. With the rise of early-nineteenth-century museums in New England and the mid-Atlantic, objects of scientific inquiry were collected from overseas trading ventures in addition to the imported goods sold to the public. Born from eighteenth-century European curiosity cabinets that housed natural and ethnographic objects, institutions like the

East India Marine Society Museum fostered this spirit of discovery through active collecting practices. In a similar expression as the cabinet of curiosity, the pursuit for global objects during the early nineteenth century was tied to larger formulations of American national character, one that took shape in relation to the young nation's citizenship in the world. As a port city with two active marine societies, Salem was uniquely positioned to project this identity as American traders went out and foreign goods entered, fortifying the nation's connection to the seas and lands beyond it. Collecting articles of curiosity like Knapp's piña thus served a dual purpose of advancing scientific knowledge as an implicit declaration of national standing.[24]

As a museum founded and maintained by its members, the East India Marine Society charged both the mariners and its institution with this mission for scientific advancement, conflating both mariner and institutional knowledge of these objects. The traders who had set out from Salem were the first individuals through which knowledge of these items passed. Not only was this expectation clearly stated in the Society's bylaws, but the journals that each ship was expected to keep also gave detailed instructions regarding object collection. At the tail end of several paragraphs that instruct the daily recording of wind quality, latitude, longitude, and distance traveled, the directions conclude with criteria for object collection:

> *There should be collected for the Museum, specimens of various kinds of vegetable substances, earths, minerals, ores, metals, volcanic substances, &c. There should also be preserved (according to the directions hereafter given) such parts of birds, insects, fish, &c. as serve most easily to distinguish them. . . . Inquiry should be made for any remarkable books in use among any of the eastern nations, with their subjects, dates and titles. Articles of the dress and ornaments of any nation, with the images and objects of religious devotion, should be procured.*[25]

For mariners like Captain J. J. Knapp, this commission translated into an experiential knowledge of the objects. As men who had set foot in these distant isles and countries, even if for a moment compared to the months spent at sea, East India Marine Society members collected these materials through a direct experience that most did not have of the lands and societies in which these objects originated. In other words, unlike the many who mistook fabrics like cotton or silk as piña, and vice versa, Knapp knew that his cloth was made from pineapple leaf fibers because he had seen the fabric during his time in Manila and was informed of its material.

However, this experiential knowledge must be qualified, as it was not the same as that possessed by those who made and wore piña. For one, though Knapp had physically been in the Philippines, his vocation was not one that allowed him to stay in one place for too long. Unlike the expatriate who resided in a given location for several years, captains and supercargoes spent more time on the ocean than at their destinations.[26] As a result, his experiential knowledge was limited to what he could learn about piña from local informants during his short stay in one location. Furthermore, it is also possible that Knapp might have learned more than what he shared with the East India Marine Society. The brief record that made it onto the cloth and into the East India Marine Society catalog might be more reflective of cataloging convention rather than Knapp's complete understanding of the material. Nevertheless, while Knapp might have learned that the fabric was indeed made with pineapple leaf fibers, his knowledge did not extend beyond what he saw and heard during his time in Manila. As a mariner, Knapp received an incomplete knowledge of piña cloth, returning to Salem unaware of where the cloth was woven and the purposes for which it was used.

Nevertheless, this partial understanding of piña fulfilled the scientific inquiry requested by the East India Marine Society, and it was this object knowledge that became institutional through Knapp's donation of the cloth to the museum. In the 1831 object catalog, the description written on Knapp's piña bore more empirical language. Rather than simply "Made of the fibers of the Pine Apple," as was written on the cloth, Knapp's piña became a "Specimen of Cloth manufactured from the fibres of the Pine Apple, from Manilla."[27] While the language of the description alone evokes the scientific meaning that Knapp's cloth had taken on, its context within the rest of the museum's collection of Philippine objects emphasizes this transformation. Several other objects from the Philippines were labeled as specimens, such as a volcanic pitchstone and ammonite from Luzon, the northern island region where Manila is located.[28] Many items were not given the descriptor "specimen," but they did not deviate too far in nature from objects like the pitchstone and ammonite. Examples include a Muraena fish, iron ore, pearl nautilus cups, and a species of pigeon called *Columba cruenta*.[29] There were a few objects that might have been classified as more cultural than natural, such as a pair of women's slippers, swords, and cigars, so it is possible that Knapp's cloth may have been understood as examples of both Philippine culture and natural history.[30] Regardless, by the time of its acquisition, piña's material was stripped of its associations with early histories of craft and cosmopolitan fashion in the Philippines. In the hands of the institution, piña, in its partial understanding and scientific use, along with the other Philippine objects in the museum's collection, became a material metonym for the Philippines, filling the museum's metaphorical display case of global knowledge. Cut from the world, Knapp's cloth remains an archive of the world, weaving together multiple histories and cultural meanings in its pineapple leaf materiality.

Notes

1. At the Peabody Essex Museum, I am grateful to Karina Corrigan and George Schwartz for access to the museum's piña collection.

2. East-India Marine Society of Salem, *The East-India Marine Society of Salem* (Salem Press, Palfray, Ives, Foote & Brown, 1831), 11, https://archive.org/details/eastindiamarines00east/page/n3/mode/2up. The thirteenth article states specifically that "members shall collect such useful publications, or articles of curiosity, as they think will be acceptable to the Society, either as donations therefore, or to be held in their own private right for the temporary use of the Society, under such terms may be agreed on with the President and Committee."

3. George H. Schwartz, *Collecting the Globe: The Salem East India Marine Society Museum* (University of Massachusetts Press, 2020), 44–45.

4. See Abigail Lua, "Interrogating Translucence: Clarifying Philippine Piña Materiality" (master's thesis, University of Delaware, 2023), 1–13.

5. While trade between the Philippines and Salem was frequent during this period, scholarship on the exchanges between Manila and New England is relatively new. See Florina Capistrano-Baker, "Beyond Hemp: The Manila–Salem Trade, 1796–1858," in *Global Trade and Visual Arts in Federal New England*, ed. Patricia Johnston and Caroline Frank (University of New Hampshire Press, 2014), 251–64. See also Benito Legarda Jr.'s and Capistrano-Baker's essays in *Transpacific Engagements: Trade, Translation, and Visual Culture of Entangled Empires (1565–1898)*, ed. Florina H. Capistrano-Baker and Meha Priyadarshini (Ayala Foundation, Inc., Getty Research Institute, and Kunsthistorisches Institut in Florenz, 2020), 247–67.

6. Lourdes R. Montinola, *Piña* (Amon Foundation, 1991), 26–27. Montinola's volume continues to be the authority for most scholarship on the pineapple's history in the Philippines. Here, she writes of different pathways that the pineapple could have taken in the hands of fifteenth-century Portuguese and Spanish explorers. Elena Phipps cites other sources in her essay on the international trade of silk, cotton, banana fiber, and piña textiles, but these sources also look primarily to Montinola's volume for the history of the pineapple in the Philippines. With the exception of Antonio Pigafetta's text from 1521, Montinola's evidence draws mostly from twentieth-century US sources. A deeper study of the pinapple's botanical history would enrich future scholarship on piña cloth. Elena Phipps, "Silk, Cotton, Wild Banana, and Piña: Luxury Cloth and Their Materials—Connecting Worlds," in *Transpacific Engagements*, 181–95; Luís Mendonça de Carvalho, Francisca Maria Fernandes, and Stephanie Zabel, "The Collection of Pineapple Fibers—*Ananas comosus* (Bromeliaceae)—at the Harvard University Herbaria," *Harvard Papers in Botany* 14, no. 2 (2009): 105–09, https://doi.org/10.3100/025.014.0202.

7. Most bast and leaf fibers within the Asian-Pacific context require hand-knotting to create thread. Roy W. Hamilton and B. Lynne Milgram, ed., *Material Choices: Refashioning Bast and Leaf Fibers in Asia and the Pacific* (Fowler Museum, 2007), 34.

8. In the original Spanish: *De las hojas de estas plantas sacan los indios hilos finisimos, de los cuales hacen camisas de una delicadeza portentosa.* The term *indios* reflects the racial taxonomical language of the Spanish colonial period. Manuel Blanco, *Flora de Filipinas:*

Segun el sistema sexual de Linneo (Imprenta de Santo Thomas, 1837), 231.

9. See Henry F. Funtecha, "Iloilo's Weaving Industry During the 19th Century," *Philippine Quarterly of Culture and Society* 26, no. 1/2 (1998): 81–88.

10. See Montinola, *Piña*; and Lua, "Interrogating Translucence." Montinola, for instance, documents the contemporary techniques of weaving piña in her monograph, explaining the endurance of these processes into the twentieth century. In 2022, I was also able to visit these piña weaving communities to learn about the material and their craft. In particular, I thank the weavers of Dela Cruz House of Piña, Raquel's Piña Cloth Products, and La Herminia for their generosity in time and expertise. I also thank Anna India Dela Cruz Legaspi. I draw from this fieldwork for my discussion of Knapp's cloth.

11. A note on the technological continuity of piña production is important here. Before my fieldwork, I was suspicious of many publications' assumption that the tools and processes of making piña remained unchanged. However, as I met with artisans and observed their craft, the nuances between change and continuity became more evident. While there are certainly a few processes that are now mechanized for greater efficiency, the delicate nature of piña fiber has mostly resisted the use of other tools that might damage the material. See Lua, "Interrogating Translucence," 25–26.

12. Carlos Eliserio, in conversation with the author, July 12, 2022; Montinola, *Piña*, 53. The washed-out fibers were used to make objects like ropes or the hair of religious icons. In Aklan, the washed-out fibers would be used specifically for Ati-Atihan costumes, which are the costumes worn for the annual Ati-Atihan festival in Kalibo, Aklan.

13. In addition to a plain-weave structure, weavers also wove a more open plain-weave structure called *rengue*. Rengue patterns feature a more open, gridlike weave structure where one warp thread and one weft thread cross each grid square. See Lua, "Interrogating Translucence," 40.

14. Stephanie Coo, *Clothing the Colony: Nineteenth-Century Philippine Sartorial Culture, 1820–1896* (Ateneo de Manila University Press, 2019), 72–83.

15. The following embroidery techniques were observed and taught to me during a visit to the embroidery centers in Taal, Batangas, where they actively embroider *nipis* garments like piña.

16. Coo, *Clothing the Colony*, 80. See also Maria Luisa Camagay, *Working Women of Manila in the 19th Century* (University of the Philippines Press, 1995); Patricia Justiniani McReynolds, "The Embroidery of Luzon and the Visayas," *Arts of Asia* 10 (January 1980): 128–33; Marlene Ramos, "The Filipina Bordadoras and the Emergence of Fine European-Style Embroidery Tradition in Colonial Philippines, 19th to Early-20th Centuries" (master's thesis, Mount Saint Vincent University, 2016). In addition to their current focus on the embroidery tradition in Lumban, Laguna, these authors have written about the beginnings and development of embroidery in Manila *beaterios* (convent schools) and *asilos* (orphanages).

17. Coo, *Clothing the Colony*, 30–31, 240.

18. In using tipos del pais images to explain the sartorial distinctions in nineteenth-century Philippine lowland fashion, I want to acknowledge the voyeurism that might be inherent in this genre of painting. Tipos del pais, which are paintings that depict the different attire across socioeconomic class and race, were products made as souvenirs for international visitors to Manila. As such, these images might not capture the nuanced and lived connections between cloth, fashion, socioeconomic class, and race.

19. Patricio N. Abinales and Donna J. Amoroso, *State and Society in the Philippines*, second edition (Rowman & Littlefield, 2005), 75–76.

20. Coo, *Clothing the Colony*, 64.

21. Nathaniel Bowditch, Mary C. McHale, and Thomas R. McHale, *Early American-Philippine Trade: The Journal of Nathaniel Bowditch in Manila, 1796* (Yale University, Southeast Asia Studies, 1962), 21.

22. See Elizabeth Potter Sievert, *The Story of Abaca: Manila Hemp's Transformation from Textile to Marine Cordage and Specialty Paper* (Ateneo de Manila University Press, 2009).

23. *Salem Gazette*, June 22, 1824.

24. Schwartz, *Collecting the Globe*, 17, 45.

25. Printed Journal Directions from the East India Marine Society of Salem in Joseph J. Knapp Jr., *Joseph J. Knapp, Jr.'s journal in the Phoenix (Brig)*, 1823–1824, MH 88, vol. 10, no. 87, 503. Phillips Library, Peabody Essex Museum, Rowley, Massachusetts, https://archive.org/details/mh88v10n87/.

26. Dane A. Morrison, *True Yankees: The South Seas and the Discovery of American Identity* (Johns Hopkins University Press, 2014), 138.

27. *The East-India Marine Society of Salem*, 173.

28. Ibid., 66, 69.

29. Ibid., 87, 106, 129, 139, 173.

30. Ibid., 43, 52, 69, 90, 94.

An Ocean of Blue and White: Archaeological Excavations at the Port of Acapulco

Roberto Junco, Deputy Director, SAS-INAH

Acapulco is a famous vacation destination today, especially for people from Mexico City. Its appeal began in the 1950s, when Hollywood actors and the international jet set flocked to its sunny shores. However, relatively few people outside academic circles know about the Acapulco–Manila Galleon trade route and the renowned Acapulco Fair, where silver from the Americas traded for a wide range of luxurious and exotic goods from across the ocean. Although Acapulco was a small port until the second half of the twentieth century, it was a nodal point in sixteenth- to early nineteenth-century global commerce. First, it was the designated American port for the Acapulco–Manila route (the name depending on whether the ship was sailing to or from Manila or Acapulco), bridging both sides of the Pacific. Second, it was also connected to the ports of Panama and Callao, Peru, with merchants arriving with South American silver. Mexico City was a short way from Acapulco, connecting to Puebla, Veracruz, and then on to the Atlantic and Caribbean.

Much archaeological research has been undertaken in the last decade, feeding into what can be called an "archaeology of the Manila Galleon." The most significant body of work concentrates on ceramics, including style, provenance, distribution, and consumption studies. For many years, archaeological evidence from different shipwrecks and excavations has contributed to our understanding of transpacific trade. Archaeological work has revealed production centers and even specific kiln sites, as well as studies of porcelain commercialization, use, and influence in Mexico and Manila, among others.[1] Since 2015, archaeological excavations at Acapulco have yielded an interesting collection of porcelain. This brings to light new evidence about the port's commercial activity and a better understanding of the types of pieces available for commercialization in New Spain and beyond. Some of the sherds tell individual stories and contribute to our understanding of the early modern world and the Manila Galleon.

Acapulco

Designated in 1573 as the official origin and terminus of the Acapulco–Manila Galleon route, Acapulco's well-protected harbor became the entry and exit point for galleons traveling along this crucial commercial route for over 250 years. In 1565, the first galleon, the *San Pedro*, under the direction of *fray* Andrés de Urdaneta, discovered the *tornaviaje*, or return route, from the Philippines, following the northern Pacific currents to the American continent and then sailing south to reach Acapulco. This development made it possible to establish a continuous connection between Acapulco and Manila. Manila itself was part of a preexisting network of Asian commercial routes. The Spanish Crown protected this trade route from competing interests, such as the merchants from Seville or Lima. Under the direction of the Casa de la Contratación, the merchants of Mexico controlled the trade, fighting with the irregular Peruvian ships and merchants that made the voyage yearly for the best products and prices. Taxation on imported products helped finance the administration of the Philippines and supported the Church in the islands. Historical accounts mention the luxurious items that passed through Acapulco, including silks, cotton, and other textiles from India, China, and the Philippines;

spices and precious woods from Southeast Asia; lacquerware and screens from Japan; and ceramics from China.

Several historical figures testify that Acapulco was an ideal port, as William Lytle Schurz pointed out in his famous 1939 book on the Manila Galleon:

> *Domingo Fernández de Navarrete, a much-traveled friar, called it "the best and safest harbor in the world, as was duly asserted by those who have seen many others." Of the size of the harbor Dampier remarks: "The Port of Acapulco is very commodious for the reception of Ships, and so large, that some hundreds may safely Ride there without damnifying each other." Lord Anson considered it "the securest and finest in all the northern parts of the Pacific Ocean." Malaspina, one of the most skilled of Spanish navigators of the later eighteenth century, a scientific seaman of the type of Cook and Bougainville, favored the further development of Acapulco as a Spanish naval base for the northern Pacific and a great commercial port. He thought it much superior to San Blas. "No one can deny," he said, "that Acapulco has great advantages which are found together in very few ports of the globe." Humboldt, who saw the place in 1803, thus describes the harbor, which he called "the finest of all those on the coast of the great ocean," and again "one of the finest ports in the known world:" "The port of Acapulco forms an immense basin cut in granite rocks."*[2]

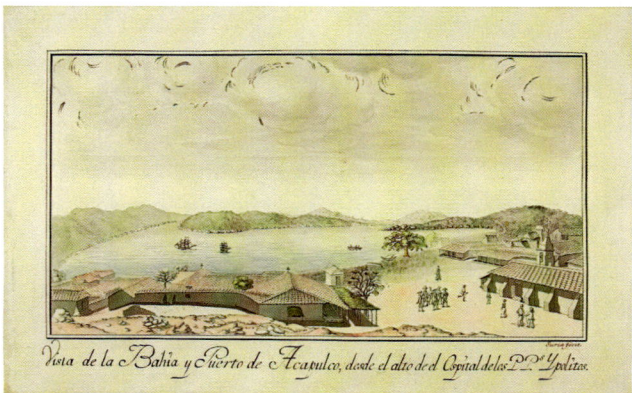

Fig. 1 Tomás de Suría (1761–1844), *Acapulco Bay and Port*, from the expedition of Malaspina (1789–1794), Mexico, 1791. Laid paper, ink, sepia, and colored gouaches, 11⅝ × 19¼ in. (29.5 × 49 cm). Biblioteca Virtual de Defensa, Archivo Histórico de la Armada - J.S. de Elcano [AHA JSE Ms. 1726 (44)].

Despite the galleons, the annual fair, and the arrival of Peruvian ships and merchants from the interior, Acapulco remained modest throughout its historical period (fig. 1). Its most prominent structure was the Fort of San Diego. Other notable buildings included the cathedral church, a Franciscan convent, the San Juan de Dios Hospital, and the Royal Contaduría. None of them were significant or strongly built. In 1598, some 250 tiny houses existed, made of wood, adobe, and palm. The hot climate, the mosquitos and animals, and the lack of food, among other reasons, made it hellish for a population to develop. Many accounts from travelers and administrators attest to this.[3]

In 1578, fear spread through New Spain as it became known that Francis Drake passed northward through the viceroyalty, attacking the town of Huatulco. The same happened when Thomas Cavendish, in 1587, captured the galleon *Santa Ana* at the tip of Baja California. However, it was the

Dutch attack on Acapulco in 1615 by Joris van Spilbergen that prompted the viceroy, Diego Fernández de Córdoba, 1st Marquess of Guadalcázar, to commission the construction of a new redoubt from the engineer Adrian Boot, who oversaw the drainage works in Mexico City. However, the viceroy rejected the initial proposal because it was small and insufficient. Boot then sent a fortification project consisting of five towers joined together with projections to give a pentagonal shape, which was approved. Work started in 1616, on top of a promontory dominating the bay to prevent attacks by pirates and enemies of the Crown who entered the bay. It was completed by February 1617. The fortress remained impregnable throughout the colonial period, except for a brief attack by Dutch pirates in 1624. However, a severe earthquake on April 2, 1776, caused substantial damage, leading to reconstruction efforts that commenced in 1778 and concluded in 1783. The rebuilt fortress, made of stone and surrounded by a moat, could accommodate up to two thousand people with ample provisions for a year. Initiated in 1810, the independence movement in Mexico became interested in capturing Acapulco. General José María Morelos sieged the Fort of San Diego for two years. The War of Independence ended the route; the last ship sailed off into the Pacific in 1815, ending a long, prosperous line. Acapulco remained sleepy until new opportunities came in the form of tourism and it regained its celebrated name.

Manila Galleon Archaeology

The archaeological interest in the colonial period of Acapulco arose from broader interest in the archaeology of the Manila Galleon, a theme and an approach that explores all aspects of the galleons, such as infrastructure, maritime and nautical aspects, trade, cultural influences, distribution, etc. and which has been developing through several papers and archaeological interventions over time.[4] As José Luis Gasch-Tomás has noted: "Unfortunately, the archaeological studies of the Manila galleons have not developed as much as their histories. Apart from a few excavated underwater sites and several studies of the material culture transported in the galleons, especially Chinese porcelain and to a lesser extent Chinese silk and Japanese furniture, experts have undertaken few archaeological researches of the Manila galleons."[5] Among the few projects focused on shipwrecks recently conducted are the search for the galleon *San Francisco* in Japan by archaeologist Jun Kimura and several in the Philippines by Bobby Orillaneda and his team.[6]

In 2000, the Underwater Archaeology Office (SAS) of the National Institute of Anthropology and History of Mexico (INAH) began researching the remains of a sixteenth-century Manila galleon, wrecked on the journey from the Philippines to New Spain, on the coast of Baja California at the 38th parallel. This desolate, desert-like region by the ocean holds remains of the ship's cargo scattered along eleven kilometers of the shoreline. A reference to the shipwreck site appeared in George Kuwayama's *Chinese Ceramics in Colonial Mexico* (1997).[7] His book presented images of Chinese porcelain sherds from an "unpublished site off the Baja California coast." This citation aroused the interest of maritime historian Edward Von der Porten, who contacted him for more information. Kuwayama revealed that beachcombers had collected porcelain sherds from the site. In 1999, with this knowledge and under the supervision of INAH, Von der Porten, along with archaeologists Jack Hunter and Edward Ritter, organized the first expedition to the site thanks to the beachcombers' information (fig. 2). SAS-INAH subsequently established the archaeological project "Manila Galleon, Baja California," providing financial support for ongoing excavations, conservation, and research until Von der Porten's passing in 2019. To date, 3,787 artifacts have been documented at the site, with extensive finds from the Chinese Wanli period (1573–1620), totaling 1,923 pieces. The collection primarily includes underglaze blue-and-white plates, bowls, cups, bottles, and boxes, alongside polychrome pieces studied by Von der Porten. The porcelain was manufactured in Jingdezhen (Jiangxi province) and Zhangzhou (Fujian province), and it significantly resembles the pieces from the sunken Chinese vessel *Nan'ao 1*, thought to have been en route to Manila in the early stages of the trade route.[8] Additionally, at least five different types of stoneware sherds and complete pieces from southern China and Southeast Asia (possibly northern Vietnam) have been identified

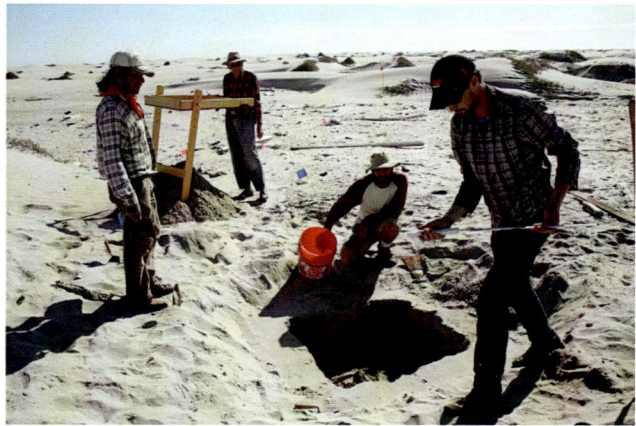

Fig. 2 Archaeologists Edward Von der Porten and Peter Von der Porten, from SAS-INAH, at the site of a Manila Galleon, Baja California, Mexico, 2015. Courtesy the author.

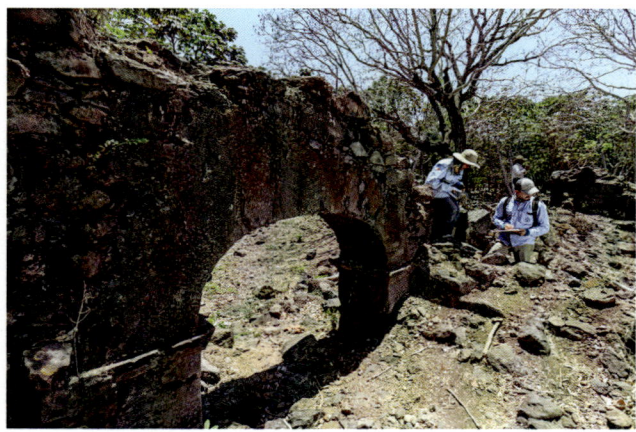

Fig. 3 Archaeologists from SAS-INAH prospecting the Contaduria complex in San Blas, Nayarit, Mexico, 2017. Courtesy A. Martinez, SAS-INAH.

and were likely used as containers during the voyage. Other significant finds include fragments of Spanish olive jars, cloisonné plates, Mexican silver coins, a Chinese coin, small lead objects, pieces of beeswax, lead shot, metal fittings, a bronze incense burner cover shaped like a Fu dog, and compass gimbals.[9] These artifacts provide crucial insights into the cargo carried aboard the galleons and the ship construction technology of that era.[10]

In 2006, an archaeological survey along the north coast of the state of Guerrero indicated possible smuggling activities related to the Manila Galleon route. Ming dynasty (1368–1644) porcelain sherds and a type of maiolica known as Romita Sgraffito were recorded. Around the same time, neutron activation analysis revealed this type of slipware was made in the region of the lakes of Michoacán. Therefore, the hypothesis is that some smuggled porcelain was destined for this region as part of an exchange route not documented in the historical record, revealing that not all Asian merchandise arrived in Acapulco

before traveling to Mexico City as was the norm. Alternative, lesser-known routes were utilized for trade. The coastal area of Petatlán, to the north, was ideal for ships to anchor and load water, facilitating the unloading of select cargo items.[11]

In 2016 and 2017, SAS-INAH conducted an archaeological inspection of the Port of San Blas on the Pacific coast of Mexico, which yielded a collection of Chinese porcelain sherds linked to the transpacific trade (fig. 3). Although officially active only for a few decades in the eighteenth century, this port served as a stop along the Manila Galleon route. The predominant type of porcelain in the collection is landscape designs produced in Jingdezhen, which later developed into the "willow pattern." The second most common type is blue-and-white Jingdezhen porcelain, followed by red-overglaze bowls known as Guanzai, dated from the mid-seventeenth to nineteenth centuries, indicating a continued movement of Asian goods even prior to San Blas's establishment as a maritime department. As Gasch-Tomás mentions, "Remains of shipwrecks and Chinese porcelain are becoming as important as archival documents to write the history of the Manila galleons."[12] Indeed, porcelain has been archaeologically reported in the past in Mexico as elsewhere by authors like Goggin, Lister and Lister, López Cervantes, Pierson, and Fournier, among others.[13] A distribution map showing archaeological finds of these ceramics was published in 2019 by Fournier and Junco.[14] Many noteworthy archaeological works have been published since, some about specific sites like the kilns in China, new wrecks found in the Philippines, and ports and cities along the route. It would be another type of undertaking to be able to cite them all, but allow me to highlight some notable contributions, such as the work of Guanyu Wang, who characterized the porcelain traded by the Manila Galleon in the early part of the trade, during the Ming dynasty, describing three key moments.[15] In the same book, Nida Cuevas writes about Fujian and Hizen wares found in the Philippines, Tai-Kang Lu addresses Kraak pieces from Macau and Taiwan linked to the Manila Galleon, and Etsuko Miyata describes the ceramics at Nagasaki and their relation to the Galleon.[16] Archaeology is in an interesting position from which to study not simply the design, distribution, and evolution of porcelain but also the preferences of consumers. Furthermore, symbolic aspects (as mentioned in the work of Skowronek) and stylistic influences on Mexican ceramics from the imported Chinese porcelain appear in shape, color, and style (as in the work of Castillo and

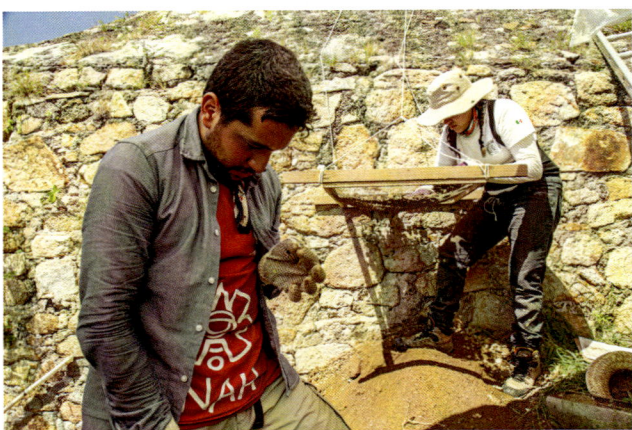

Fig. 4   Archaeologists from SAS-INAH excavating at the walls of the Fort of San Diego, Acapulco, Mexico, 2018. Courtesy A. Soto, SAS-INAH.

Fournier).[17] It also allows us to reconstruct lesser-known aspects of the past, such as in San Blas, where porcelain reveals smuggling routes, which by nature are little documented, or as in Acapulco, where the distribution of porcelain permits us to make inferences on the location of the fair and where the galleon was unloaded. In recent years, a vibrant study of these topics has emerged and will contribute significantly to understanding the Manila Galleon from a material perspective.

Manila Galleon Archaeology in Acapulco

Historically, archaeological research in Acapulco has primarily focused on prehispanic remains around the bay. The area is home to various recorded archaeological sites, petroglyphs, and ceramic artifacts, some of which are among the oldest ceramics in Mesoamerica.[18] However, little attention had been given to the colonial period, and no materials were reported until 2015. That year, excavations at the Fort of San Diego uncovered enough evidence to initiate a long-overdue project focused on the colonial period (fig. 4). In 2015, the SAS-INAH responded to a report in Acapulco Bay and documented some historical objects that divers retrieved from the water. Also, excavations in Acapulco commenced as a rescue effort linked to maintenance work on the outer wall of the San Diego fortress, which is now the History Museum of Acapulco, recovering archaeological materials from the prehispanic, early contact, colonial, and republican periods. This excavation found various materials such as ceramics, metal, glass, stone, and bone. Among the ceramics are sherds of prehispanic and local wares, Spanish olive jars, Chinese porcelain, English transfer-printed pottery, and Asian stoneware. Archaeological research focusing on the colonial period in Acapulco has led to the development of a comprehensive project that includes underwater and land investigations at the port, the "Proyecto de Arqueología Marítima del Puerto de Acapulco" (PAMPA, or Maritime Archaeology Project at the Port of Acapulco), which aims to reconstruct historic Acapulco's maritime activity. One of the main goals of PAMPA is to understand the relationship between archaeological materials and trade dynamics over time, examining how these evolved and changed. Since Acapulco was the gateway between New Spain and the Pacific Ocean, investigating the archaeological remains at the port is key to understanding commercial dynamics of the colonial period. The project also involves documenting shipwrecks and the remains of vessels to catalog all historical elements

found within the bay. The project employs a variety of theoretical approaches, including historical archaeology and maritime archaeology, to interpret these findings.

A second archaeological excavation took place in downtown Acapulco in 2016, where the local government initiated a thirty-meter-long ditch for a water system replacement adjacent to the Cathedral on Francisco I. Madero, La Paz, and José María Iglesias streets. This two-meter-deep ditch unveiled thousands of blue-and-white porcelain fragments, primarily of the Kraak porcelain style produced in various private kilns in Jingdezhen. Given the site's central location, it is hypothesized that it may have been where the traditional Acapulco Fair was hosted annually just after the arrival of the Manila Galleon every December or January. The similarities in motifs on the porcelain sherds and their size suggest that many pieces sustained damage during the long five- to six-month voyage from Asia to Acapulco, with some items likely breaking en route and being discarded upon arrival.[19] Three test pits on the slopes of Fort San Diego were excavated. Many materials were recovered during this season, including over five thousand pieces of Chinese porcelain, mainly from the sixteenth and seventeenth centuries.

In 2017, further archaeological rescue was conducted in the town center, focusing on several streets, especially parts of La Quebrada street. In 2018, excavations were carried out at Fort San Diego, with four excavation units recovering material and documenting an architectural element before a section of the fort wall. In 2019, restoration work was performed on the mentioned part of the old fort, and it was reburied. This project has recovered over ten thousand colonial-period artifacts, including Chinese porcelains, maiolica and colonial ceramics, English earthenware, metal artifacts, and glass.

In the 2020 season, activities were proposed related to the organization of the information generated, as well as documentary research efforts, highlighting access to digital collections for the creation of a digital and physical library of maps and plans of the port of Acapulco and Fort San Diego from the colonial era. Additionally, dissemination talks were planned for primary schools and carried out remotely. Once normal post-pandemic activities resumed in 2023, office work focused on analysis of the recovered porcelain collection and creating a database for information and consultation. Finally, in 2024, along with Dr. Ivan Valdéz of UNAM, we curated the restructuring of the museography content at Fort San Diego, displaying some of the pieces recovered from the excavations conducted there (fig. 5).

An Ocean of Blue and White

While Chinese porcelain had not been previously documented archaeologically in Acapulco, the more than 6,500 fragments identified to date are noteworthy. Preliminary analysis indicates that, within the fortress, most of the porcelain dates to the eighteenth and nineteenth centuries, whereas the porcelain found in downtown Acapulco belongs to the sixteenth and early seventeenth centuries; some of the sherds appear to be from very early in the route, the 1560s and 1570s. This discrepancy can be attributed to the fortress's destruction during an earthquake in 1766, followed by its reconstruction. In contrast, the downtown area, where more than 90 percent of all porcelain was recovered, mainly from the Wanli period (1573–1620) of the Ming dynasty (1368–1644), may well be the site of the cargo offloading, the area for opening containers, and where the Acapulco Fair was held annually. Some of the pieces in the collection point to this fact. For example, over a dozen fragments of a delicate plate representing deer in the park from the Ming dynasty can be said to have come from the same hand (fig. 6). When we overlap the fragments, we see they are almost identical in the paintwork. As with a puzzle, the fragments that could not be joined belong to at least four plates, maybe six or more. Having been made and packed in Jingdezhen, they traveled to the coast, sailed to Manila, then sailed to Mexico, and arrived partially broken in Acapulco (fig. 7). They were likely discarded in the same place where the unpacking was done during the Acapulco Fair. A dozen plates were bundled together, and a few cracked. Whatever the fact, they are also important as they are the finest example of a considerable number of plates with a deer-in-the-park design. There is also a plate from around the same period from Zhangzhou, somewhat reconstructed, and it has a lower-quality design of a deer in the park in the collection (fig. 8).[20] This

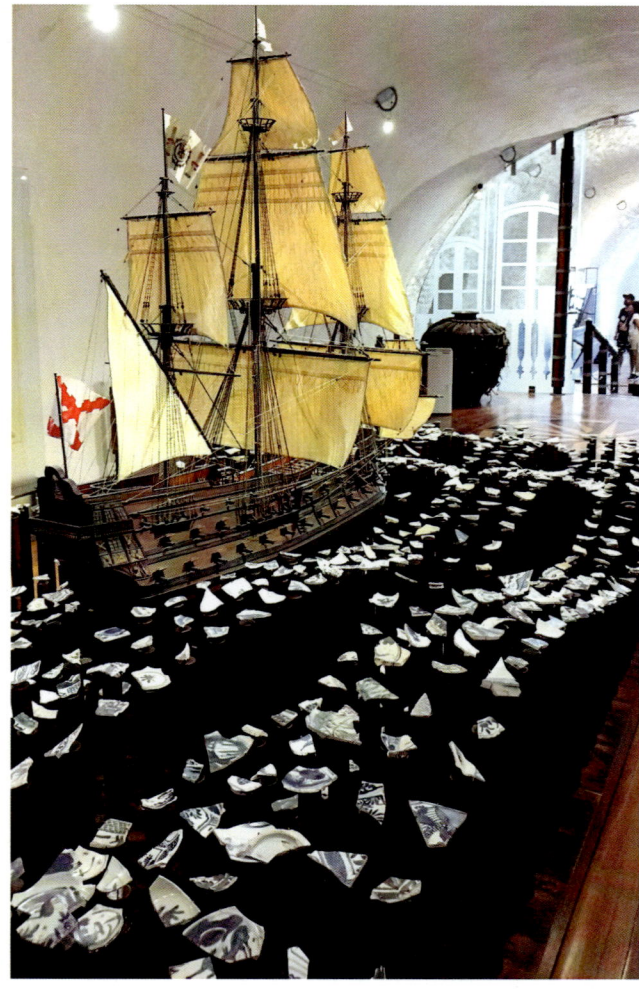

Fig. 5 A replica of the Manila Galleon *N.S. de Guía*, on blue-and-white ware, Mexico. Museum of Acapulco at the Fort of San Diego. Courtesy the author.

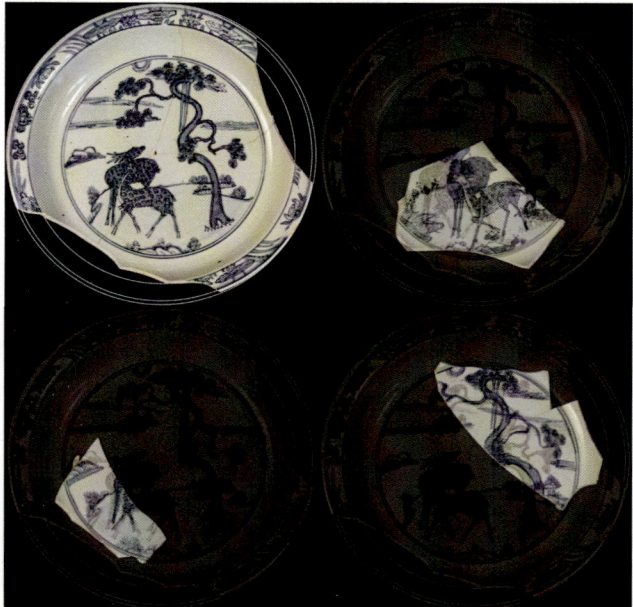

Fig. 6 View of the fine deer-in-the-park plate with overlapping sherds showing the differences and similarities. It is possible they were done in the same shop at the same time and broke together, about 1580–95. Courtesy the author and F. Troncoso, SAS-INAH.

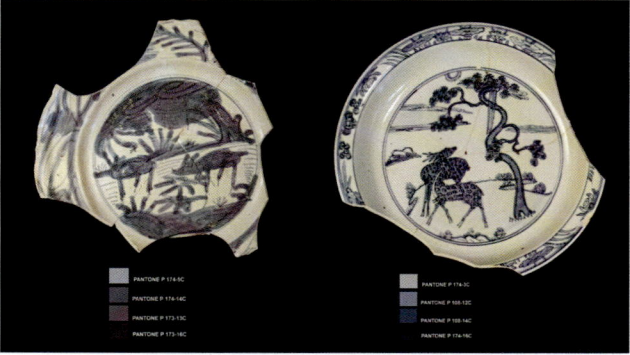

Fig. 8 Comparison of two plates with the same deer motif. One is from Jingdezhen the other from Zhangzhou. They demonstrate the range in qualities aboard the galleons. Courtesy the author and F. Troncoso, SAS-INAH.

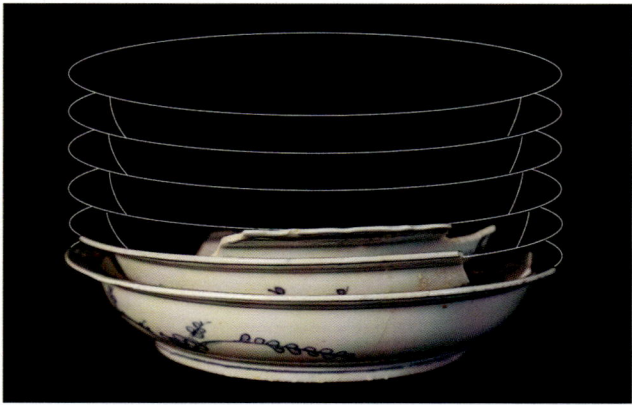

Fig. 7 Reconstruction of the fine deer-in-the-park plates from the available sherds. There are at least four plates (maybe even six) from the sherds recovered. Courtesy the author and F. Troncoso, SAS-INAH.

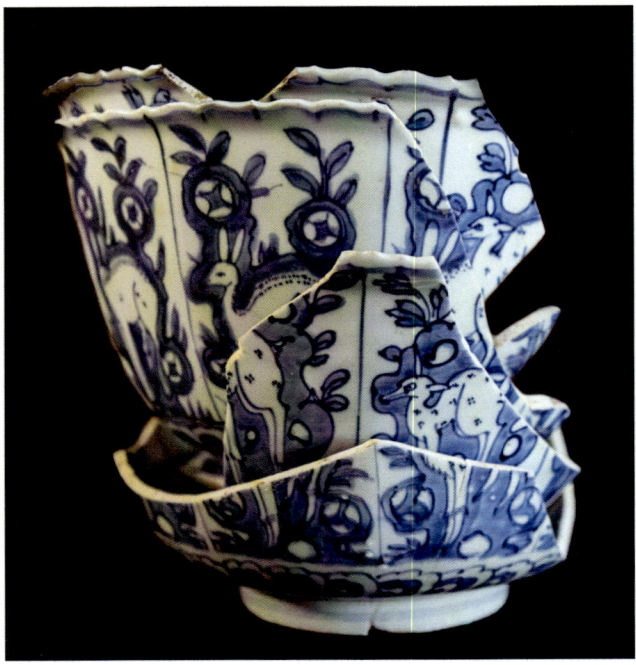

Fig. 9 Large bowls with the same deer motif, a popular Wanli (1573–1620) export design. Courtesy the author and F. Troncoso, SAS-INAH.

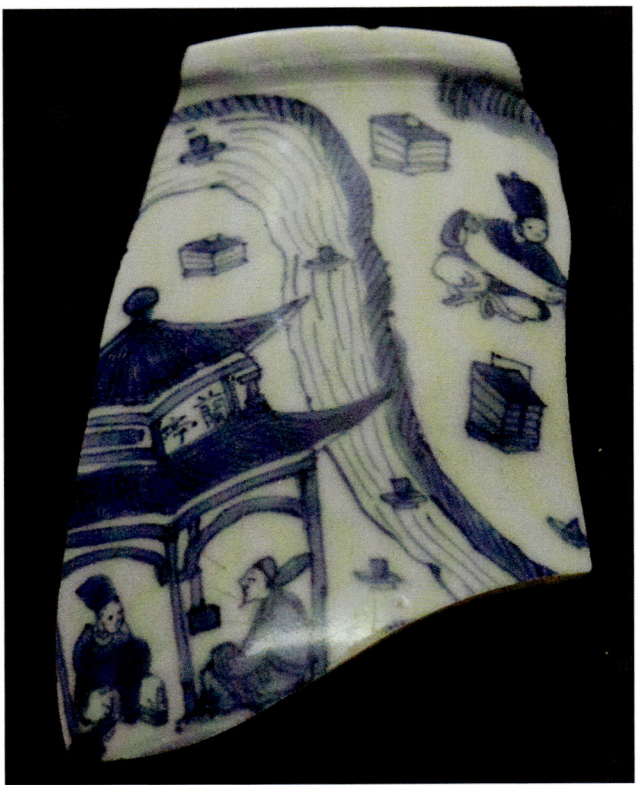

Fig. 10 Sherd of a large cup in blue-and-white porcelain from the Wanli (1573–1620) period, depicting the celebrated "Lanting Xu." This scene is represented broadly in the late Ming dynasty (1368–1644) on different media. Courtesy the author and F. Troncoso, SAS-INAH.

comparison gives us a range of what the consumers in New Spain acquired.

As mentioned, there is a large quantity of this motif in plates, bowls, and large vessels.[21] As with the plates mentioned earlier, around two dozen fragments of large bowls with deer (ca. 1580–95) suggest items discarded when unpacked (fig. 9). Although the deer are not identical in all (some are), they are the same shape and design with slight variations; for instance, the dotting in the deer is sometimes in clusters of four and in other instances is in lines. The interior base presents, in all but one, a rabbit. A few small bowls also repeat the deer motif in a smaller version. The same thing occurs with the typical cups decorated with a crow motif (ca. 1590–1600). There are a dozen bases with this motif, with slight variations of the bird

in the interior bottom of the cup and the exterior decoration.

A fascinating example of the porcelain that arrived in Mexico is a sherd identified by Etsuko Miyata as the well-known scene of the poem "Lanting Xu." The famous Chinese poem narrates an event that took place in 353 CE during the Jin dynasty (265–420) when the poet and calligrapher Wang Xizhi (303–361) gathered with fellow literati at the Orchid Pavilion to celebrate the Spring Purification ritual. They collectively composed thirty-seven poems, among which Wang wrote the "Lanting Xu," serving as a preface to their work.[22] The poem has become one of China's masterpieces of calligraphy. Over a

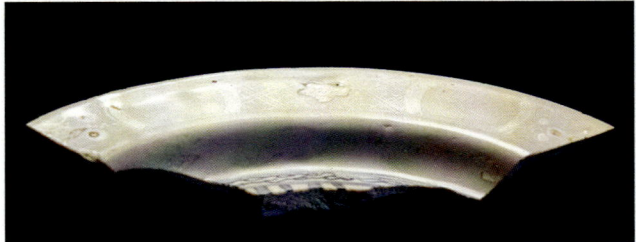

Fig. 11 A blue-and-white Wanli (1573–1620) plate with the phoenix design and overglaze enamel, which has disappeared, but the imprint can still be seen under certain angles. Examples of this design can be found in Lima and the *Nan'ao 1* wreck. Courtesy the author and F. Troncoso, SAS-INAH.

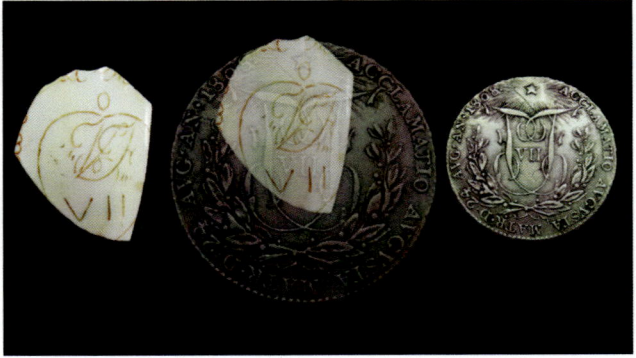

Fig. 12 Fragment of a white chocolate cup with the monogram of Ferdinand VII, king of Spain, possibly, and the coin of his proclamation with his monogram. The execution of the decoration is poor. Courtesy the author and F. Troncoso, SAS-INAH.

millennium later, this story was depicted on a blue-and-white porcelain bowl produced in Jingdezhen at the end of the Ming dynasty (fig. 10). Like many other goods, the understandings of these objects varied among the individuals who crafted them in China, those who traded them in the Philippines, and those who bought them in New Spain and beyond. Exploring these perspectives can provide a more comprehensive understanding of the interconnected societies involved.

Overall, the downtown segment of the collection contains early blue-and-white Zhangzhou pieces, fine early Wanli, typical export wares (such as the phoenix plates), and some polychromed plates and bowls, which are very similar to the ones found in Baja California and the *Nan'ao 1* wreck (fig. 11). Fragments of Kraak saucer dishes, plates, small plates, bowls, bottles, dishes, ewers, *klapmuts* (a type of vessel), cups, boxes, and jars are present.[23] One sherd was identified as having been reused as a tool for cutting. On the bottom of a phoenix plate, the foot and base were flaked on both sides to make a cutting implement. Few chocolate cups appear, a design that would

become very common. Few Qing dynasty (1644–1911) pieces were recovered. No *Imari* or enameled pieces are present as are in Mexico City, for example. The end of the Ming dynasty in the seventeenth century interrupted porcelain production and flow to New Spain, with the Galleon bringing fewer porcelains compared to textiles, though perhaps fewer objects have been found due to different packing, unloading cargo into other spaces in the port, or having larger, more stable ships. These thoughts are inquiries to make sense of the pattern.

The sherds from the fort are very different. European decorations are abundant, as are some blue-and-white Canton wares. A few white "Dehua" pieces, such as cups, boxes, and the foot of a lion, are present. Armorial designs are but two so far: One is a small fragment, likely from a plate with a heraldic composition of a lion behind a red and gold flag; another is the body of a chocolate cup with what appears to be Ferdinand VII's monogram (fig. 12). The design is in oxide red and gold, clearly depicting the Roman numeral VII above the letter F. A similar monogram appears in the commemorative coin of his coronation. The extraordinary thing is that Ferdinand VII became king in 1808 and had to abdicate to Napoleon's pressure shortly thereafter. After commissioning a porcelain set in his honor, the chocolate cup would have arrived two or three years later. He became king again in late 1813, only two years before the last galleon departed Acapulco in 1815. It is almost certain that these commemorative works would have arrived in New Spain after Ferdinand's abdication and would have thus been discarded.

Conclusions

The port of Acapulco, the origin and terminus of the Acapulco–Manila Galleon route, has been the focus of extensive archaeological work since 2015. Inspired by Manila Galleon studies, this maritime archaeology project seeks to explore the material aspects of this trade route. The project, conducted by the Underwater Archaeology Office (SAS) of INAH, has completed several field seasons and recovered a significant collection of objects. In the first five field seasons (2015–19), it recorded more than 6,500 sherds of Chinese porcelain, Asian stoneware, olive jars, Mexican majolica, and local wares, illustrating Acapulco's trading significance and daily life through ceramics. Excavations at the fort have incorporated test pits and geophysical explorations to locate the original fort structure that collapsed in 1766 due to an earthquake. Analysis of archaeological materials has provided insights into their provenance and exchanges during this period. Preliminary analysis of the porcelain suggests that while most of it belongs to the eighteenth and nineteenth centuries in the Fort of San Diego, in downtown Acapulco it belongs to the sixteenth and first half of the seventeenth centuries. In the case of downtown, it could be the area of the cargo offloading, the opening of containers, and where the Acapulco Fair took place. Most of these sherds were likely pieces that arrived broken from the long journey and discarded in situ. The collection of Chinese porcelain excavated by PAMPA in Acapulco features a variety of types imported to New Spain that makes it a unique catalog of the different shapes and designs that traversed the Pacific Ocean. A detailed catalog of the collection is forthcoming.

Notes

1. Meha Priyadarshini, *Chinese Porcelain in Colonial Mexico: The Material Worlds of an Early Modern Trade* (Springer, 2018), 107; Ellen Hsieh, *The Archaeology of Early Colonial Manila: A Hybrid City in Global History* (Florida University Press, 2025), 41.

2. William Lytle Shurz, *The Manila Galleon* (E. P. Dutton, 1939), 372.

3. Ibid., 373–75.

4. Roberto Junco, "The Archaeology of Manila Galleons," in *Proceedings on the Asia-Pacific Regional Conference on Underwater Cultural Heritage*, ed. Mark Staniforth, Jennifer Craig, Sheldon Clyde Jago-on, Bobby Orillaneda, and

Ligaya Lacsina (Asian Academy for Heritage Management, 2011), 877.

5. José Luis Gasch-Tomás, "The Manila Galleons in Perspective: Notes on the History and Archaeology of the Transpacific Trade," in *Heritage and the Sea. Volume 2: Maritime History and Archaeology of the Global Iberian World (15th–18th centuries)*, ed. Ana Crespo Solana, Filipe Castro, and Nigel Nayling (Springer, 2022), 243.

6. Jun Kimura, "Searching for the *San Francisco* (1609), a Manila Galleon Sunk off the Japanese Coast," in *Archaeology of Manila Galleon Seaports and Early Maritime Globalization*, ed. Chunming Wu, Roberto Junco, and Liu Miao (Springer, 2019), 173; Sheldon Clyde B. Jago-on and Bobby C. Orillaneda, "Archaeological Researches on the Manila Galleon Wrecks in the Philippines," in *Archaeology of Manila Galleon Seaports*, 129.

7. George Kuwayama, *Chinese Ceramics in Colonial Mexico* (Los Angeles County Museum of Art and Hawaii University Press, 1997).

8. Chunshui Zhou, "The Investigation and Preliminary Analysis of *Nanao No. I* Shipwreck in Guangdong," in *Archaeology of Manila Galleon Seaports*, 49.

9. Edward P. Von der Porten, *Ghost Galleon: The Discovery and Archaeology of the* San Juanillo *on the Shores of Baja California* (Texas A&M University Press, 2019).

10. Roberto Junco, "On a Manila Galleon of the 16th Century: A Nautical Perspective," in *Early Navigation in the Asia-Pacific Region: A Maritime Archaeology Perspective*, ed. Chunming Wu (Springer, 2016), 103.

11. Roberto Junco, "Smuggling Porcelain from the Manila Galleon," in *The Archaeology of Manila Galleons in the American Continent: The Wrecks of Baja California, San Agustín, and Santo Cristo de Burgos (Oregon)*, ed. Scott Williams and Roberto Junco (Springer, 2021) 93.

12. Gasch-Tomás, "The Manila Galleons in Perspective," 235.

13. For an overview of Chinese porcelain in Mexico as a research topic, see Patricia Fournier and Roberto Junco, "Archaeological Distribution of Chinese Porcelain in Mexico," in *Archaeology of Manila Galleon Seaports*, 220.

14. Ibid., 222.

15. Guanyu Wang, "Chinese Porcelain in the Manila Galleon Trade," in *Archaeology of Manila Galleon Seaports*, 93.

16. Nida T. Cuevas, "Fujian and Hizen Ware: A 17th Century Evidence of the Manila Galleon Trade Found from Selected Archaeological Sites in the Philippines," in *Archaeology of Manila Galleon Seaports*, 115; Tai-Kang Lu, "The Kraak Porcelains Discovered from Taiwan and Macao, and their Relationship with the Manila Galleon Trade," in *Archaeology of Manila Galleon Seaports*, 147; Etsuko Miyata, "Ceramics from Nagasaki: A Link to Manila Galleon Trade," in *Archaeology of Manila Galleon Seaports*, 161.

17. Russell K. Skowronek, "Cinnamon, Ceramics, and Silks: Tracking the Manila Galleon Trade in the Creation of the World Economy," in *Early Navigation in the Asia-Pacific Region*, 59; Karime Castillo and Patricia Fournier, "A Study of the Chinese Influence on Mexican Ceramics," in *Archaeology of Manila Galleon Seaports*, 220.

18. Rubén Manzanilla López and Arturo Talavera González, *Las manifestaciones gráfico rupestres en los sitios arqueológicos de Acapulco* (INAH, 2008), 25.

19. Roberto Junco, "Archaeological Discoveries: The Baja California Shipwreck and the Port of Acapulco," in *Across the Pacific: Art and the Manila Galleons*, ed. Alan Chong and Benjamin Chiesa (Asian Civilisations Museum, 2024), 209.

20. Teresa Canepa, *Zhangzhou Export Ceramics: The So-Called Swatow Wares* (Jorge Welsh Books, 2006).

21. For an in-depth look at these bowls and many pieces in the collection, see Teresa Canepa, *Jingdezhen to the World: The Lurie Collection of Chinese Export Porcelain from the Late Ming Dynasty* (Ad Ilissum, 2019), 154. See also William R. Sargent, *Treasures of Chinese Export Ceramics from the Peabody Essex Museum* (Peabody Essex Museum, 2012).

22. A fragment of Wang Xizhi's famous preface: "I am often moved by the ancients' sentimental lines, which lamented the swiftness and uncertainty of life. When future generations look back to my time, it will probably be like how I now think of the past. What a shame! Therefore, when I list out the people that were here, and record their musings, even though times and circumstances will change, as for the things that we regret, they are the same. For the people who read this in future generations, perhaps you will likewise be moved by my words."

23. Teresa Canepa, *Kraak Porcelain: The Rise of Global Trade in the Late 16th and Early 17th Centuries* (Jorge Welsh Books, 2008), 17.

Name that Pot! Viceregal Potters and Workshops of Puebla de los Ángeles

Margaret E. Connors McQuade, Vice President of Collections, Museum of the City of New York

It is impossible to walk through the historic center of the city of Puebla de los Ángeles (known as Puebla) without encountering the myriad shops lined with colorful glazed pottery, popularly known as *talavera poblana*.[1] In addition to vibrant tableware, ceramic tiles adorn the walls and floors of religious and civic buildings including the endless church domes that define the city's skyline. These colorful remnants speak to the long tradition that began nearly five hundred years ago with the founding of the city.

During the viceregal period of New Spain (1519–1821)—as Mexico was known—Puebla pottery gained widespread popularity across the Americas, reaching regions throughout Central and South America, the Caribbean, and present-day southeastern and southwestern United States. Despite fluctuations in production over the centuries, the tradition has persisted without interruption. Today, Puebla's ceramic tradition is celebrated internationally; however, little attention is given to the individuals who created these renowned wares. This essay aims to shed light on the artisans behind Puebla's famed ceramics and to associate specific pieces with the potters and their workshops.

The tools and techniques for producing tin-glazed earthenware were introduced to New Spain by Spanish potters, building upon the rich legacy of ceramic production that had flourished in Mesoamerica for thousands of years. Pottery in Mesoamerica was hand-built or mold-made, often adorned with colored slip and stamped designs, burnished for a smooth finish, and fired in pit kilns. The pottery of Cholula—located close to the city of Puebla—was particularly well developed by the time of the arrival of the Spanish and had enjoyed widespread circulation throughout Mesoamerica.[2]

Despite the appeal of Indigenous pottery, Spanish settlers sought the wheel-thrown, tin- and lead-glazed earthenware (also known as *maiolica*) they were accustomed to using in Spain. Initially, Spanish glazed ceramic ware was imported to the Americas from Spain; it met the demand of recent settlers and served as excellent ballast for transatlantic galleons. However, as the settler population grew, Spanish workshops could no longer supply sufficient wares. By the mid-sixteenth century, Spanish potters began to migrate to New Spain, bringing essential tools—such as the potter's wheel, tin- and lead-based glazes, and updraft kilns—necessary for achieving a vitreous glazed ceramic ware.

The first known workshops of glazed ware in the Americas were established in Mexico City before 1537 by Spanish potters Francisco de la Reyna and Francisco Morales.[3] While production continued in Mexico City, Puebla quickly emerged as the dominant center of ceramic manufacture by the end of the sixteenth century. Founded in 1531 as the second city of New Spain, Puebla was designed as an urban model for Spanish settlement and an industrial center for the manufacture of European-style goods. In addition to tin-glazed ceramics, the city produced soap, glass, and textiles.

If the location of Puebla was influenced by potters, they chose wisely. The climate was mild, the soil was rich, and there were extensive clay beds and raw sodium

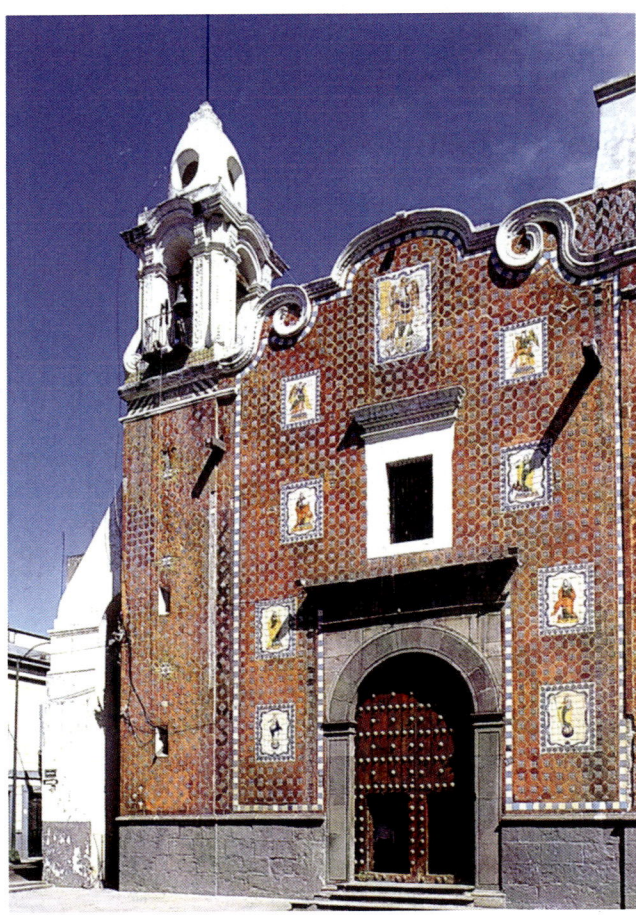

Fig. 1 Facade with tile panels, church of San Marcos, Puebla de los Ángeles, Mexico, about 1797. Photograph by Carlos Varillas.

essential for glaze preparation. Ceramic workshops clustered in the center of the city, within blocks of the cathedral and central square. By 1653, when the potters' guild was officially established, the church of San Marcos had become the seat for the trade. The town council (*ayuntamiento*) first designated the site as the parish church San Antonio Abad in 1538, long before the present facade of the church of San Marcos was completed in 1797 (fig. 1).[4] While the name of the church changed a couple times before it was dedicated to San Marcos in the seventeenth century, it is believed to have always been the location where the potters' confraternity and guild held meetings and celebrated festivities.[5] The church of San Marcos is also named as a reference point for the location of workshops, underscoring the importance of the site as central area for Puebla potters. For example, in 1647 and 1660, the workshop locations of master potters Alfonso Sevillano and Nicólas de la Cueva were listed in operation "on the street of Plaza Publica, at the church of the Evangelist San Marcos."[6]

The first workshops in Puebla were situated on Calle los Herreros ("street of the blacksmiths"), indicating the proximity to other essential trades. As the industry expanded in the seventeenth century, workshops congregated along Poniente 700, including the workshops (*lozerías*) of Cabezas, Zayas, and Alfaro, which continued to operate for over two hundred years.[7] The workshop of Cabezas, one of the largest workshops in the eighteenth century, was likely abandoned after a fire in the early twentieth century. Its two-story structure, adorned with brickwork, tiles, and cherubic figures, suggests its prominence. Nearby, the more modest Zayas workshop housed generations of potters dating back to 1674. Matrimonial records identify Nicólas de Zayas as a mestizo (a person of Spanish and Indigenous descent) and an "official potter of white ware" (*oficial locero de lo blanco*), with subsequent generations continuing the craft.[8] Other known members of the Zayas family who became master potters include José de Zayas (active ca. 1714–30), Nicólas de Zayas (active ca. 1734), Sebastián de Zayas, the elder (*el viejo*) (died 1746),

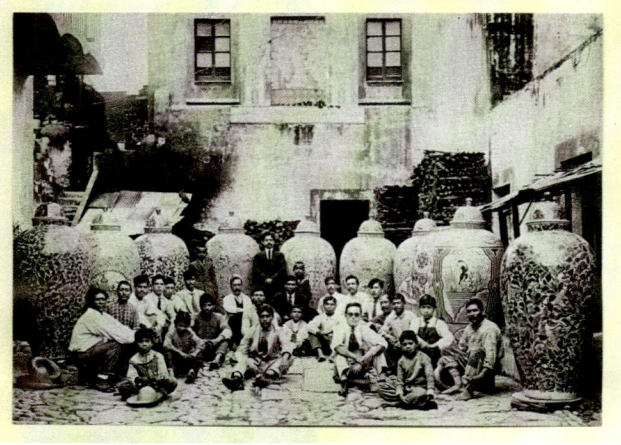

Fig. 2 Padierna ceramic workshop featuring tin-glazed earthenware, Puebla de los Ángeles, Mexico, ca. 1917–18. Enrique Luis Cervantes Collection, Mexico City.

Sebastián de Zayas, the younger (*el mozo*) (born 1715, active ca. 1750), and Antonio de Zayas (active ca. 1772).[9] A photograph from 1918 shows the building when it was owned by Pedro Padierna and his brother, visible behind a group of twenty-five members of their ceramic workshop proudly positioned in front of nine oversized jars made at the end of the Mexican Revolution (fig. 2).

Puebla potters were sufficiently organized by the last quarter of the sixteenth century, with their appointment of aldermen and inspectors. In 1573, Juan Vázquez served as alderman (*alcalde*) and Francisco Trujillo served as inspector (*veedor*).[10] The alderman was the administrator and a link to city authorities, and the inspector was responsible for making periodic inspections of workshops to ensure the observance of required rules and regulations.

Production in Puebla became substantial enough by the mid-seventeenth century for the potters to formalize a guild in 1653. Together, they petitioned the viceroy to use the municipal ordinances to establish standards of production and distribution that would serve to control the trade. The ordinances outlined ten articles specifying requirements for guild membership, prerequisites for master potters, steps for processing clay and glaze mixtures, and the manner in which pieces were to be decorated. The three potters designated to lead the guild in 1653 were Diego Salvador Carreto, Damián Hernández, and Andrés de Haro. Carreto was appointed inspector, Hernández for white ware (*diputado para lo blanco*), and Haro for common or yellow ware (*diputado por lo amarillo*).[11]

To regulate production, the ordinances specified three types of pottery: cooking ware, common ware, and fine ware (*loza amarilla*, *loza común*, and *loza fina*). Later a refine ware (*loza refina*) was added, stipulating that it was reserved for blue-and-white Chinese-style decoration. Those who produced common ware could not produce fine ware unless they had passed an exam and were confirmed by the guild as a master potter.

The city was dominated by Spaniards, and thus, the ordinances decreed only men of pure Spanish parentage could be considered for the master potter examination. However, while the guild was largely controlled by Spaniards, there is adequate evidence to suggest that Indigenous, mestizo, and free and enslaved African men also contributed to production. Franciscan historian Jerónimo de Mendieta (1525–1604), in his book *Historia eclesiástica indiana* (1595), documents

Indigenous expertise in pottery and their eventual mastery of glazing techniques introduced by Spanish craftsmen. He wrote:

[The Indigenous] were masters of pottery and clay hollowware for eating and drinking. Their pottery was finely painted and well made. And although they were not familiar with glazing, they learned this process later from the first masters who arrived from Spain, no matter how much he guarded and protected it from them.[12]

In 1579, Gerónimo Pérez de Salazar agreed to finance the opening of the ceramic workshop of Antonio Xinovés and "feed Xinovés, the other journeymen, and the Indians employed."[13] Other examples support the presence of Indigenous men employed by workshops; however, because they were barred from taking the exam required to become master potters, they were unable to move beyond the role of journeyman. Thus, regardless of proficiency, racial restrictions limited advancement for many potters. Mestizo potters were, however, ultimately permitted to rise to the rank of master potter, such as Francisco Martín, who had worked since 1666 on the street of Traje de la Santa Iglesia Catedral.[14]

One of the earliest documented potters in Puebla, Gaspar de Encinas (ca. 1537–1619), migrated from Seville, Spain, and established a workshop near the cathedral on Calle los Herreros. Born in Seville around 1537, Encinas married María Gaitan from Talavera de la Reina, and they had four sons before he departed for Mexico without his family between 1587 and 1590. Encinas had worked in Talavera de la Reina before moving to New Spain. In New Spain, Encinas produced ceramic tableware, water pipes, and likely the first glazed tiles. In 1602, he received a commission to produce tiles for the first cathedral of Mexico City.[15]

Mexican historian Guillermo Tovar de Teresa attributed to Encinas two rare basins with a lace design in monochrome manganese that he acquired from the Pérez de Salazar collection (one is illustrated in fig. 3).[16] As the decoration likely originated in Talavera de la Reina, it was more likely Encinas's son, Gaspar Encinas, el mozo, who introduced the lace design to Puebla as the style of decoration had not yet been developed before Encinas, el viejo, left for New Spain.[17] Encinas, el mozo, came to Puebla from Talavera de la Reina with his mother at the very end of the sixteenth century, along with a number of supplies his father had requested.[18] Once settled in Puebla, he continued the family tradition by becoming a master potter. A document from 1619 indicates that he and his second wife, Ursula de Espindola, lived on Calle los Mesones, where they kept a store.[19]

Despite the strong resemblance to the lace design from Talavera de la Reina, the decoration of the Puebla basin also evokes its local manufacture with an image of a *guajolote* (Mexican turkey) at the center.[20] The lace decoration evolved significantly from its Spanish roots by the mid-seventeenth century, introducing cobalt and reimagined to create a web-like pattern. To archaeologists, this decoration is

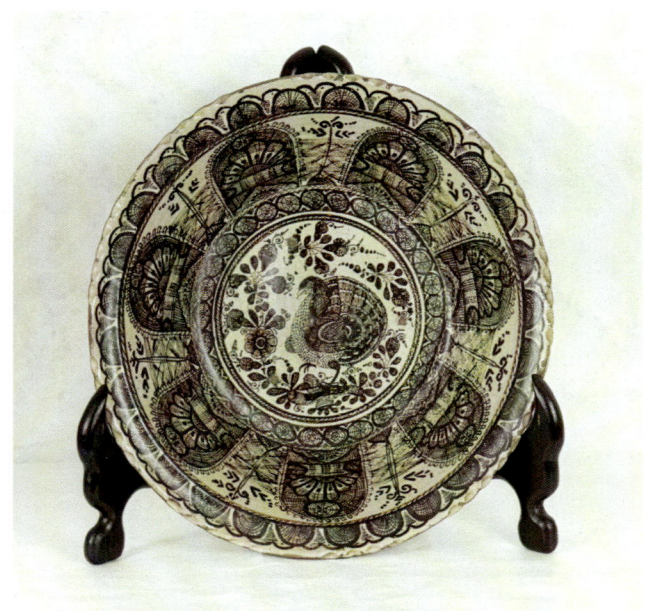

Fig. 3 Attributed to Gaspar de Encinas, the younger, Basin with Guajolote, Puebla de los Ángeles, Mexico, ca. 1600. Tin-glazed earthenware. Guillermo Tovar de Teresa House Museum, Museo Soumaya, Mexico City.

referred to as Puebla Polychrome, characterized by its cobalt-blue-and-manganese design.[21] While intact pieces from the seventeenth century are rare, the number of fragments found in archaeological excavations in Central America, the Caribbean, Georgia, Florida, and New Mexico suggest that it enjoyed a wide appeal.[22] A rare extant example from The Metropolitan Museum of Art includes an inscription: "I am for washing the purificators and nothing else" (*Soy para labar los puryfycadores y no más*), indicating that it was made for washing the altar napkin used to clean the chalice following communion (fig. 4). On the outer wall of the vessel appears the letter "A," referencing a potter's mark that was required by all master potters (fig. 5). Without the existence of a ledger or document correlating the mark to a specific potter or workshop, we must rely on the

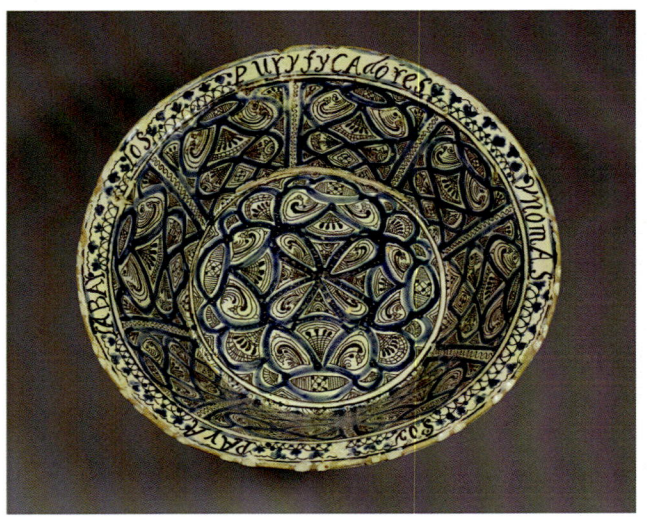

Fig. 4 Basin with inscription "Soy para labar los puryfycadores y no más," marked "A." Puebla de los Ángeles, Mexico, ca. 1625. Tin-glazed earthenware. Image © The Metropolitan Museum of Art. Image source: Art Resource, NY.

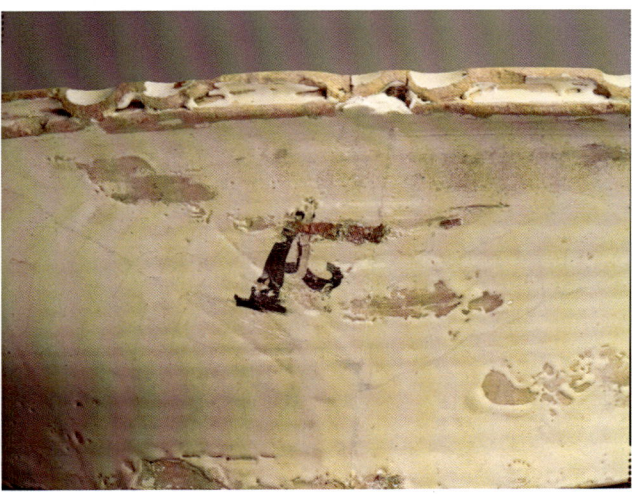

Fig. 5 Basin with inscription "Soy para labar los puryfycadores y no más," (detail of mark "A"), Puebla de los Ángeles, Mexico, ca. 1625. Tin-glazed earthenware. Image © The Metropolitan Museum of Art. Image source: Art Resource, NY.

names we find in historic records that correspond to the dates identified by archaeologists, which for this design span from approximately 1650 to 1680. Using those dates, we may surmise that the mark "A" may be associated with the workshop of Domingo de Aguilar, Jose Anaya, or Antonio de Arteaga, all of whom were master potters from the early to mid-seventeenth century.[23]

The "A" mark also appears on another type of tin-glazed earthenware from Puebla known as Abo Polychrome, which has a distinct combination of orange, yellow, green, and manganese thin lines (fig. 6).[24] Abo polychrome is likely the product of a stipulation in the potter ordinances that specifies "in order that there be variety, the other style of decoration for this fine ware shall be in imitation of Talavera [de la Reina] ware or figures and designs in colors shading them with all the five colors used in the art."[25] Given the strong correlation to

the design tradition of Talavera de la Reina, we might assume that the potter who helped popularize it had worked in Talavera de la Reina or was familiar with the style. Figure 6 is one of the few extant examples. While it is unmarked, it is typical of many of the fragments found with a mark.

By the mid-seventeenth century, Puebla potters began responding to the increasing demand for vessels inspired by Asian designs as a result of transpacific trade between 1565 and 1815 that brought millions of goods from Manila to New Spain—an important topic covered by Diego Javier Luis in this volume.[26] This shift likely took place prior to the issuance of amendments to the ordinances in 1682, one of which specified that one of the decorations shall be in "imitation of Chinese ware, very blue, finished in the same style."[27] A pair of identical blue-and-white jars marked "he" held by the

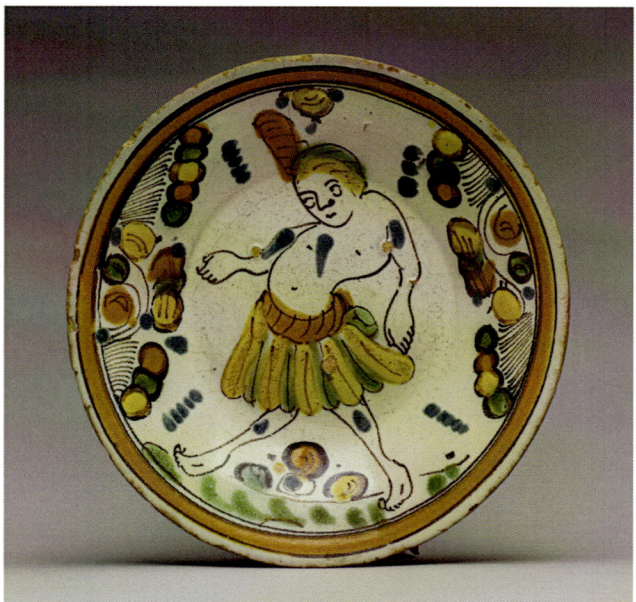

Fig. 6 Plate with figure, Puebla de los Ángeles, Mexico, ca. 1625–75. Tin-glazed earthenware. Hispanic Society Museum & Library, New York.

Hispanic Society Museum & Library (fig. 7) and the Philadelphia Museum of Art represent two of the finest examples of how Puebla potters responded to the growing enthusiasm for Chinese style while also maintaining a unique style of their own. The mark "he" on the lower register has been attributed to master potter Damián Hernández. As a founding member of the potter's guild and one of its first inspectors, the attribution is logical. Born in Spain, Hernández settled in Puebla at a young age and learned the art of tin-glazed earthenware in Mexico from Antonio de Vega y Córdoba. Hernández's name appears in documents as early as 1607, which suggests that he was older and well-established professionally when he founded the guild with his colleagues.[28] The use of blue and white, cloud forms, and male figures with queue hairstyle all characterize the Chinese style. However, the narrative scene better reflects the

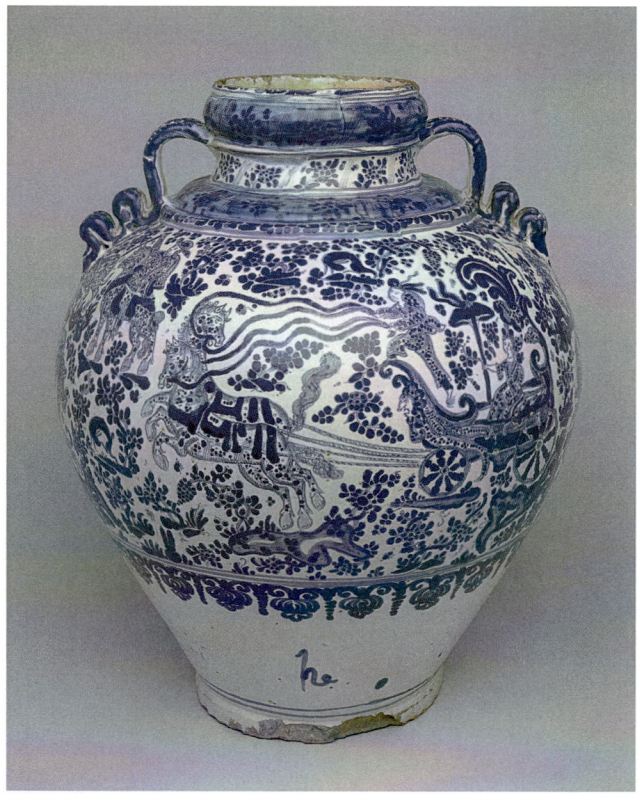

Fig. 7 Attributed to Damián Hernández (active 1607–1653), Jar with festival scene marked "he," Puebla de los Ángeles, Mexico, ca. 1660. Tin-glazed earthenware. Hispanic Society Museum & Library, New York.

dramatic festivals that took place in Puebla and other cities, where individuals dressed in costumes from different parts of the world, bullfights took place, and triumphal chariots processed in a theatrical fashion. One such event occurred in 1649 on the occasion of the consecration of the cathedral of Puebla, when people "dressed as Spaniards and Indians of all nations . . . and performed *cañas y toros* (lance and bullfighting) all ending with the dramatic appearance of a triumphal chariot dedicated to the Immaculate Conception."[29]

Whether the mark "he" represents Hernández, his workshop, or even another potter altogether, the number of sophisticated examples signed "he" suggest that the production was important.[30] A basin from the Franz Mayer Museum (figs. 8 and 9) and a pharmacy jar from The Metropolitan Museum of Art (figs. 10 and 11) are among the wide variety of extant pieces marked "he." The decoration of these and other works fully embraces another article in the 1682 amendment to the ordinances specifying that one decoration shall "be painted in the manner that we call *aborronado*," a term used to describe blurred or blotted dots. The jar (fig. 10) is decorated with a density of decoration surrounding a rectangular void for a removeable label or inscription naming the medicinal contents of the jar. Woven within crowded blurred dots and foliage of the basin (fig. 8) appear a quetzal bird and feline, both important animals in Mesoamerican cosmology and iconography. It is not known if the image was requested as part of a commission or if it was a subject that the painter was familiar with. It does, however, suggest the influence of Mesoamerican imagery endured through the viceregal period. The use of local and Mesoamerican references appears in other vessels, such as the bird on a cactus popularized on blue-and-white jars from about 1700 (fig. 12) and ocelots found on blue-and-white tiles (fig. 13).[31]

Of all the marks known today, "C.S." is one found most frequently on blue-and-white Puebla pottery from the viceregal period (figs. 14 and 15). Edwin Atlee Barber, former director of the Philadelphia Museum and School of Industrial Art (present-day Philadelphia Museum of Art), attributed the mark to Diego Salvador

Carreto, who was active in 1649 and died between 1670 and 1671, and like Hernández was one of the founders of the potters' guild.[32] While the attribution is a logical choice given the quality of the pieces and Carreto's rank in the guild, the letters would then be in reverse order. In current practices, it is not uncommon for workshops to require painters of vessels to sign their initials in reverse, so it is possible that the tradition has been perpetuated over time; however, there is nothing to indicate that this was a common practice during the viceregal period. Another possible attribution is Cristobal Sánchez de Hinojosa, el viejo, who was a master potter documented in 1653.[33] The C.S. mark appears on a wide variety of pieces that span from the mid-seventeenth century through the eighteenth century, which supports the idea that the mark represents a family workshop that continued to use it for generations.

The letter "F" is another important mark found on vessels and a series of tiles representing different trades (see fig. 13). These tiles are among the most finely painted works produced in Puebla during the seventeenth century. Not all the tiles from the series have the "F" mark, although the frequency of the mark and the repetition of the scenes suggest that these were produced at the same workshop. There are a number of artists from the last quarter of the seventeenth century whose names contain the letter "F," such as Juan de la Feria, Luis Fernández Lechuga, and Miguel Fernández Palomino. While the decoration of the tiles is entirely unique,

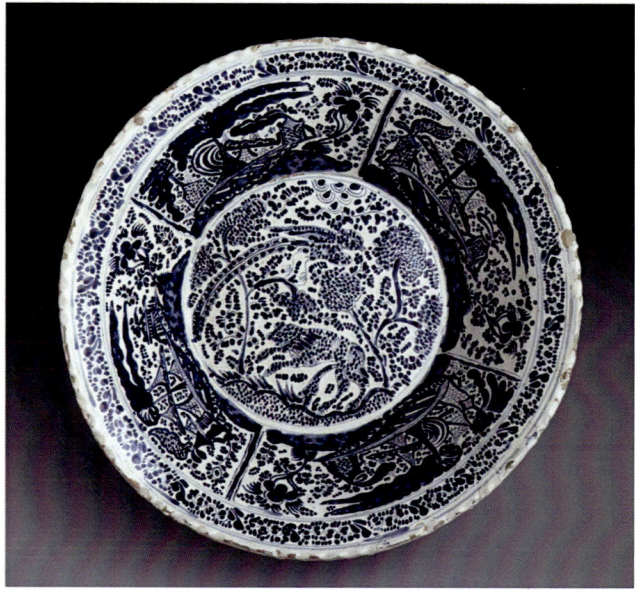

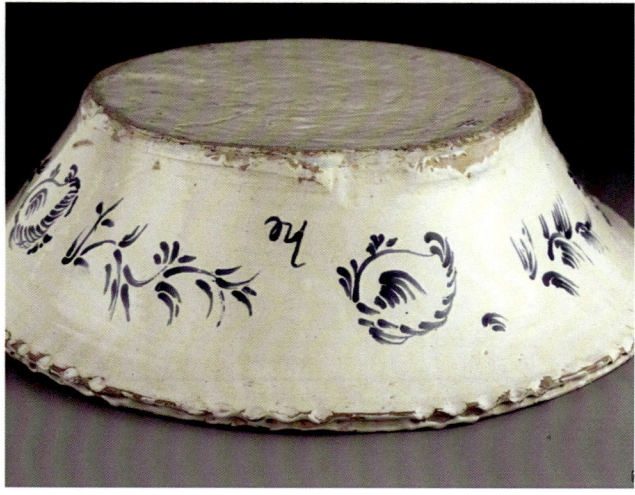

Fig. 9 Attributed to Damián Hernández (active 1607–1653), Basin with quetzal and spotted feline (detail of mark "he"), Puebla de los Ángeles, Mexico, ca. 1660. Tin-glazed earthenware. Franz Mayer Museum, Mexico City.

Fig. 8 Attributed to Damián Hernández (active 1607–1653), Basin with quetzal and spotted feline, marked "he," Puebla de los Ángeles, Mexico, ca. 1660. Tin-glazed earthenware. Franz Mayer Museum, Mexico City.

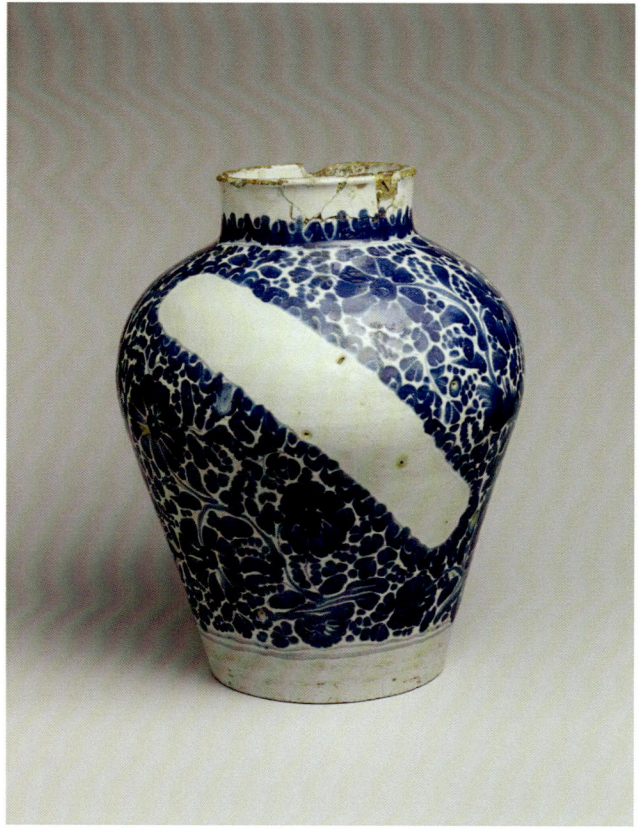

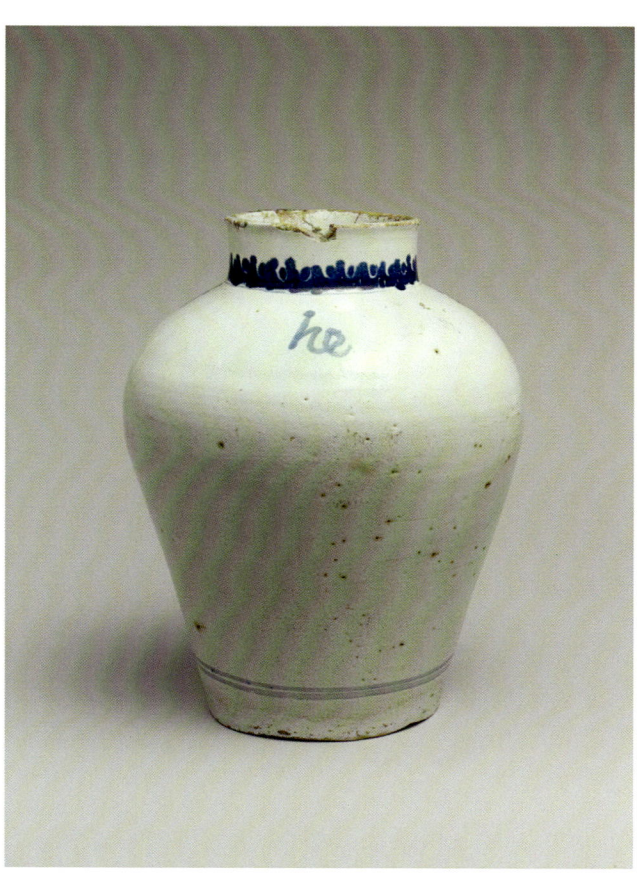

Fig. 11 Attributed to Damián Hernández (active 1607–1653), Pharmacy Jar (detail of mark "he"), Puebla de los Ángeles, Mexico, ca. 1660. Tin-glazed earthenware. Image © The Metropolitan Museum of Art. Image source: Art Resource, NY.

Fig. 10 Attributed to Damián Hernández (active 1607–1653), Pharmacy Jar, marked "he," Puebla de los Ángeles, Mexico, ca. 1660. Tin-glazed earthenware. Image © The Metropolitan Museum of Art. Image source: Art Resource, NY.

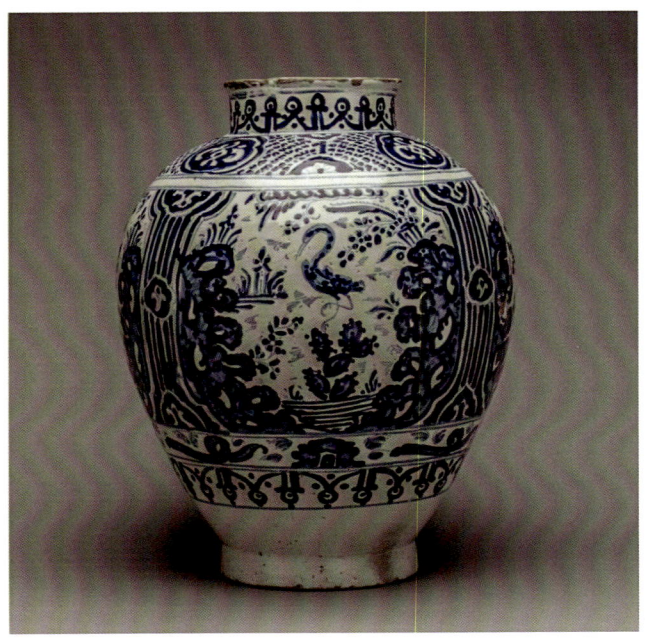

Fig. 12 Jar with cactus and bird, Puebla de los Ángeles, Mexico, ca. 1660–75. Tin-glazed earthenware. The Hispanic Society of America, New York.

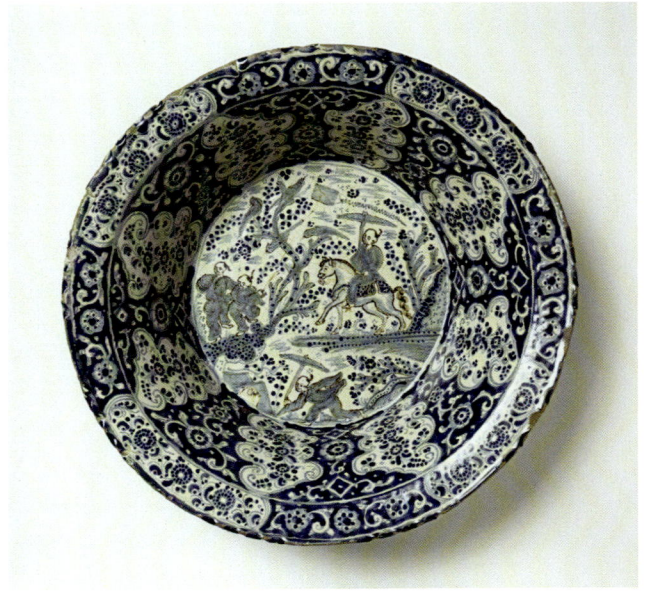

Fig. 14 Attributed to Diego Salvador Carreto (active 1649, died 1670 or 1671), Basin, Puebla de los Ángeles, Mexico, ca. 1649–71. Tin-glazed earthenware. Philadelphia Museum of Art: Purchased with the Joseph E. Temple Fund, 1908.

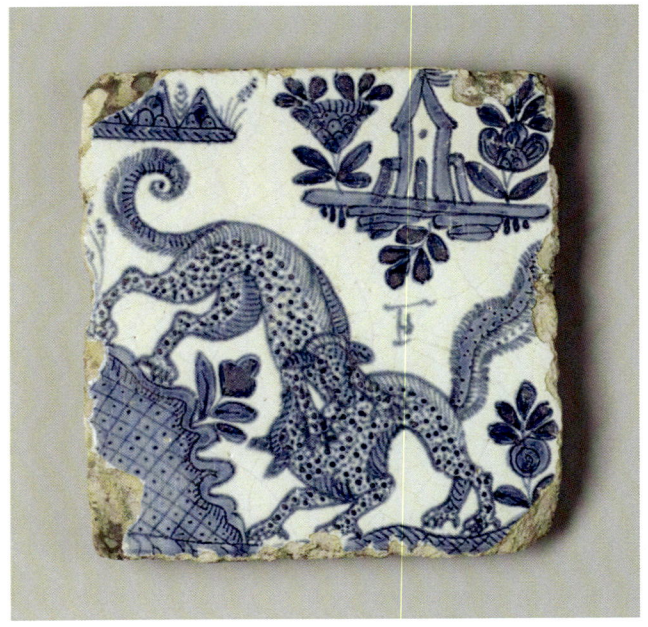

Fig. 13 Trade tile, Puebla de los Ángeles, Mexico, ca. 1660–75. Tin-glazed earthenware. Philadelphia Museum of Art: Purchased with the Joseph E. Temple Fund, 1908.

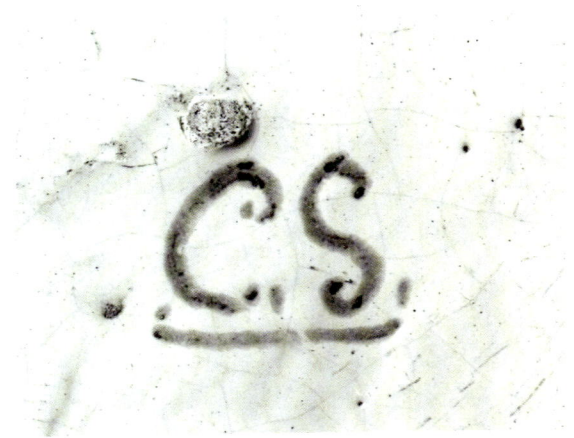

Fig. 15 Attributed to Diego Salvador Carreto (active 1649, died 1670 or 1671), Basin (detail of mark "C.S."), Puebla de los Ángeles, Mexico, ca. 1649–71. Tin-glazed earthenware. Philadelphia Museum of Art: Purchased with the Joseph E. Temple Fund, 1908.

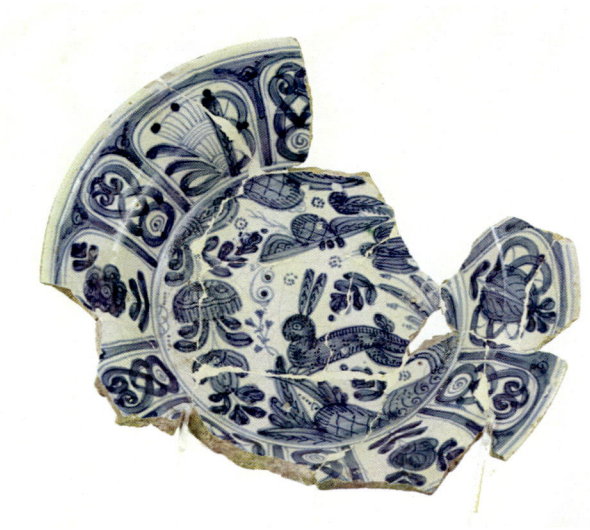

Fig. 16 Plate, Puebla de los Ángeles, Mexico, ca. 1680–1700. Tin-glazed earthenware. Franz Mayer Museum, Mexico City.

they resemble the style of decoration found in Kraak porcelain from the Ming dynasty (1368–1644)—a style that became increasingly popular among Puebla workshops by the turn of the eighteenth century. An excellent example of this type of design was uncovered from a site excavated during the renovation of the Franz Mayer Museum in Mexico City (fig. 16).

Master potter Diego de Santa Cruz de Oyanguren y Espinola (also spelled Espindola) was considered one of the most important producers of tin-glazed earthenware during the eighteenth century. Espinola was appointed alcalde of the guild numerous times between 1734 and 1761.[34] He was married to Maria de Zayas, whose family had operated a prominent ceramic workshop in Puebla since the seventeenth century (and was mentioned earlier in the text). Like his wife's family, Espinola became so well known that the street where the workshop was located carried

the family name of "street of Espinola" (calle de Espinola). The lawyer to the Royal Audience, Manuel Caro, presented Espinola to the viceroy in 1762 as having "invented" the Chinese style in Puebla.[35] He continued to promote Espinola by boasting that "most experts were not able to distinguish his work from that of China or Japan" and that his ware was "not only the most polished but also the most durable."[36] Depending on how one defines the "Chinese style," it is unlikely that Espinola invented it in Puebla; however, he and his workshop certainly may have specialized in the decoration. A late-eighteenth-century or early-nineteenth-century plate signed "Espindola" on the back suggests that the workshop was in operation for multiple generations.[37]

In 1813, a new constitution for the Spanish empire, promulgated by an anti-monarchical assembly at Cádiz, eradicated the potter's guild and revoked the ordinances. Mexican ceramicists were free to create new styles of their own, but the lack of regulations led to a decline in the quality for which Puebla potters were known. Also at this time, workshops in other parts of Mexico began producing less expensive alternatives. The lifting of import restrictions allowed for a variety of European ceramic types to enter New Spain. The demand for Asian-style pottery declined alongside the weakening of transpacific trade, which ultimately ended in 1815, just as independence movements were emerging in the Americas.

Despite numerous attempts by the guild to require master potters to mark their work, most of the extant viceregal vessels remain without a mark, leaving much of Puebla's ceramic history anonymous. This may have been the result of market constraints during the viceregal period as the demand for ceramic ware grew and the guild's rigid regulations became increasingly difficult to enforce, particularly concerning the exclusive right of master potters to use costly cobalt blue.

The success of Puebla's ceramic production beginning in the viceregal period is a testament to the city's role as a major center of artistic and commercial exchange. While the potters' guild established strict regulations to maintain quality and control production, the anonymity of many artisans—due in part to social hierarchies and guild restrictions—has left gaps in our understanding of individual contributions. The marks that do exist provide crucial insights into the workshops and stylistic evolution of Puebla's ceramics, but they represent only a fraction of the story. For example, marks are typically signed by the painter of the vessels and most workshops involve specialists for each area of production. The dissolution of the guild in the early nineteenth century led to both artistic liberation and a decline in the standardized quality that had defined Puebla pottery for centuries. Nevertheless, the tradition adapted and endured. The revival efforts of the late nineteenth and early twentieth centuries—with potters such as Ysauro Uriarte Martínez, Enrique Luis Ventosa, J. Miguel Martínez, Antonio Espinosa, and Pedro Padierna—had a lasting impact on the regrowth of the industry and development into new directions that would ultimately lead to the enforcement of new authenticity standards and establishment of the trademark of the term "talavera." By reassessing the historical record and recognizing the collaborative nature of these workshops, we gain a deeper appreciation for the artistry, labor, and cultural significance embedded in Puebla's famed pottery. Today, potters continue to draw inspiration from historical forms while innovating within the medium to create unique works of art. This has ensured that the legacy of Puebla's potters remains a vital part of the city's heritage.

Notes

1. This tradition takes its name from Talavera de la Reina, a city in central Spain where many of Puebla's first potters originated. The term *talavera* eventually became synonymous for the glazed pottery by 1824 when Ysauro Uriarte opened his workshop as Fabrica de Loza de Talavera.

2. Examples of the prehispanic pottery known as Cholula ware or Mixteca-Puebla ware can be found at the National Museum of Anthropology in Mexico City and Amparo Museum in Puebla, among other museums. For example, see the pedestal bowl in the collection of The Metropolitan Museum of Art in New York, 1979.206.365, https://www .metmuseum.org/art/collection/search/ 312587.

3. Florence C. Lister and Robert H. Lister, *Sixteenth Century Maiolica Pottery in the Valley*

of Mexico (University of Arizona Press, 1982), 89.

4. Hugo Leicht, *Las Calles de Puebla: Estudio Historico* (Junta de Majoramiento Moral, Civico y Material del Municipio de Puebla, 1986), 412; Margaret E. Connors McQuade, "Loza Poblana: The Emergence of a Mexican Ceramic Tradition" (Ph.D. diss., City University of New York, 2005), 77.

5. Enrique Cervantes, *Loza Blanca y Azulejo de Puebla,* 2 vols. (Puebla de los Ángeles: Privately printed, 1939), 1:112–19.

6. *"En la calle que va de la Plaza Pública a la iglesia del Evangeslista San Marcos."* Ibid, 2:185. This and all translations are by the author.

7. McQuade, "Loza Poblana," 70–71.

8. Sagrario Angelopolitano, Puebla, Libros de Matrimonio, March 11, 1674. Cited in Cervantes, *Loza Blanca*, 2:238.

9. Cervantes, *Loza Blanca*, 2:324–25.

10. Archivo Histórico Municipal de Puebla (AHMP), December 5, 1573, Libro de Actas de Cabildos, no. 10, fol. 118.

11. Cervantes, *Loza Blanca*, 2:174.

12. Jerónimo de Mendieta, *Historia eclesiástica indiana* (Editorial Porrúa, 1980), 4:404.

13. Agreement between Antonio Xinovés and Gerónimo Pérez de Salazar, 1579. Collection of Francisco Pérez de Salazar, Mexico City. I am grateful to Mr. Francisco Pérez de Salazar for providing this document and his support of my research.

14. AGNP, 1666, fojo 1399. Cited in Cervantes, *Loza Blanca*, 2:218.

15. Archivo de la Catedral de Puebla, Fábrica Municipal, Legajo II. Cited in Cervantes, *Loza Blanca*, 2:15; Lister and Lister, *Sixteenth Century Maiolica*, 231; Rose Gpe. de la Peña V., "Azulejos encontrados *in situ*: primera catedral de México," in *Ensayos de Alfareria Prehispánica e Histórica de Mesoamérica: Homenaje a Eduardo Noguera Auza*, Serie Antropológia 82, ed. Mari Carmen Serra Puche and Carlos Navarrete Cáceres (Universidad Autónoma de Mexico, 1988), 437–38.

16. The attribution was suggested to me via email in late 2018 by Guillermo Tovar de Teresa, who acquired the pieces from the Pérez de Salazar family. The basins are currently held in the Guillermo de Tovar House Museum, operated by the Museo Soumaya in Mexico City.

17. See, for example, Alfonso Pleguezuelo, "Center of Traditional Spanish Mayólica," in *Cerámica y Cultura: The Story of Spanish and Mexican Mayólica*, ed. Robin Farwell Gavin, Donna Pierce, and Alfonso Peguezuelo (University of New Mexico Press, 2003), pl. 1.11.

18. Archivo General de las Indias, Seville (AGI), "Gaspar de Encinas a su mujer Maria Gaitán en Triana," April 30, 1596 (Puebla), Indiferentes. Cited in McQuade, "Loza Poblana," 57.

19. AGNP, Notaria no. 4, Protocolos de 1619, folios 183–186r. It is worth noting that Espindola is another important family name among ceramic workshops in Puebla who continued the tradition into the nineteenth century.

20. See Donna Pierce's entry in *Mexico: Splendors of Thirty Centuries*, exh. cat. (The Metropolitan Museum of Art, 1990), 461.

21. John M. Goggin, *Spanish Majolica in the New World: Types of the Sixteenth to Eighteenth Centuries* (Yale University Press, 1968), 173.

22. Kathleen Deagan, *Artifacts of the Spanish Colonies of Florida and the Caribbean, 1500–1800* (Smithsonian Institute Press, 1987), 83–84.

23. Cervantes, *Loza Blanca*, 2:199–200.

24. Lister and Lister, *Sixteenth Century Maiolica*, 241.

25. Cervantes, *Loza Blanca*, 1:28–29.

26. See also Diego Javier Luis, *The First Asians in the Americas: A Transpacific History* (Harvard University Press, 2024).

27. Cervantes, *Loza Blanca*, 1:29; McQuade, "Loza Poblana," 148.

28. Cervantes, *Loza Blanca*, 1:112, 114, 116, 118. See also Margaret E. Connors McQuade's entries in *The Arts in Latin America, 1492–1820,* ed. Joseph J. Rishel and Suzanne L. Stratton-Pruitt, exh. cat. (Philadelphia Museum of Art, 2006), 140–41.

29. Antonio Tamariz de Carmona, *Relación y descripción del templo real de la ciudad de Puebla de los Ángeles en la Nueva España y su catedral: Que de orden de su magestad acabó y consagró a 18 de abril de 1649* (Puebla de los Ángeles, s.n.).

30. Examples can be found at the Franz Mayer Museum in Mexico City, José Luis Bello y González Museum in Puebla, Soumaya Museum in Mexico City (formerly from the collection of the Pérez de Salazar family), as well as The Metropolitan Museum of Art in New York, Philadelphia Museum of Art, and Hispanic Society Museum & Library in New York, among others.

31. I am grateful to Roberto Junco of the Instituto Nacional de Antropología e Historia in Mexico City for bringing this to my attention.

32. Edwin Atlee Barber, *The Maiolica of Mexico (Art Handbook of the Pennsylvania Museum and School of Industrial Art)* (Pennsylvania Museum and School of Industrial Art, 1908), 50.

33. Cervantes, *Loza Blanca*, 2:229.

34. Ibid, 2:303–04.

35. Ibid, 1:42.

36. Ibid.

37. Ibid, 2:190–91.

For the Consolation of Manila: A Case Study of a New Spanish Image of Christ

Ronda Kasl, Curator of Latin American Art, The Metropolitan Museum of Art

On March 3, 1653, a celebrated image of the ecce homo departed Acapulco for Manila on the galleon *San Francisco Xavier* in the custody of Augustinian Recollect missionaries. Known as the *Christ of Humility and Patience*, the sculpture, which was venerated in the monastic church of San Nicolás de Tolentino, was destroyed in the bombardment of Manila in 1945 (fig.1). A prewar photograph preserves a blurry record of its appearance, but early written sources vividly describe it as a life-size image of the scourged and humiliated Christ, crowned with thorns and holding a reed scepter (fig. 2).[1] Official histories of the Recollects narrate the story of its origin, its translation from Mexico City to Manila, and its festive reception there in mid-October 1653.[2] Chronicles and eye-witness reports by members of other religious orders corroborate many details of the sculpture's history.[3] While the documentary and explanatory value of these sources is considerable, they are far from neutral. Recognition of the aims and biases of those who recorded the details amassed in this case study is crucial, not only in the interest of objectivity but because it illuminates attitudes toward the making, use, and mutable resonances of sacred images in movement. The first objective of this investigation is to document the existence of a sculpture sent from New Spain to the Philippines in the mid-seventeenth century and the second is to reconstruct its context to understand how it functioned in the practice of belief under circumstances described by contemporaries as both miserable and calamitous. The analysis of written sources foregrounds the contention that a sacred image made in Mexico City had the capacity to console a divinely castigated community on the other side of the world.

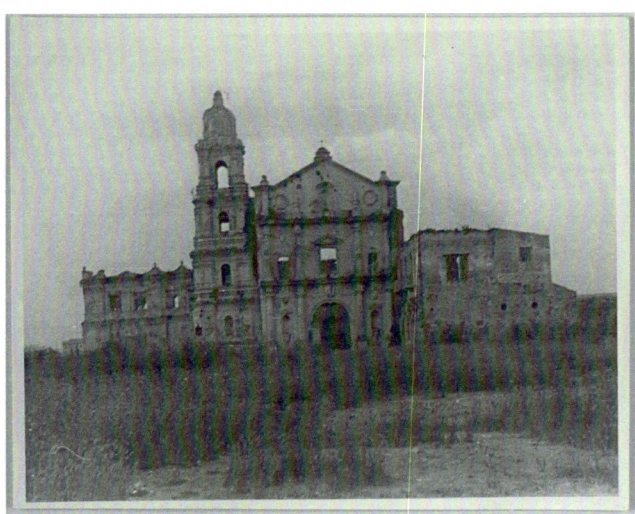

Fig. 1 Church of San Nicolás de Tolentino, Manila, about 1945. Courtesy the author.

The principal sources for this study are histories of the Order of Augustinian Recollects, also known as "Discalced or Unshod Augustinians," a Spanish mendicant reform order that sought a return to the primitive observance of the Rule of St. Augustine.[4] The Recollects were one of the last orders established in the Philippines, where they were instrumental in efforts to reform the regular Augustinians, who were implicated in a series of scandals. The first mission arrived there in 1606.[5] Chronicles emphasize successes in the evangelization of the archipelago, recounting the foundation of missions, narrating the deeds of illustrious friars, and enumerating miracle-working cult images and their origin stories.

The Origin Story

Fray Diego de Santa Teresa published an extended version of the origin story of the *Ecce homo* in 1743, writing that it was made for Juan de Araus, a Mexico City priest who sought a representation of Christ's humility

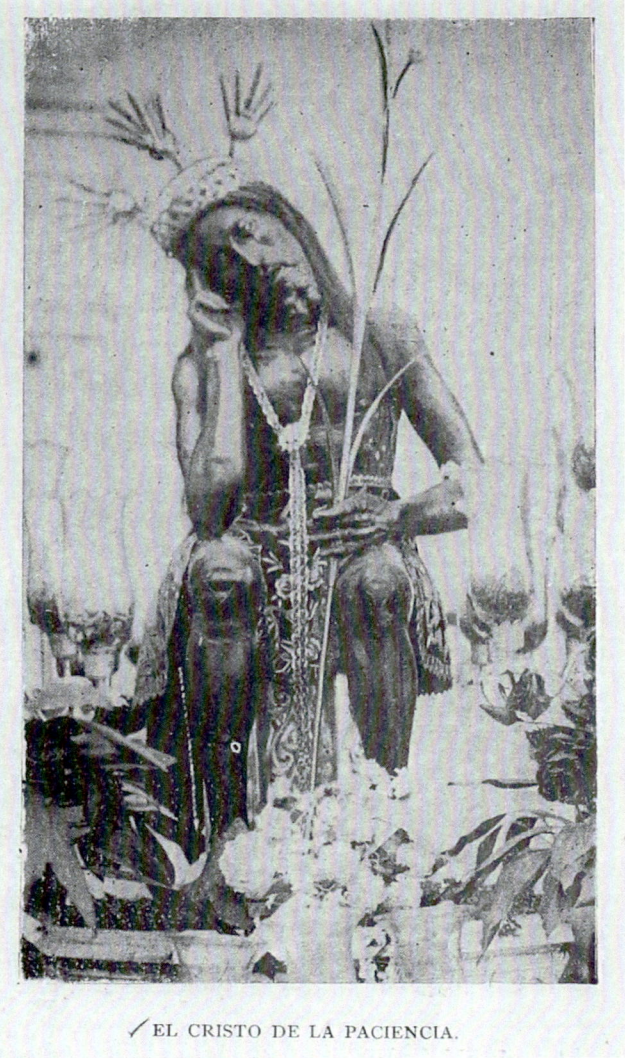

EL CRISTO DE LA PACIENCIA.

Fig. 2 *El Santo Cristo de la Paciencia*, in *Excelsior: Revista decenal ilustrada*, vol. 4, no. 72 (April 20, 1908), 1067. Courtesy the Filipinas Heritage Library.

and patience to help subdue his fiery disposition (fig. 3). According to Santa Teresa, Araus commissioned the image from an unnamed sculptor whom he described as "a most exquisite and devout Artist" (*un Artífice primorossimo, y devoto*). In advance of making the image, both the priest and the artist prepared themselves through prayer and fasting. For the three years during which the work was in progress, they were sustained by frequent Communion, readings from the Gospel, and contemplation of the works of Christian mystics, including St. Gertrude and St. Bridget of Sweden. The chronicler also specifies that the material used to make the image is *pasto*, likely cornstalk paste (*caña de maíz*), a lightweight material well-suited to processional images. He goes on to describe an improbable artistic process of "adding and taking away" until it was finished to the priest's liking. Araus venerated the image on an altar in his private quarters until fray Jacinto de San Fulgencio, en route to the Philippines with twenty-four Augustinian Recollect missionaries, asked him to give it up "for the consolation of Manila." After his initial refusal to part with the image, Araus was stricken with unbearable pain, relieved only when he reversed his decision.[6] The calamitous state of Manila, ruined by natural disasters, conflict, and economic collapse, called for both material and spiritual remedies. The inference was that an image of Christ in an attitude of patient submission to his torments could aid the city's beleaguered residents.

This origin story is largely invented, but key details can be confirmed through other sources. Juan de Araus was indeed a priest of the parish church of Santa Catarina Mártir in Mexico City. He was a benefactor and *hermano mayor* of the Augustinian Recollects, and his gift of the image to the Manila mission is recorded in other sources.[7] His allegedly passionate temperament, which led to "grave encounters with the powerful," is consistent with accounts of his involvement in a bitter dispute over the administration of the

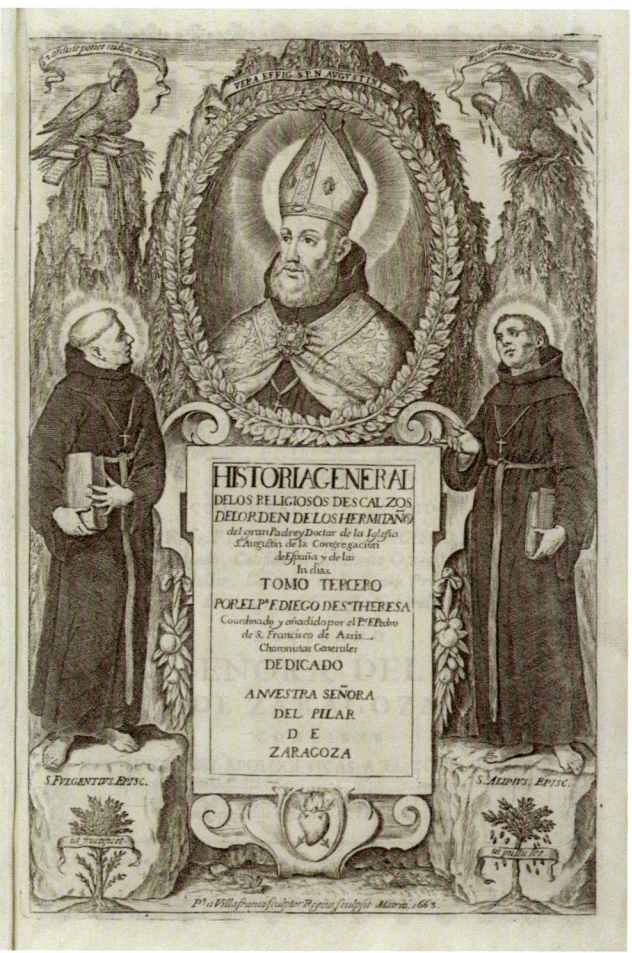

Fig. 3 Pedro Villafranca Malagón, Frontispiece, 1633. Diego de Santa Teresa, *História general de los religiosos descalzos del orden de los ermitaños del gran padre, y doctor de la Iglesia San Agustin* (Barcelona, 1743). Biblioteca Nacional de España, Madrid.

Recollect Hospice in Mexico City, a clash in which fray Jacinto de San Fulgencio was also implicated.[8] The Recollect friar had traveled to Spain in 1649 as a delegate (*comisario*) of the Philippine province to recruit missionaries and secure royal financing. He returned in the spring of 1652, encountering Araus in Mexico City on his way to Acapulco, where he embarked for Manila a year later, in 1653.[9]

Even though not every detail of Santa Teresa's story is credible, it is nonetheless consistent with prevailing attitudes toward the making of sacred images. That is, the sacred resides in images made by devout artists, inspired by prayers, penances, and spiritual exercises. In his account of the making of the image of Christ, Santa Teresa specifically references the writings of St. Gertrude and St. Bridget of Sweden, whose vivid revelations of Christ's suffering have long been recognized as sources for visual representations of the Passion.[10] What is most striking about the friar's account, however, is its emphasis on the spiritual preparation required for the making of a "devout" image imbued with the quality of sacredness or divinity. That the preparatory exercise is jointly undertaken by the priest and the artist recalls other histories of sacred images, such as a copy of *Nuestra Señora de la Soledad* carved by Gaspar Becerra, who was aided by the prayers, alms, and penances of Minim friars in Madrid.[11] In a similar story, Mariana de San José, founder of the Augustinian Recollect order of nuns, commissioned a sculpture of Christ at the Column for her convent in Madrid and stipulated that the artist should commence work on it while the nuns received Communion in order to ensure that the image was especially devout.[12]

Early written sources consistently refer to the Manila image as an ecce homo, although it was properly known as the *Christ of Humility and Patience*. In 1664, the Recollect chronicler Andrés de San Nicolás referred to it by that name and declared that it was one of the most venerated images in the islands. He described it as life-size and praised its manufacture as the "best that is known in those distant

hemispheres." The image of Christ, seated on a stone and resting his hand on his cheek, he wrote, "moved the hard heart of the most lost to trembling and devotion."[13] In 1743, Diego de Santa Teresa elaborated on its appearance:

> The Holy Image is the natural size of a man; represented seated on a pedestal; his entire body is purple, signifying the cruel lashes he suffered because of the human race: His cheek rests on his right hand, his head tilted, and his body slightly turned to one side, so that his shoulders show many pitiful wounds; he is crowned with very thick, woven rushes; and in his left hand he holds the reed cane. The eyes, which are beautiful, seem to weep and gaze in all directions. The physique and symmetry of the body are most perfect, with every part a sum of beauties; and the hearts of those who look at it are moved to pity, even those who are adorned with diamonds.[14]

Augustinian Recollect writers were not the only ones to describe the image, although others focus less on its visual appearance than on subjective responses to it. The Dominican friar Domingo Fernández de Navarrete saw the image in the 1650s and wrote that it "moves all who see it to pious compassion."[15] In 1660, Alonso del Valle wrote that it was "the living impression of the scandals of Jerusalem . . . the sculpted consolation of the sinner's afflicted tears."[16]

The subject of Christ's humility, with its emphasis on quiet self-negation, was eminently suited to the mental prayer methods of the Recollects, but devotion to

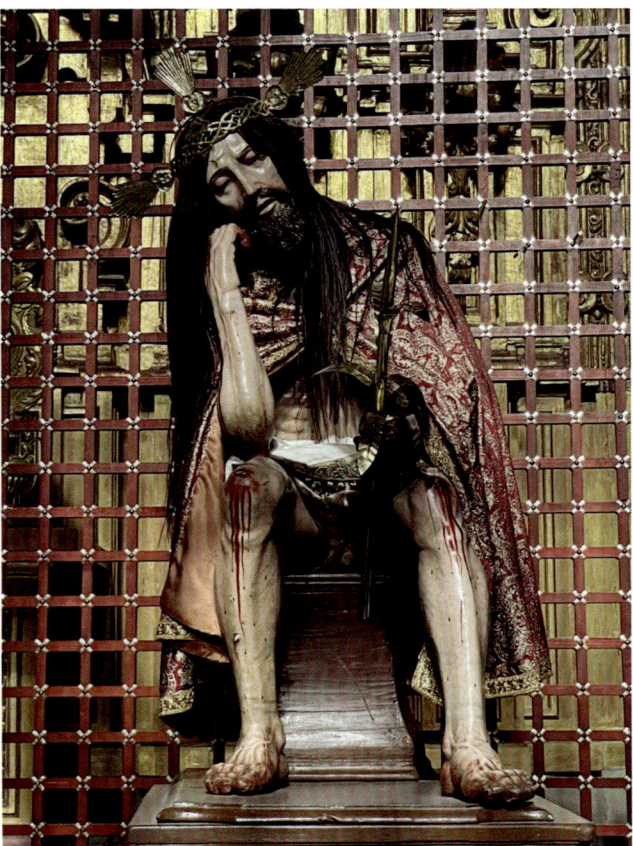

Fig. 4 Unknown artist, *El Señor del Cacao*, Metropolitan Cathedral, Mexico City, 1600s. Polychromed *caña de maíz* (cornstalk paste, gesso, and oil paint). Courtesy the author.

Translation and Reception

In the early spring of 1653, after overwintering in Acapulco, the nine-hundred-ton galleon *San Francisco Xavier* prepared to depart for Manila with six hundred passengers, silver to sustain the colony and exchange for merchandise, dispatches and correspondence, trade goods, and personal belongings. The ship's cargo included the image of Christ given to the Augustinian Recollects by Juan de Araus as well as a number of other works of art.[20] Passengers included many high-ranking officials and clerics, including Sabiniano Manrique de Lara (1609–1679), the new governor and captain general of the Philippines, and Miguel de Poblete (1602–1667), the incoming archbishop. Other passengers included an infantry company of one hundred soldiers and fifty Augustinian and Jesuit missionaries.[21] The new governor-general, Manrique de Lara, was a Knight of Santiago descended from a noble family of Málaga. His military career included five years of imprisonment in Portugal following the dissolution of the Iberian union in 1640. After his release, he was made *castellan* of the fortress that guarded the Port of Acapulco. He was the highest authority of the port, in charge of receiving and dispatching the Manila galleons and overseeing the fair where imported merchandise was traded.[22] After being named governor of the Philippines in June 1651, Manrique de Lara left Acapulco for Mexico City, where he spent the next two years making preparations and procuring funds for the journey to Manila, which was delayed until March 1653 for

the ecce homo was prevalent throughout the Spanish world. The most notable example in Mexico City is the so-called *Señor del Cacao*, a life-size image venerated in the Metropolitan Cathedral (fig. 4). Like the Manila *Christ of Humility*, it is made of cornstalk paste.[17] The fabrication of the Manila image in paste as an episode (*de pasto en un passo*) representing Christ's humility is stipulated by Santa Teresa and points to its having been conceived from the outset for processional use.[18] The previously cited prewar photograph shows the image on a silver platform with lanterns to illuminate it during nighttime processions.[19]

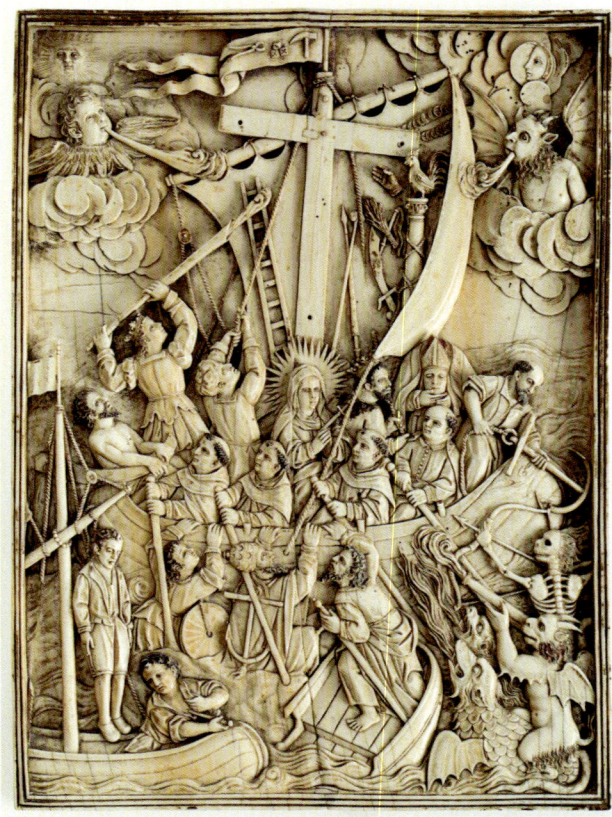

Fig. 5 Hispano-Philippine artist, *Nave Typus Religionis (Ship of Religion)*, 1600s. Ivory, 10⅛ × 8½ in. (25.7 × 21.5 cm). Museo Nacional de Artes Decorativas, Madrid. Photo courtesy of Ansorena.

lack of a ship to transport him.[23] Poblete, born in Mexico, was the first creole archbishop of Manila, a post to which he was named in 1647. He was not consecrated until 1650 and did not take possession of the seat until his arrival in Manila in 1653.[24] Poblete had previously been *maestrescuela* of Puebla Cathedral, whose powerful bishop, Juan de Palafox y Mendoza, was his protector.[25]

While passengers waited to depart for Manila, the image of *Christ of Humility* was venerated in the Acapulco parish church of San Pablo. On March 2, 1653, the afternoon prior to their embarkation, the Recollects, accompanied by the governor, archbishop, missionaries, and townspeople, carried the *Christ of Humility* in procession to the beach, where it was received with artillery salvos and then loaded onto the ship. During the transpacific crossing—a journey of almost five months—the image of Christ was used to arouse the devotion of passengers and petition for divine aid and protection. By the time the ship arrived in Manila, it had already been acclaimed as a miracle-worker, credited with curing gravely ill passengers and rescuing the ship from violent storms. According to Diego de Santa Teresa: "They put it on board the ship *San Francisco Xavier*, in a place where everyone could have it in their presence and ask it for help from the recurring perils of the waves; which they did, with many pious petitions and fervent novenas."[26] The same missionaries, on the transatlantic leg of their journey, had performed spiritual exercises as if they were in their convent. They preached in the afternoons, persuaded sailors to pray the rosary, gave the Sacrament of Penance to sinners, and provided instruction in Christian doctrine.[27] The ship's transformation into a place of worship and religious instruction is a recurring theme in histories of religious orders with overseas missions.[28] While it attests to actual religious practice, the chronicler's narrative is also informed by Christian allegories of the Ship of the Church, endangered by demons and tempests. In a late seventeenth-century Hispano-Philippine ivory, the Ship of Religion is rowed by members of religious orders (three friars and a Jesuit), whose labors propel it through dangerous waters toward the safe harbor of Salvation (fig.

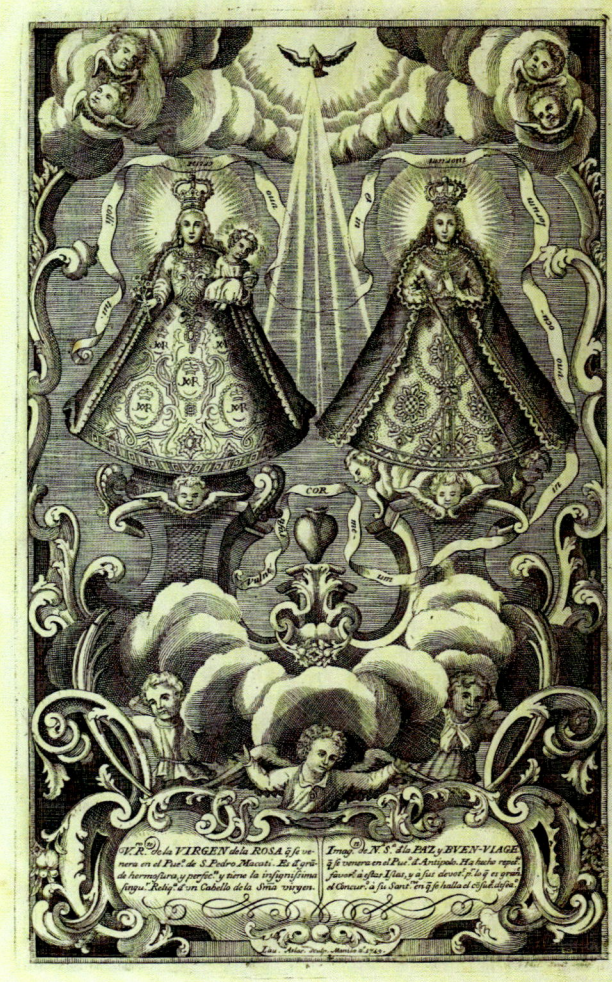

Fig. 6 Nuestra Señora de la Rosa of Makati and Nuestra Señora de la Paz y Buen Viaje of Antipolo, Frontispiece, Pedro Murillo Velarde, *Historia de la provinica de Philipinas de la Compañia de Jesús* (Nicolás de la Cruz Begay, 1749). Courtesy of the John Carter Brown Library.

5).[29] The Cross serves as the ship's mast, and symbols of the Passion emblazon the pennant and sail. The Virgin Mary, her head encircled by a radiant halo and her heart pierced by the sword of sorrow, is a passenger.

Sacred images often aided religious practices and rituals intended to assure the safe passage of ships, and passengers on the Manila-bound galleon in the spring of 1653 were accompanied by at least two: *Christ of Humility and Patience* and *Our Lady of Good*

Voyage and Peace (also known as *Our Lady of Antipolo*) (fig. 6). According to the Jesuit chronicler Diego de Oña, the image of Christ was placed next to that of his mother on the ship, and under their watch, there was nothing to fear.[30] The latter image is said to have come from a church in Acapulco, where Juan Niño de Tavora, governor-elect of the Philippines, encountered it in 1626 and took it with him to Manila. The diminutive image of the Virgin Mary protected that galleon during the transpacific crossing, and the grateful governor gave it to the Jesuits for their church in Antipolo (in the mountains east of Manila). After miraculously escaping destruction during the *sangley* uprising of 1639, the image was taken to Manila's Royal Chapel. In 1646, it was moved to Cavite, Manila's harbor, to safeguard the city from Dutch attacks. The image purportedly crossed the Pacific eight times as protectress of the galleon. In gratitude for the safe arrival of the *San Francisco Xavier* in 1653, the incoming governor and archbishop vowed to restore the Virgin to her church in Antipolo and bestowed the title *Nuestra Señora de la Paz y Buen Viaje*.[31]

On June 26, after almost four months on the open sea, the *San Francisco Xavier* entered the waters of the Philippine archipelago through the Strait of San Bernardino. Up to this point, the voyage had been miraculously uneventful. Diego de Oña observed that only three passengers had died en route and took it as a sign that the ship brought good health to the islands. He attributed the successful voyage to higher causes, specifically to "God made human, adored in a most tender image of the ecce homo, a precious treasure brought by the Recollect fathers for their church, and his Holy Mother, adored in the admirable image of Antipolo."[32] The ship was nearly lost before reaching Manila, but on July 23, it cast anchor at Cavite, the first Spanish vessel to do so in fourteen years.[33] The significance of the occasion was accentuated by the fact that Cavite had ceased to be the principal port of the archipelago during the 1640s, as the galleon was diverted to Lampón (Lamon Bay) to avoid the Dutch blockade.[34] The governor and the archbishop disembarked the day before, and on the beach, Poblete blessed the land and then blessed Manrique de Lara, who had symbolically ceded primacy to him (and to the Church) in the act.[35] This was the first in a series of public acts, both civil and religious, that followed the arrival of the galleon. The archbishop and governor, as heads of church and state, made public entries into the city of Manila on July 24 and 25. The splendor of these events (which the city could ill afford) confirmed the power and continuity of the Spanish monarchy and the Catholic church in a distant city imperiled by acute political, economic, and spiritual crises.[36] The public spectacle of Manrique de Lara's entry stood in stark contrast to his own assessment of the dire situation on taking possession of the government. In a report to King Philip IV, he wrote, "I found these islands in a miserable state and in their final gasp."[37] At the time of Poblete's entry, the episcopal seat of Manila had been vacant for twelve years. His predecessor, Hernando Guerrero, who was banished from Manila by the

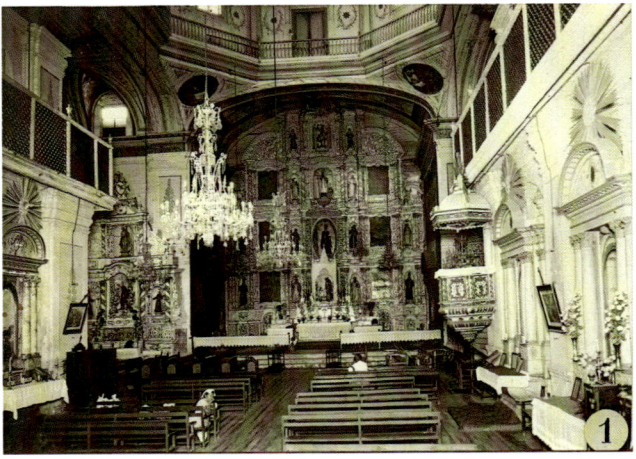

Fig. 7 Interior of the church of San Nicolás de Tolentino, about 1930. Archivo General de la Orden de Agustinos Recoletos, Rome.

governor in 1636, died in 1641; his would-be predecessor, Fernando Montero de Espinosa, died en route to Manila and entered the city in 1645 as a cadaver.[38] The exile of Archbishop Guerrero was pinpointed by some chroniclers as the shameful cause of Manila's castigation by God.[39] Archbishop Poblete delivered a remedy in the form of a papal brief by Innocent X absolving inhabitants of the Philippines of their sins and conceding plenary indulgences to those who sincerely confessed them.[40]

On arrival in Manila, the *Christ of Humility* was initially taken to the monastic church of St. John the Baptist in Bagumbayan, located just outside the city walls. The monastery was the first one established by the Recollects in the Philippines.[41] The miracle-working image was placed on an altar, where it attracted the devotion of the local community and that of the governor and archbishop, who were said to have visited it daily in gratitude for their safe passage from Acapulco.[42] It remained in

Bagumbayan for almost three months, until it was carried in procession to its permanent location in the *intramuros* church of San Nicolás de Tolentino, the Recollect Province's patron saint. The church was newly rebuilt, having collapsed in the earthquake of 1645.[43] On October 16, the governor prayed an all-night vigil in the Bagumbayan church and the next morning received the Sacrament of Penance. Festivities continued with dancing, artillery salvos, and the gunfire of both Indigenous and Spanish militias. On October 18, the image was carried beneath a canopy of branches in a solemn procession led by the archbishop to the church of the Misericordia (which served as a provisional cathedral). The next morning, the Recollect fathers carried it on their shoulders in procession to the church of San Nicolás and placed it on a side altar.[44] There, the image became the focus of the daily devotions of the governor, whose public displays of piety were praised by chroniclers and emulated by other worshippers (fig. 7).[45] The eighteenth-century Recollect historian Juan de la Concepción observed that, following the governor's example, devotion to the *Christ of Humility* was universal, and feasts were celebrated annually with costly brilliance. In his own time, he noted that "this fervor has greatly diminished; fashion also has its use in devotions, and the most flamboyant ones attract attention."[46] Indeed, the image with the most prominent cult in the church of San Nicolás was not the *Christ of Humility*, but *Christ the Nazarene*, said to have been brought from New Spain to the Philippines in 1606 by the first Augustinian Recollects. The San

Nicolás–based confraternity of *Nazarenos* carried it in procession on Holy Thursday, taking it out at midnight, and on Holy Monday, in the afternoon.[47] The *Ecce homo* was the focus of passional devotion on Good Friday, but in a measure adopted by the provincial chapter in 1663, the *Nazarenos* were forbidden to carry it in processions except in the case of "most urgent necessity."[48] The injunction points to the use of the image in Rogation processions in connection with extraordinary emergencies and calamities, such as those organized during the previous year, when the city was threatened by the Chinese archpirate Zheng Chenggong (known to the Spanish as Koxinga).[49]

Calamity and Consolation

In 1654, on assuming his duties as the new governor of the Philippines, Manrique de Lara reported to Philip IV that he found the islands "in tears from calamities and miseries."[50] Another informant, Magino Sola, the Jesuit Procurator General of the Philippines, contrasted Manila's former splendor with its current ruin: "Today you look so abused, so oppressed, so poor, and so lacking in the strength you used to have, that if you once had enough to aid and enrich other kingdoms, today you do not have enough to sustain yourself . . . with reason then you weep over so many calamities, so many misfortunes, and so much poverty."[51] The catastrophic earthquake that occurred on November 30, 1645, during the feast of San Andrés, patron saint of the city, was of such magnitude that it caused the literal collapse of the city. Most of the city's principal buildings were destroyed or badly damaged, including the cathedral, governor's palace, Real Audiencia, *colegio* of Santo Tomás, and the convents of Santo Domingo and San Nicolás de Tolentino. According to one eye-witness report, "Only a shadow of Manila remained."[52] Bleak assessments detailing Manila's misfortunes and miseries—conflict, earthquakes, typhoons, shipwrecks, epidemics—routinely attributed them to God's displeasure with its sinful populace, likening it to the biblical city of Nineveh.[53]

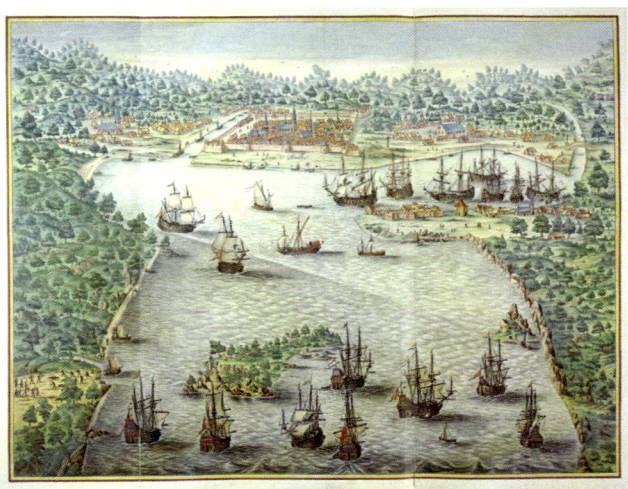

Fig. 8 Johannes Vingboons (and/or workshop), *The Dutch Attack on Cavite in 1647*, in Laurens Van der Hem, *Atlas Blaeu-van der Hem*, 50 vols. (Amsterdam, about 1670). Pen and brush drawing. Österreichische Nationalbibliothek, Vienna.

Descriptions of Manila in which colonial officials and clerics describe the city's degraded situation have no visual equivalents, with the possible exception of a seemingly serene view of Manila attributed to the Amsterdam cartographer Johannes Vingboons (1616/17–1670) (fig. 8). The scene includes a blockade fleet of Dutch ships at the entrance to Manila harbor. Dutch harassment of Spanish shipping, which culminated in attacks on Manila in 1646 and 1647, sparked a severe economic crisis, exacerbated by a series of maritime disasters that disrupted the provision of an already inadequate *situado* or *socorro*—the financial subsidy sent from New Spain to maintain the colony.

The Dutch were not the only threat faced by the Spanish in the Philippines. Other external threats included ongoing confrontations with regional sultanates (called *moros* by the Spanish) and the danger posed by Chinese and Japanese piracy. Internally, dependence upon and distrust of the large Chinese population of the Parián (so-called sangleyes) hastened violent uprisings and brutal repression in 1603, 1639, and 1662.[54] The looming threat of an attack by Koxinga, whose demand for tribute was refused in 1662, provoked panic and interethnic violence in Manila. Rumors of sangley collusion with the Chinese underlie a miracle story in which a surprise attack was thwarted by Manrique de Lara thanks to warnings communicated by the *Christ of Humility*. According to Juan de la Concepción, a message was found at the feet of the image: "Governor, take care of your city, they want to surprise you." The next day a more explicit message was discovered in the same place: "Governor, take care of your city, remove the scaffolding from the walls, do not trust anyone, you have enemies very near."[55] According to the story, Manrique de Lara promptly removed scaffolding that could have aided seditious sangleyes in scaling the city walls. In fact, the threat of imminent attack did cause the governor to strengthen the city's fortifications and demolish buildings outside the walls, including churches and convents, that were close enough to serve as enemy positions.[56] These defensive measures proved unnecessary when Koxinga died unexpectedly. Manrique de Lara evoked Celtiberian resistance to Roman conquest when he reported that "if the barbarian had not died nothing would have remained of we Spanish who inhabited the Philippines but memories, like those of Numancia."[57]

Manrique de Lara's personal devotion to the *Christ of Humility* is routinely cited by witnesses and repeated by later sources. By all accounts, the governor was genuinely devout, but his public acts of atonement and reparation were manifestly performative ones, enacted as the representative of a distant Catholic monarch. Military chaplain Alonso del Valle vividly recounted one such act in a festival book commemorating celebrations in Manila of the birth of Felipe Próspero (1657–1661).[58] In August 1659, the galleon from Acapulco brought news of the long-awaited birth of an heir to the Spanish throne, assuring the continuity of the monarchy at a critical moment in the Philippines. The short-lived prince was born in Madrid in November 1657, almost two years before reports reached Manila. Church bells announced the news in Manila, followed by the celebration of a Mass in the Royal Chapel. Twenty days of festivities followed, with both solemn and

joyful proceedings, including sermons and processions, as well as bullfights, mock jousts, and fireworks.[59] On the day the governor received the news, he rushed by carriage to the church of San Nicolás, where he humbled himself before the image of Christ and gave thanks to "the daily guarantor of his government."[60] According to Alonso del Valle:

> *Prostrate, he gave thanks to the holy* Ecce homo; *miraculous carved figure of devotion, living impression of the scandals of Jerusalem, exact image of the painful sorrows of the Just, sculpted consolation of the sinner's afflicted tears. To this celestial wonder of earth, which he reverently visits every day, to whom he commends the discreet prayers of human error, with whom he sweetens the bitterness of high command, from whom he recognizes the advent of mild successes, he made exemplary sacrifice of his joys in order to guarantee the credit of eternal ones in faith.*[61]

The burden of the office of governor and captain general of the Islands consoled by a sacred image of Christ is not only an evocative representation, in this case, it is also poignant. Manrique de Lara's corporeal mortification and performative disengagement from worldly affairs anticipated his actual withdrawal. Initially hailed as "Governador Deseado," by mid-1656, he had petitioned to be relieved of the post, citing poor health, which he traced to his imprisonment in Portugal and the rigors of Manila's climate.[62] He was silent about other tribulations, which only grew worse as he awaited a successor, who was not destined to arrive until 1663.[63] Manrique de Lara returned to his native Málaga, having renounced its governorship, and became a priest.[64]

The festivities that celebrated the birth of Felipe Próspero in 1659 were staged in a ruined city. The earthquake of 1658 had wrecked many of the buildings constructed after the devastation of 1645, including the Recollect church of San Nicolás. When the governor went there after receiving news of the royal birth to prostrate himself in prayer before the *Christ of Humility*, it was in a provisional church not rebuilt until after 1666.[65] The ruinous state of the church of San Nicolás, the departure of the governor, and the diminished fortunes of the Recollects in Manila all likely contributed to the waning fervor of devotion to the *Christ of Humility and Patience*.[66] At the beginning of the eighteenth century, the Augustinian chronicler Casimiro Díaz observed that the value of the governor's example was magnified in a land where even devotions were changeable and, like a style of clothing, everyone dressed in what the governor was wearing.[67] During Manrique de Lara's ten years as governor of the Philippines, religious engagement with Christ's Passion, aroused by a celebrated image from Mexico, was inextricably bound to a political culture shaped by economic precarity and spiritual crisis. Recognized as a miracle worker from the moment of its transfer to Manila, the image was enshrined on altars and paraded in the streets and plazas of the city in public rituals of salutation, petition, and atonement. These acts of performative piety, whether individual or collective, were also acts of governance that linked the expiation of sin to the consolation and repair of Manila.

Notes

1. "El Santo Cristo de la Paciencia," *Excelsior: Revista decenal ilustrada* 4, no. 72 (April 20, 1908): 1067. I am grateful to Regalado Trota José for sharing this reference.

2. Andrés de San Nicolás, *Historia general de los religiosos descalzos del orden de los hermitaños del Gran Padre de la Iglesia San Agustín, de la Congregación de España y de las Indias*, vol. 1 (Madrid, 1664), 441–42; Diego de Santa Teresa, *Historia general*, vol. 3 (Barcelona, 1743), 241–45, 365; Juan de la Concepción, *Historia general de Philipinas. Conquistas espirituales y temporales de estos españoles dominios, establecimientos, progresos, y decadencias*, 14 vols. (Sampaloc, 1788–89), 6:387–94, 7:49–51.

3. Domingo Fernández de Navarrete, *Tratados históricos, políticos, ethicos y religiosos de la monarchia de China* (Madrid, 1676), 324; Diego de Oña, *Labor evangélica. Ministerios apostólicos de los obreros de la Compañía de Jesús, segunda parte (ca. 1701) del Padre Diego de Oña, SJ (1621-1755)*, ed. Alexandre Coello de la Rosa and Verónica Peña Filiu (Silex, 2020), 762, 775; Casimiro Díaz, *Conquistas de las Islas Filipinas; la temporal, por las armas de nuestros Católico Reyes de España, y la espiritual, por los religiosos de la orden de San Agustín* (Manila, 1718; reprint Valladolid, 1890), 529; Pedro Murillo Velarde, *Historia de la provincia de Philipinas de la Compañía de Jesús* (Manila, 1749), 210.

4. Ángel Martínez Cuesta, "Recolección agustiniana: origen, historia y espiritualidad," *Revista Agustiniana* 48, no. 145 (2007): 57–76.

5. Pedro Luengo, *The Convents of Manila* (Ateneo de Manila Press, 2018), 94.

6. Santa Teresa, *Historia general*, 242–43; Concepción, *Historia general*, 387–90.

7. San Nicolás, *Historia general*, 441; Santa Teresa, *Historia general*, 196–200.

8. Both fray Jacinto and Juan de Araus had ties to Juan de Palafox y Mendoza, bishop of Puebla. Santa Teresa, *Historia general*, 195–200, 242; Ricardo Fernández Gracia, *En las entrañas del atardecer de Palafox en Puebla. Deberes y afectos encontrados* (Idea, 2020), 92–94.

9. Santa Teresa, *Historia general*, 174–75.

10. Antonio Rubial García and Doris Bieñko de Peralta, "La más amada de Cristo. Iconografía y culto de santa Gertrudis la Magna en la Nueva España," *Anales del Instituto de Investigaciones Estéticas* 83 (2003): 5–54.

11. Javier Portús, "Verdadero retrato y copia fallida. Leyendas en torno a la reproducción de imágenes sagradas," in *La imagen religiosa en la Monarquía hispánica. Usos y espacios*, ed. María Cruz de Carlos Varona, Pierre Civil, Felipe Pereda, and Cécile Vincent-Cassy (Casa de Velázquez, 2008), 241–42.

12. Luis Muñoz, *Vida de la venerable M. Mariana de S. Joseph, fundadora de la recolección de las Monjas Augustinas, priora del Real Convento de la Encarnación* (Madrid, 1645), 318–19.

13. San Nicolás, *Historia general*, 441.

14. Santa Teresa, *Historia general*, 242.

15. Navarrete, *Tratados históricos*, 324.

16. Alonso del Valle, *Prensados fastos, descriptivos mapas de festivas acclamaciones, y ponposos jubileos, con que inundo en perenes alegrias a la insigne, y siempre leal Ciudad de Manila, Diadema de las Philipinas* (Manila, 1660), 3v.

17. Manuel Toussaint, *La Catedral de México y el Sagrario Metropolitano: su historia, su tesoro, su arte* (Porrúa, 1973), 96, 156, figs. 1 and 65; Andrés Estrada Jasso, *Imágenes de caña de maíz* (Universidad Autónoma de San Luis Potosí, 1996), 98.

18. Santa Teresa, *Historia general*, 242.

19. "El Santo Cristo de la Paciencia," 1067.

20. The personal belongings taken to Manila in 1653 by Archbishop Miguel de Poblete included forty-two paintings and three sculptures. Cayetano Sánchez Fuertes, "Biblioteca, pinacoteca, mobiliario y ajuar de Don Miguel de Poblete, arzobispo de Manila," *Archivo agustiniano* 95, no. 213 (2011): 399–444.

21. Libro de cartas de Sabiniano Manrique de Lara, July 19, 1654, AGI, Filipinas, 285, N. 1, fols. 4r–v.

22. William Lytle Schurz, "Acapulco and the Manila Galleon," *The Southwestern Historical Quarterly* 22, no. 1 (1918): 24–25; for the biography of Sabiniano Manrique de Lara, see Navarrete, *Tratados*, 310–14; Luis de Salazar y Castro, *Historia genealógica de la Casa de Lara* (Madrid, 1696), 2:776–80; Ana María Prieto Lucena, *Filipinas durante el gobierno de Manrique de Lara (1653-1663)* (Consejo Superior de Investigaciones Cientificas, 1984).

23. Libro de cartas, AGI, Filipinas, 285, N. 1, fol. 16r.

24. AGI, Filipinas, 2, N. 79; Gregorio Martín de Guijo, *Diario, 1648-1664*, ed. Manuel Romero de Terreros, 2 vols. (Porrúa, 1952), 1:126–27.

25. For the biography of Miguel de Poblete, see Oña, *Labor evangélica*, 876–80; Eduardo Juliá Martínez, "Notas sobre El Dr. D. Miguel de Poblete, arzobispo de Manila," *Revista de Indias* 3, no. 2 (1942): 223–49; Sánchez Fuertes, "Biblioteca," 399–444.

26. Santa Teresa, *Historia general*, 243.

27. Ibid., 175.

28. See "Voyage of Fr. Diego de Bobadilla to the Philippines (Manila, August 6, 1643)," in *History of Micronesia: A Collection of Source Documents*, vol. 4, *Religious Conquest, 1638–1670*, ed. Rodrigue Lévesque (Lévesque Publications, 1995), 64–70.

29. Margarita Estella, "La representación de la Nave de la Iglesia en un relieve de marfil," *Traza y baza* 8 (1983): 97–101.

30. Oña, *Labor evangélica*, 775.

31. Ibid., 762, 766–75; Murillo Velarde, *Historia*, 210r–215v. For a recent study of the image, see Christina H. Lee, "Our Lady of Antipolo, Our Lady of the Tree," in *Saints of Resistance: Devotions in the Philippines under Early Spanish Rule* (Oxford University Press, 2021), 100–26.

32. Oña, *Labor evangélica*, 762.

33. Ibid., 762–63; Díaz, *Conquistas*, 528; Santa Teresa, *Historia general*, 243.

34. Libro de cartas, AGI, Filipinas, 285, N. 1, fol. 4r-v.; María Baudot Monroy, "Lampón, puerto alternativo a Cavite para el galeón de Manila," *Vegueta: Anuario de la Facultad de Geografía e Historia* 20 (2020): 21–48.

35. Oña, *Labor evangélica*, 763.

36. The public entries of the archbishop and governor are described in ibid., 764–66.

37. Libro de cartas, AGI, Filipinas, 285, N. 1, 4v.

38. Alexandre Coello de la Rosa, "Interregnos en el cabildo metropolitano de Manila (1641-1653)," *Colonial Latin American Review* 32, no. 3 (2023): 369, 380–83.

39. Oña, *Labor evangélica*, 780–81.

40. Ibid., 778–81; Díaz, *Conquistas*, 531–32.

41. María Lourdes Díaz-Trechuelo Spínola, *Arquitectura española en Filipinas (1565-1800)* (Escuela de Estudios Hispano-Americanos de Sevilla, 1959), 27–28.

42. The translation of the image to Bagumbayan is described by San Nicolás, *Historia general*, 441–42; Santa Teresa, *Historia general*, 244.

43. The first church of San Nicolás was built in 1614–19. Díaz-Trechuelo, *Arquitectura española*, 251–53.

44. The translation of the image to the church of San Nicolás is recounted in San Nicolás, *Historia general*, 442; Oña, *Labor evangélica*, 775; Santa Teresa, *Historia general*, 244–45.

45. This photograph of the interior of the church (rebuilt in 1780) appears in Ricardo Jarauta Fuentes de la Consolación, *Album de la Orden de Agustinos Recoletos: con motivo del XV centenario del glorioso transito de San Agustín* (1931). I am grateful to Fr. Rene Paglinawan,

OAR, for providing the image and sharing the reference.

46. Concepción, *Historia general*, 6:394.

47. Valeriano Sánchez Ramos and Carlos Villoria Prieto, "La cofradía de Jesús Nazareno de Manila (Filipinas)," in *Las cofradías y hermandades de Jesús Nazareno y Nosso Senhor dos Passos: Historia, arte y devoción*, ed. Manuel Peláez del Rosal (Asociación Hispánica d Estudios Franciscanos, 2019), 1–16.

48. *Actas y determinaciones del capítulo Intermedio del año 1663 de la Provincia de San Nicolás de Tolentino* (Orden de Agustinos Recoletos, 1663), https://agustinosrecoletos.org/wp -content/uploads/library/76-capitulos-de-la -provincia/861-cappsnt-1663.pdf.

49. Prieto Lucena, *Filipinas*, 140; Dana Leibsohn, "Dentro y fuera de los muros: Manila, Ethnicity, and Colonial Cartography," *Ethnohistory* 61, no. 2 (2014): 242.

50. Libro de cartas, AGI, Filipinas, 285, N. 1, 33r.

51. Magino Sola, *Memorial y carta del Padre Magino Sola de la Compañía de Jesús, Procurador general della, por la Provincia de Philipinas, para el señor Don Sabiniano Manrique de Lara, Governador y Capitán general de dichas Islas* (Mexico City, 1652), 8v.

52. *Verdadera relación de la grande destruicion, que por permission de nuestro Señor, ha avido en la Ciudad de Manila* (Madrid, 1649), unpaginated; Murillo Velarde, *Historia*, 138v–142r.

53. Oña, *Labor evangélica*, 664; Díaz, *Conquistas*, 531–32; Murillo Velarde, *Historia*, 229v–230r.

54. Jean-Noël Sánchez, "A Prismatic Glance at One Century of Threats on the Philippine Colony," in *The Representation of External Threats: From the Middle Ages to the Modern World*, ed. Eberhard Crailsheim and María Dolores Elizalde (Brill, 2019), 343–65; Ostwald Sales and Colín Kortajarena, "Apuntes para el estudio de la presencia 'holandesa' en la Nueva España: una perspectiva mexicano-filipina, 1600-1650," in *Memorias e historias compartidas. Intercambios culturales, relaciones comerciales y diplomáticas entre México y los Países Bajos, siglos XVI-XX*, ed. Laura Pérez Rosales and Arjen van der Sluis (Iberoamericana, 2009), 149–76.

55. Concepción, *Historia general*, 7:49–51.

56. Prieto Lucena, *Filipinas*, 128–33.

57. Ibid., 139.

58. Valle, *Prensados fastos*. For empire-wide celebrations of the birth, see Inmaculada Rodríguez Moya, "La esperanza de la monarquía. Fiestas en el imperio hispánico por Felipe Próspero," in *Visiones de un Imperio en Fiesta*, ed. Inmaculada Rodríguez Moya and Víctor Mínguez Cornelles (Fundación Carlos de Amberes, 2016), 93–119.

59. Valle, *Prensados fastos*.

60. Ibid., 3v.

61. Ibid., 3v–4r.

62. Francisco Combés, *Governador Deseado* (ca. 1654), University of Indiana, Lilly Library, Philippine Mss II; *Petición de renuncia al cargo de Manrique de Lara*, Cavite, July 15, 1656, AGN, Filipinas, 22, R. 10, N. 59.

63. Prieto Lucena, *Filipinas*, 34–38.

64. Díaz, *Conquistas*, 527.

65. Díaz-Trechuelo, *Arquitectura española*, 251–53; Luengo, *Convents*, 94–103.

66. Concepción, *Historia general*, 394.

67. Díaz, *Conquistas*, 529.

The Other Silver Flow: Liturgical Objects in the Philippines

Kathryn Santner, Assistant Curator of Latin American Art, Denver Art Museum

In 1750, the Dominican Order in the Philippines made an inventory of the many *alhajas* (religious ornaments) and jewels found in its convent, *beaterio*, college, and the numerous provincial churches spread across what was then known as the Province of the Holy Rosary (fig. 1).[1] The inventory extends over more than 150 folios and details the profusion of liturgical silver, religious statuary, and jewelry encrusted with diamonds, rubies, emeralds, sapphires, topazes, and pearls found in these Dominican institutions. Many of the pages are left blank or only partly filled in anticipation of future pious donations, bequests, and purchases that would arrive in coming years to further adorn altarpieces and enhance the Eucharistic experience. While never as wealthy as its Augustinian counterparts, the convent of St. Dominic had among its riches twenty-five lamps and chandeliers, nearly sixty candlesticks, nine chalices, four altar frontals, and eleven crucifixes all wrought in silver and silver-gilt. The jewelry alone went into the hundreds of items. So where did this impressive store of treasure originate?

While a significant thread of research in the last few decades has considered the flow of silver into the Philippines, it has focused on the prodigious quantities of coins mined and minted in Mexico or Potosí that found their way into Chinese coffers.[2] Little has been conducted on the flow of finished silver goods into Manila, nor on local facture in the Philippines, which had a rich tradition of Indigenous goldsmithing and was later home to sangley (Chinese) silversmiths. This, in part, results from the paucity of surviving objects: War, natural disasters, and the vagaries of time have resulted in a small number of colonial art objects in all media—let alone silver, which is both desirable and fungible. During the

British occupation of Manila during the Seven Years' War (1756–63), for example, the defending governor issued a mandate to collect and bury silver ornaments from religious institutions to prevent them from falling into the hands of the invading navy, which would soon go on to capture the silver cache onboard the galleon *Santísima Trinidad*.[3] These measures were limited in their success; in October 1762, the British sacked the Dominican church, where they not only looted dozens of silver vessels but also the abundant silver adorning statues like *Our Lady of the Rosary*, known as *La Naval*, including her *rostrillo* (halo or sunburst encircling the face) and gem-studded crown. Not content to simply steal, they desecrated the image, shattering the glass that protected her, cutting off her ivory head and throwing it to the floor, rending her vestments to shreds, and severing the limbs of the Christ Child in her arms. As they rampaged through Manila's churches, British troops dismantled silver reliquaries, burned nativity scenes, cast the Eucharistic host to the ground, and tied clerical stoles to their horses' tails.[4] Crucially, the 1750 inventory allows us to see a snapshot of the order's silver before these depredations and the equally devastating losses that would come with the Second World War.[5]

Despite the rapacity with which it was sought after by Spain's trading partners and political enemies alike, silver objects are less desirable to modern collectors of Filipinana than locally produced ivories and wooden santos. Only two large public collections of silver can be viewed in

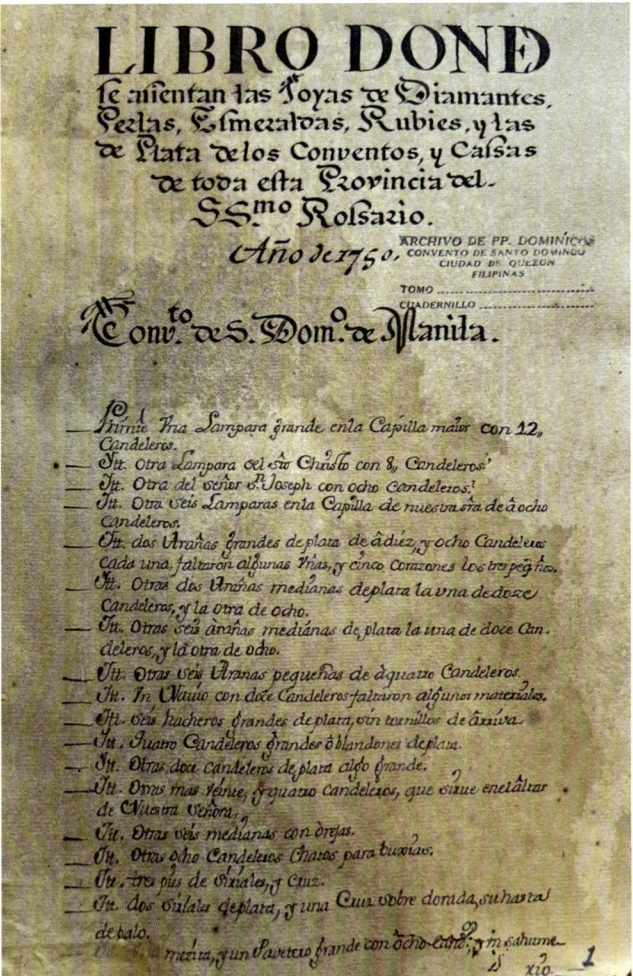

Fig. 1 *Libro donde se asientan las Joyas de Diamantes, Perlas, Esmeraldas, Rubies, y las de Plata de los Conventos, y Casas de toda esta Provincia del Ssmo Rossario, Año de 1750*. Archivo de la Provincia del Santísimo Rosario, Avila. Photo by author.

Manila today: those of the San Agustin and Intramuros museums. Silver maintains a generally fusty reputation. As Helen Hills observes in her work on Neapolitan silver, "Scholarship and gallery displays are overwhelmingly connoisseurial, drily technical, narrowly specialist, and aridly drained of political engagement," which belies the complex relationship between the cruelty of silver's extraction and its exalted position as a substance that "bestowed and conveyed immaculacy and polished sophistication."[6] And yet, silver was not simply the fulcrum of global maritime trade but the very stuff of the sacred. On both sides of the Pacific, it was the preferred material for liturgical objects, saints' reliquaries, and votive offerings. It was the substance from which the infants of Lal-lo (Cagayan) made their first contact with the sacred through the application of holy water from a silver *bernegal* (drinking vessel) pressed into service as a baptismal shell; it was the same material used to fashion the spectacular, white sapphire-studded armor of *Nuestra Señora de la Consolación* in the nineteenth century that aided her in her spiritual mission; it was silver that housed a relic of the True Cross in the church of los Santos Reyes del Parián, where it was hoped that this holy shard might inspire Chinese immigrants to adopt the Catholic faith.

If, to invoke the words of seventeenth-century Spanish chronicler Juan Grau y Monfalcón, Asian goods were "desired and sought by the rest of the world"—what goods were in turn desired by the Spanish, particularly religious communities, living amongst these immediately available and luxurious export goods?[7] While the vast majority of cargo on Manila-bound galleons was specie, that is silver *reales* that could be exchanged for porcelain, silk, ivory, and other fineries, the Spanish also imported gold, olive oil, wine, glass, European clothing and textiles, and art objects. It would seem natural, then, that galleons would also ferry many splendid Mexican and Spanish silverworks bound for Philippine churches: a parallel flow of silver. I had initially hoped to tell a story of silver in Asia as more than a mere commodity and consider artistic influence of the galleon trade that focused on the Philippines rather than Latin America: Mexico in Asia instead of Asia in Mexico. Instead it seems that the landscape is a bit more complicated, especially given the dearth of extant silver objects as well as documents that record them. Despite the difficulty of tracing the course of silver's importation from abroad, there is a compelling narrative of local creation by sangley artisans to be told.

Silver in the Philippines

Whether imported as finished objects or, as was more common, wrought locally, silver in the Philippines began its life in the bowels of the Cerro Rico in Potosí or the mountainous regions of Mexico. The quantity of silver mined at Potosí in particular was so immense that chroniclers reported that "it was considered easier and cheaper to arm men and shoe horses with silver than with iron."[8] So too did they describe with openmouthed awe the mind-bending splendor to which this Mexican and Bolivian silver was put for local celebrations: formed into cobblestones for viceregal entries and forged into triumphal arches, images of the Virgin, and miniature silver mountains for religious processions.[9] And yet, *potosino* silver was famously extracted through a brutal system of forced labor known as the *mita*. After extraction, silver ore was locally processed through smelting or amalgamation, assayed, and formed into silver bars or minted into coins.[10] It was then transported to various artistic centers where it was worked by *plateros* who forged it into objects both sacred and profane, from processional crosses and chalices to inkstands and chamber pots. In the process, it lost its association with the cruelty of the extractive process and became associated with both secular refinement and religious majesty.[11]

When the mendicant orders first came to the Philippines in the sixteenth century, they brought with them from Spain the necessary objects to conduct mass.[12] A royal decree promulgated by Philip II in 1579 provisioned each new mission in the Philippines with an "ornament," chalice, paten, and bell from the royal treasury.[13] This basic service would later be augmented by both imported goods from Mexico and Spain and objects forged locally. In the early days of the colony, however, few churches were able to adequately outfit their altars; reports from colonial officials in Manila often lamented the lack of necessary and beautifying *orfebrería* in the city's cathedral.[14] This was seen as a matter of some urgency; adequate silver was necessary to maintain the dignity of mass, to minister to the faithful, and to convert a new flock.[15] Some priests took on the cause of ornamenting provincial churches themselves rather than relying on their orders or the Crown to do so, such as *fray* Fernando Cabrera, who furnished the church of San Pablo de los Montes (Laguna) with such a surfeit of liturgical silver that it was said to outshine the cathedrals of Spain, and its most exceptional object (a silver tabernacle described below) was

subsequently redistributed to the Augustinian convent in Manila a few miles away.[16] While the influx of silver coins via the Manila Galleon was significant, the Crown placed limitations on the importation of wrought silver to the colony.[17] Private citizens and public officials could submit a formal request to the Crown to import wrought silver and jewels for their personal use.[18] Yet private citizens, government and church officials, and institutions imported silver objects from Mexico with regularity, often clandestinely.[19] At the time of his death in 1667, the archbishop of Manila, Miguel de Poblete, had some forty-six items of *plata labrada* (wrought silver) in his possession valued at nearly 4,350 pesos, much of it likely brought from his homeland of Mexico. Among them were sacred objects like chalices and a silver-gilt bishop's crosier but also luxury goods including a set of coconut cups with silver mounts, a perfumer, and three elaborate fountains.[20]

As in other colonies, arriving missionaries relied on local artists and artisans to create religious objects for newly constructed Catholic churches. The skill of sangley artisans was more than sufficient to meet this need: So talented were they in replicating European statuary that, by 1590, bishop Domingo de Salazar wrote to Philip II that "soon we shall not even miss those made in Flanders." Salazar praised the quality of smithing in particular: "Although the silversmiths do not know how to enamel (for enamel is not used in China), in other respects they produce marvelous work in gold and silver. They are so skillful and clever that, as soon as there are any objects made by a Spanish workman, they reproduce it with exactness."[21] While Salazar was mistaken on the use of enamel in China, which had begun in the fourteenth century, his high opinion of sangley silversmiths' talent was widely shared. Their work was so desirable, in fact, that the *tumbaga* (an alloy of copper, gold, and silver) choir screen in Mexico City's cathedral was commissioned from Chinese artisans in Macao in the 1720s, and the Sultan of Jolo (Sulu) requested a sangley silversmith be sent to his court in 1756.[22] As commerce with New Spain became more regular at the end of the sixteenth century, imported religious objects were presumably more available, but nevertheless there remained a strong reliance on local manufacture in silver as well as indigenous materials like nacre and wood.

The first wave of Chinese silversmiths came to Manila from the provinces of Fujian and Guangdong, the latter of which became a regional center of silver production in the sixteenth century.[23] As with other artisans, they concentrated around the Parián, the market just outside Manila's walls where Asian goods were bought and sold. Some arrived with skill in smithing, while others likely learned their trade in Manila, which helped them survive in a colony hostile to *chinos*.[24] Later generations of silversmiths would be not only sangley but also Chinese-mestizo and Filipino and likewise received praise for their skill from Spanish commentators—in some cases above sangleys.[25] By 1690, there were twenty-four

sangley silversmiths working in the Parián, and fifty-seven were active in the city in 1700.[26] Unlike their counterparts in Mexico, Manila's artisans were only nominally organized under a guild system and instead operated through a series of independently run companies and workshops, which numbered forty-eight by midcentury.[27]

There is also evidence of at least one silversmith who also worked as an ivory carver in the case of Juan de los Santos, a Filipino born in the village of San Pablo de los Montes who served as the sacristan of its church. De los Santos was responsible for a variety of works in Augustinian churches in the early seventeenth century, from gilded *retablos* to ivory sculptures and elaborate objects wrought in silver. While a perhaps singular example of talent, de los Santos allows us some insight into the relationship between commissioning friars and local artisans. According to the Augustinian chronicler Pedro Andrés de Castro, "He made with his own hands all of the silver ornaments of the church, which were many and good... but everything was at the cost, zeal, direction, and care of [the prior] fray Fernando Cabrera," the silver-loving priest from above.[28] It is unlikely that any of these silver objects survives in the San Agustin museum today, as much of the museum's collection was relocated from churches in Cebu, but Castro's text provides a sense of its splendor. He describes in great detail a nine-and-a-half-foot-tall, gothic-style silver tower made by de los Santos to hold a gold monstrance, which featured five octagonal tiers with varying orders of columns and was adorned with jewels, bas-reliefs, and figures of the Apostles, Doctors of the Church, and angels. Clearly, silversmiths in Manila were capable of a remarkable degree of sophistication; as Castro noted in his text, in this instance, the "work exceeded the material" (*materiam superabat opus*).[29] As with many of Manila's most spectacular silver objects, it was seized during the British Occupation, reinforcing the importance of documents like the Dominican inventory and Castro's chronicle to understand local silver production.

Such grandiose objects were commissioned because silver was a key part of the missionizing effort, beautifying the church space and enticing new converts to Catholicism through its burnished splendor. The ornamentation of the church "heightened the magnificence of the sacred" and moved the pious to meditate on the divine.[30] The Jesuit chronicler Pedro Chirino reported that one vicar "embellished [his church] with new ornaments, very rich and curious, such as lamps and silver candlesticks, thereby augmenting the reputation and esteem of our holy religion among those new nations."[31] Laypeople likewise sought to enhance the beauty of the church through pious bequests of silver, thereby participating in the baroque theater of mass. As the Augustinian friar Juan de Medina pointed out, silver made a more attractive bequest for *manileños* because, unlike textiles, it would not become destroyed by Luzon's infamous humidity and could simply be polished to renew its former luster.[32] And, much as the tarnish

could be removed from sacred silver objects through the labor of polishing, so too would the redemptive nature of the sacraments wash away the stain of sin.

Many objects in the Dominican inventory arrived as gifts, often from Manila's ecclesiastical and secular elite. These were primarily jewels given in offering to statues, such as a large silver star set with nine diamonds placed on the forehead of a statue of Saint Dominic and given by the bishop-elect of Nueva Segovia, Juan de Arrechedera, or several jewels given to religious statues by Juana del Rosario, a Japanese mestiza.[33] Other objects—like the small silver *ramilletes* (stylized vases of flowers) donated by the marquesa doña Rita de Quijano to Our Lady of the Rosary— were intended to enhance the liturgical experience by ornamenting the altar (fig. 2).[34] Unlike in Mexico or Peru, no statue paintings survive to show us what these altars might have looked like, but written sources can help to reconstruct their appearance. For example, the devotees of *La Naval* adorned her altar with more than fifty silver lamps and candlesticks to illuminate her ivory countenance and sumptuous embroidered robes. The governor of Ternate, Pedro de Heredia, was alone responsible for donating two large candlesticks (*blandones*) valued at over a thousand pesos each, twelve smaller candlesticks (*candeleros*) at a hundred pesos apiece, and a lamp valued at 1500 pesos.[35]

It is unclear whether these objects were imported or locally produced, though the

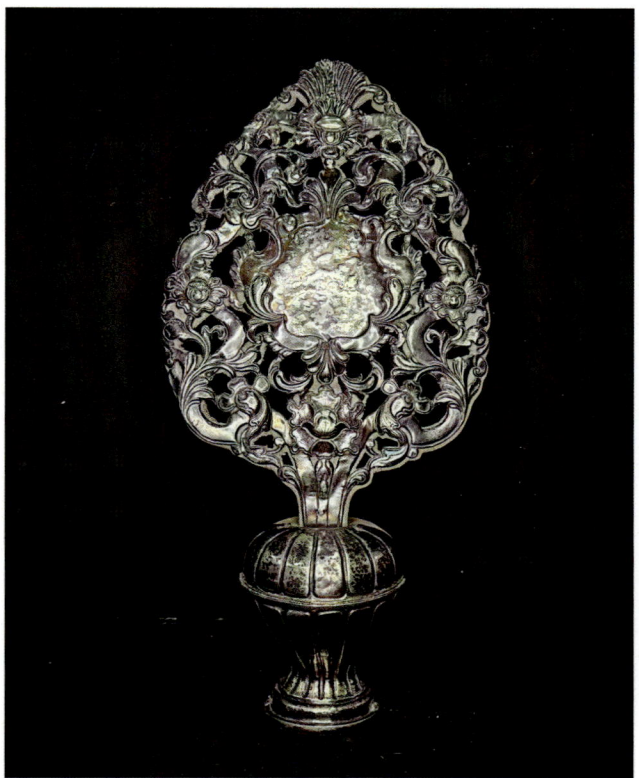

Fig. 2 Unknown artist, Ramillete, Philippines, 1700s. Silver, 18⅞ in. (48 cm). Museo de Intramuros, Manila.

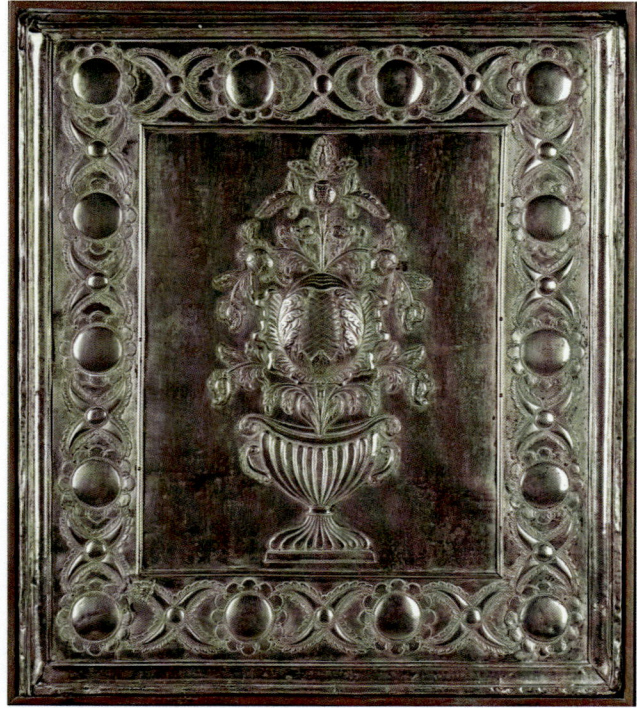

Fig. 3 Unknown artist, Silver Panel, Mexico or Philippines, about 1785. Silver, 33¼ × 29¼ × 2 in. (84.5 × 74.3 × 5.1 cm). Denver Art Museum: Gift of the collection of Frederick and Jan Mayer, 2013.301.

latter seems most likely given the availability of local talent and the time and expense of importing finished silver objects from Mexico or Spain. Philippine silver objects lack the hallmarks typically found on their Mexican and Spanish counterparts because they were often made from reworked silver pesos and therefore no royal tax (*quinto real*) needed to be paid.[36] Other scholars attribute the lack of hallmarks to the abundant use of filigree work, which left no room for stamping on its delicate designs.[37] Hallmarks indicated not simply the payment of tax but also revealed the maker, the location, the year, and the assayer who gauged the quality of the work. This leaves the objects that do survive today as orphans, unidentified in time, place, or authorship. A silver panel from the Denver Art Museum collection is a good illustration, not readily identifiable as either Mexican or Philippine, though it was acquired in Manila (fig. 3). In the nineteenth century, as the plantation economy increased the wealth of provincial towns, prominent citizens would commission silver altar frontals, which sometimes had their names inscribed on them.[38] Inscriptions like these are, other than stylistic attributions, analysis of wooden supports, and scant documentary references, among the only ways to tie works concretely to a geographic origin.[39]

Unfortunately, but predictably, the Dominican inventory is circumspect on the origins of the silver in its sacristies, with only a few exceptions. In what was then the village of Ermita, now a neighborhood in central Manila, one Padre Bernabe commissioned for the church two heavy silver chandeliers (*arañas*) weighing nine and a half pounds as well as a silver cross for the altar.[40] Across the Pasig river, in the church of los Santos Reyes del Parián, the silver chandeliers illuminating the altar of el Santo Christo del Valle had been sent from Mexico.[41] In the seventeenth century, Manila's once-impoverished cathedral was at last furnished with "a quantity of wrought silver and very rich ornaments and lamps" sent from Guadalajara by archbishop Diego Camacho y Ávila.[42] Likewise, some of the surviving works at San Agustin are thought to have been imported from Mexico, including a famous bejeweled gold and enamel chalice from circa 1600—though more recent attributions locate the work to Colombia or the Philippines.[43] Unsurprisingly, many attributions are unreliable, like a set of gold cruets at San Agustin whose serpentine handles are said to represent Quetzalcoatl, a Mexica deity.[44] In one remarkable example, a Mexican chalice was reworked in Manila and then donated to a parish in Andalucía (fig. 4). The inscription on the base of the chalice states: "To the parish of Mairena del Alcor, by Don Angel Carmona and companions (*compañeros*), [made] in Acapulco, renewed by another in Manila, 1787."[45] Stylistically, the work resembles Philippine typologies in the undulating curve of its base, the three nodes (or knops) on the stem, and the double cup separated by two rings, which suggests that it was a substantial renovation, perhaps after the original work sustained damage or simply to elaborate the original design.[46]

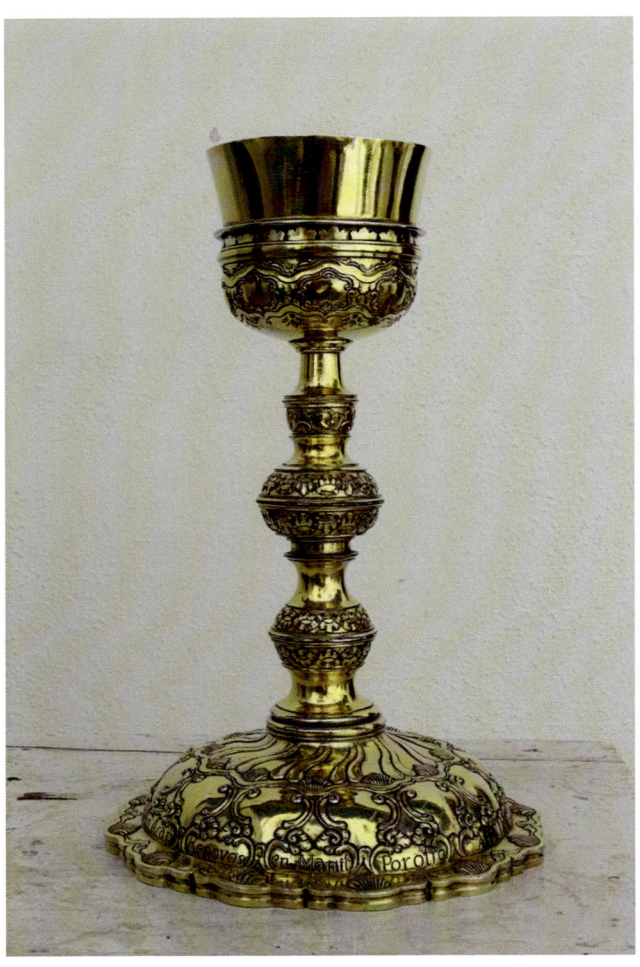

Fig. 4 Unknown artist, Chalice, Acapulco and Manila, 1787. Silver, 9 × 5⅞ in. (23 × 15 cm). Parroquia de Santa María de la Asunción, Mairena del Alcor, Sevilla, Spain.

Early works by sangley masters were often created using the *ysot*, or wriggle-work technique, in which a v-shaped chisel or burin incised designs into the silver plate. This was joined in the late seventeenth century by chasing and by repoussé, embossing, casting, and engraving in the eighteenth.[47] Stylistically, these works can have an archaizing quality, referencing earlier prototypes of Renaissance, Mannerist, and early Baroque silver. Even Juan de los Santos's nine-foot silver confection harks back to the high Renaissance in its composition of varying orders of columns.[48] Still, Philippine silver would eventually come to adopt rococo

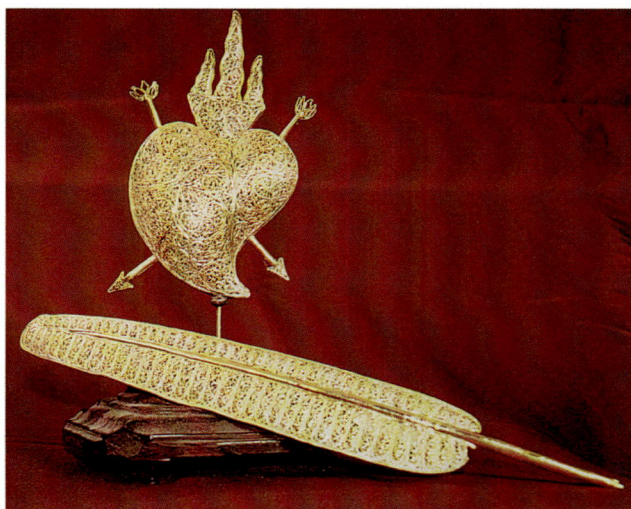

Fig. 5 Unknown artist, Heart and Pen, Philippines, 1600s. Gold, heart 6¼ × 4⅜ in. (16 × 11 cm); pen 12⅜ × 1½ in. (31.5 × 3.8 cm). San Agustin, Manila.

designs like the s- and c- scrolls and *rocalla* that were popularized in eighteenth-century Europe. As María Jesús Sanz has pointed out, many of the surviving objects at San Agustin betray simultaneous influences from Chinese, Spanish, and Mexican silver traditions, which suggests a local authorship.[49] So, too, does it bespeak the consistent importation of Mexican and Spanish objects to serve as artistic prototypes, even if these objects have been difficult to trace in the documentary record.

As mentioned, filigree was a technique favored by sangley artisans, though it was also popular in the Americas, Southeast Asia, and India. Filigree and granulation techniques had been used in prehispanic Philippine goldwork, but filigree became increasingly prominent after the arrival of Chinese smiths in the sixteenth century.[50] San Agustin's best surviving examples of the technique are in gold: a *palabra* or *sacra*, probably the most spectacular object in the collection, and a pen and heart belonging to a statue of St. Augustine (fig.

5). These latter objects may well be the same ornaments lauded by Castro in his text, where he boasts that they "could shine in Rome and Toledo for their value and workmanship."[51] Examples of filigree work were exported from the Philippines to Spain, Italy, Mexico, and Lima, while others were traded clandestinely to England via Madras (now Chennai).[52] They were found not only in private collections but in ecclesiastical and royal settings: Splendid lamps commissioned in the Philippines hung in the Dominican convent in Rome, and filigree objects belonging to a lady's dressing table (*tocador de señora*) were displayed in the recently created Real Gabinete de Historia Natural in Madrid alongside other curiosities.[53] The exquisite quality of the work was often praised by commentators, one of whom remarked that it had "astonished the Europeans" (*pasmado a los Europeos*) who beheld it and had quickly been imitated by Italian artisans—though Diego Aduarte insisted they could not achieve the mastery of their Asian counterparts.[54] A few examples of sangley filigree work have been identified in Spain, including a monstrance in Caicedo de Yuso, which came at the bequest of the *oidor* (judge) Francisco de Samaniego, who had been born there and spent much of his career in Manila.[55]

Silver, including filigree work, was often incorporated into works of ivory, not just as crowns and scepters but as the wings on sets of ivory angels or as silver overlays on the garments of religious statues.[56] But this technique was perhaps most famously used in the ivory *niños dormidos* that rest on elaborate beds trimmed with "trinkets and little pieces of silver."[57] The eighteenth-century niño dormido in the Bangko Sentral collection is the prototypical example (fig. 6). It features design elements that suggest Chinese or sangley authorship, such as phoenixes and gourds wrought in silver and kingfisher feather inlay. Its filigree work is also distinctly Chinese in style, which tended to be smaller and more delicate than contemporary Cuban or Central American examples.[58] While these objects have been primarily understood as domestic in use, the Dominican convent had four such statues in its inventory, which noted the Christ Child's gilt-wood beds dangling with silver, gold, and jewel-embellished pendants.[59]

Iglesia de los Santos Reyes del Parián

To close with a brief example from this very lengthy inventory, note the church of los Santos Reyes del Parián, founded by the Dominican order in 1617 to minister to the Chinese community, including the many artisans who sold their wares there.[60] The original structure was rebuilt repeatedly before the area was demolished in the late eighteenth century, the church along with it. In his chronicle, Diego Aduarte describes the "very well adorned" (*muy bien adornada*) church with its many edifying images.[61] It was home to numerous painted and sculpted depictions of saints and advocations of the Virgin—including *Our Lady of Consolation* and *Our Lady of Biglang Awa*—that were adorned with silver bases,

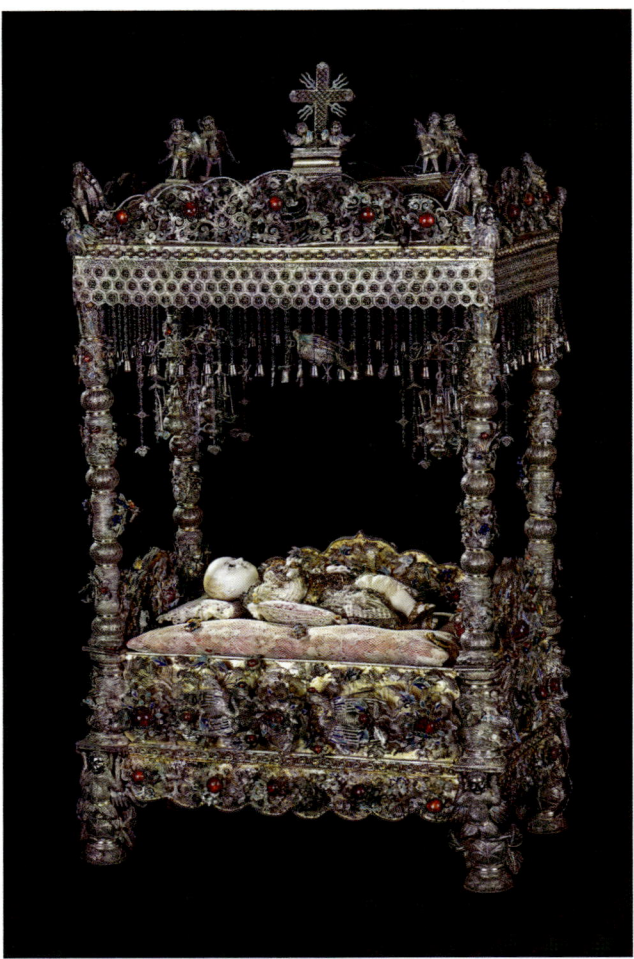

Fig. 6 Unknown artist, *Niño dormido*, Philippines, late 1600s–early 1800s. Silver, gold, ivory, cabochon gems, enamel, kingfisher feather, *piña* fiber, and lace. Figure: 7½ in. (19 cm); bed: 14⅜ × 9½ × 24⅝ in. (36.5 × 24 × 62.5 cm). Bangko Sentral ng Pilipinas Collection, Manila.

rostrillos, and crowns. In one of the lateral altars stood the Santo Christo del Valle that had received the donation of silver lanterns from Mexico.

The church was outfitted with all of the standard objects appropriate to maintain the propriety and dignity of Mass, including silver *gradillas* (small steps) to display religious images, a tabernacle (*sagrario*), an altar frontal, a pyx with its case, two monstrances, two chalices, two sets of cruets, a reliquary of the True Cross, a baptismal shell, and multiple palabras. But what is notable about this church is that it is one of the only sections of the inventory that includes reference to the weight or value of the silver objects catalogued. One wonders if this is merely the work of a singular, zealous priest with a scale or a result of the artisan population ministered to in the Parián, with their personal knowledge of the value of wrought silver.[62]

Many of the silver objects appear to have been made locally by sangley artisans, some directly at the behest of the Chinese Christian community, which remained a tiny minority in Manila. Various objects, including a silver banner for a statue of St. Dominic, were wrought from silver described as "unspendable" (ingastable), which probably meant reserve silver, meaning that the objects had been made in Manila and could be melted down if necessary. Four large candleholders were made jointly from this same unspendable silver as well as from reworked pesos given as pious donations for masses by parishioners. Other objects were commissioned specifically by the sangley community, like a large silver lamp valued at over 240 pesos and funded jointly by the Dominican house, which paid for the labor of the silversmith at a cost of twenty-five pesos.[63] These objects tell us that the Chinese converts of Manila took an active role in the beautification of their own church, commissioning a lamp and entrusting a member of their community to create this object as a devotional act. Notably, none of the jewels recorded at the church were given by sangley parishioners, which may suggest that they found platería

to be a worthier donation than the jewels often favored by Manila's peninsulars and creoles.[64] The inventory offers limited details—and may even be incomplete, as one folio appears to be missing—but it gives us a glimpse into the relationship that sangley converts had with sacred silver.

Conclusion

Across the archipelago, Philippine churches gleamed with candlelight reflected in polished silver surfaces. Despite clear evidence of their abundance, the origins—and fates—of these objects remain largely obscure. Without extended archival and collections research, it remains difficult to fully trace the history of importation and production of silver in the Philippines. In 1990, Ramon N. Villegas posed future directions for the study of Philippine silver; thirty-five years later, these questions remain largely unanswered.[65] For example, too little is known about the role of inter-Asian trade in silverworks; this essay is also guilty of trying to triangulate Philippine silver between the nodes of China, Mexico, and Spain without reference to additional influences from Southeast Asia.

What is clear is that sangley and, to a lesser extent, Indigenous artisans dominated the trade for wrought silver, producing works that were so prized as to be traded across the globe and displayed in exalted spaces from Lima to Rome. Manila's sangley artisans have been examined primarily as ivory carvers. Attending to their roles as silversmiths helps us better understand not only the kinds of work they produced but the very nature of artistic production in a city where professions were plastic and immigrants looked for economic opportunities wherever they might appear.[66]

The author would like to thank Emiliano Pérez, OP; Pedro Gil, OFM; Rev. Pe. Ramón Carmona Morillo and Mari Carmen Gavira Vara; the staff of the Archivo General de Indias; Regalado Trota Jose; Dino Carlo Santos; Ronda Kasl; Diego Javier Luis; Leslie Murrell; and Lilly Barrientos. Initial research for this essay was supported by the Leverhulme Trust.

Notes

1. Archivo de la Provincia del Santísimo Rosario (hereafter APSR), Avila, Estante 1, Tomo 164, "Libro donde se asientan las Joyas de Diamantes, Perlas, Esmeraldas, Rubies, y las de Plata de los Conventos, y Casas de toda esta Provincia del Ss^{mo} Rossario, Año de 1750."

2. See Katharine Bjork, "The Link That Kept the Philippines Spanish: Mexican Merchant Interests and the Manila Trade, 1571–1815," *Journal of World History* 9, no. 1 (1998): 25–50; Dennis O. Flynn and Arturo Giráldez, "Born with a 'Silver Spoon': The Origin of World Trade in 1571," *Journal of World History* 6, no. 2 (1995), 201–21; Flynn and Giráldez, "Cycles of Silver: Global Economic Unity Through the Mid-Eighteenth Century," *Journal of World History* 13, no. 2 (2002): 391–428.

3. Archivo-Biblioteca Provincial Franciscano (ABPF), Fondo: AFIO; Sección A-Manuscritos, Documento: 21/28, "Relación de los sucesos acaecidos en la pasada Guerra de los Yngleses por lo perteneciente solamente al convento de Sta. Clara y sus religiosas en Manila," 1764, f. 1v–2r.

4. Pedro María Jordán de Urriés y Urriés, Marqués de Ayerbe, *Sitio y conquista de Manila por los ingleses en 1762* (Ramón Miedes, 1897), 67–68; APSR, Estante 1, Tomo 380, Sección Historia Civil de Filipinas, Tomo 1, doc. 13. "En este mes el día cinco después de doze días de cercada la Ciudad por los Ingleses…," 1762; Joaquín Martínez de Zúñiga, *Historia de las islas Philipinas* (Pedro Argüelles de la Concepción, 1803), 642.

5. Frequent losses of silver ornaments also occurred during conflicts with the Muslims in Mindanao. See Emma Helen Blair and James Alexander Robertson, *The Philippine Islands, 1493–1898*, 55 vols. (The Arthur H. Clark Company, 1905), 24:117.

6. Helen Hills, "Colonial Materiality: Silver's Alchemy of Trauma and Salvation," *MAVCOR Journal* 5, no. 1 (2021): 4, 1.

7. Blair and Robertson, *The Philippine Islands*, 27:88.

8. Blair and Robertson, *The Philippine Islands*, 17:216.

9. Bartolomé Arzáns de Orsúa y Vela, *Historia de la villa imperial de Potosí*, 3 vols. (Brown University, 1965), 1:95–97, 348–49, 390; Amédée-François Frézier, *Relation du voyage de la mer du sud aux côtes du Chily et du Perou, fait pendant les années 1712, 1713 & 1714* (Jean-Geoffroy Nyon, Etienne Ganeau, Jacque Quillau, 1716), 195–96; Irving A. Leonard, ed.,

Colonial Travelers in Latin America (Alfred A. Knopf, 1972), 142–43.

10. Jorge Chapa, "The Creation of Wage Labor in a Colonial Society: Silver Mining in Mexico, 1520–1771," *Berkeley Journal of Sociology* 23 (1978): 103.

11. Hills, "Colonial Materiality," 4.

12. Blair and Robertson, *The Philippine Islands*, 7:206.

13. Archivo General de Indias (hereafter AGI), Seville, Filipinas 339, L.1, f. 156r–156v.

14. See Blair and Robertson, *The Philippine Islands*, 10:142–43, 142n12; 20:78–79; 7:70, 142–43.

15. Blair and Robertson, *The Philippine Islands*, 9:221.

16. Blair and Robertson, *The Philippine Islands*, 23:284.

17. Blair and Robertson, *The Philippine Islands*, 17:46–47; AGI Mexico 27, N. 18, f. 4r.

18. Cf. AGI Filipinas 348, L. 4, f. 344r; Filipinas 339, L.1, f. 240r.

19. AGI Filipinas 96, N. 60.

20. Cayetano Sánchez Fuertes, "Biblioteca, pinacoteca, mobiliario y ajuar de Don Miguel de Poblete, arzobispo de Manila," *Archivo Agustiniano* 95, no. 213 (2011): 428–32. My thanks to Ronda Kasl for sharing this article with me.

21. Blair and Robertson, *The Philippine Islands*, 7:226.

22. Manuel Toussaint, *La catedral de México y el Sagrario Metropolitano: su historia, su tesoro, su arte* (Editorial Porrúa, 1973), 107; AGI Filipinas 199, N. 5.

23. Susan I. Eberhard, "Metamorphic Medium: Materializing Silver in Modern China, 1682–1839" (PhD diss., University of California, Berkeley, 2023), 16; Birgit Tremml-Werner, *Spain, China, and Japan in Manila, 1571–1644: Local Comparisons and Global Connections* (Amsterdam University Press, 2015), 285n116, 289n143.

24. Jessie Park, "Made by Migrants: Southeast Asian Ivories for Local and Global Markets, ca. 1590–1640," *The Art Bulletin* 102, no. 4 (2020): 73–75; Tremml-Werner, *Spain*, 285.

25. Blair and Robertson, *The Philippine Islands*, 40:285n331; AGI Filipinas 28, N. 131, f. 970v, 972v.

26. AGI Filipinas 202, f. 385v; 435v–436v.

27. Joshua Kueh, "The Manila Chinese: Community, Trade, and Empire, c. 1570–c. 1770" (PhD diss., Georgetown University, 2014), 112–13; Pedro Luengo Gutiérrez, "Arte oriental e inquisición en Manila a principios del siglo XVIII," in *La Nao de China, 1565–1815*, ed. Salvador Bernabéu Albert (Universidad de Sevilla, 2013), 174–75; AGI Filipinas 562, "Razon Yndividual de los Gremios del Parian de Sangleyes, y consumo anual de cada gremio en el estado presente," f. 1v. Repeated attempts were made to standardize the creation of gold and silver ornaments (*alhajas*) in the Philippines and to organize silversmiths into a proper guild. See Blair and Robertson, *The Philippine Islands*, 50:103–04; AGI Filipinas 144 N. 5; Filipinas 95, N. 104; Filipinas 147, N. 2.

28. "Trabajó por su mano todas las alhajas de esta iglesia de plata, que eran muchas y buenas…; pero todo fué [sic] a costa, a celo, dirección, y cuidado del P. Fr. Fernando Cabrera," Manuel Merino, "El Convento Agustiniano de San Pablo de Manila," *Missionalia Hispanica* 8, no. 22 (1951): 105n49. However, in another of Castro's manuscripts, he mentions objects at San Pablo de los Montes of silver and gold "made in Canton." See M. Rasi Roice, "San Pablo de los Montes," *Libertas* 4, no. 816 (1902).

29. Merino, "El Convento," 105n49.

30. Brian R. Larkin, *The Very Nature of God: Baroque Catholicism and Religious Reform in Bourbon Mexico City* (University of New Mexico Press, 2010), 77.

31. Blair and Robertson, *The Philippine Islands*, 12:221–22.

32. Blair and Robertson, *The Philippine Islands*, 23:235.

33. APSR, "Libro," f. 24r. N.B. The document incorrectly notes Arrechedera's first name as Francisco and his position as archbishop-elect.

34. APSR, "Libro," f. 2v.

35. Diego Aduarte, *Tomo primero de la historia de la provincia del Santo Rosario de Filipinas, Japon y China* (Domingo Gascón, 1693), 34.

36. Martin I. Tinio, "Silver," in *Consuming Passions: Philippine Collectibles*, ed. Jaime C. Laya (Anvil Publishing, 2003), 229.

37. Pedro Luengo, personal communication, November 2024.

38. Tinio, "Silver," 227.

39. María Jesús Sanz, "Aspectos de la platería filipina. Entre la influencia española, la mexicana y la oriental," in *El sueño de El Dorado: estudios sobre la plata iberoamericana (siglos XVI-XIX)*, ed. Jesús Paniagua Pérez, Nuria Salazar Simarro, and Moisés Gámez (Universidad de León; Instituto Nacional de Antropología e Historia, 2012), 387–88.

40. APSR, "Libro," f. 124r

41. APSR, "Libro," f. 56r.

42. Blair and Robertson, *The Philippine Islands*, 37:204.

43. Pedro G. Galende and Clifford T. Chua, *The Gold and Silver Collection: San Agustin Museum, Intramuros, Manila* (National Commission for Culture and the Arts, 2003), 4–5; Clement Onn, Alan Chong, and Benjamin Chiesa, eds., *Across the Pacific: Art and the Manila Galleons*, exh. cat. (Asian Civilisations Museum, 2024), 43; Sanz, "Aspectos," 391.

44. Galende and Chua, *Gold and Silver*, 32.

45. "A la parroquia de Mairena del Alcor, por Don Ángel Carmona y compañeros, en Acapulco, renóvose en Manila por otro, año de 1787."

46. Sanz, "Aspectos," 393.

47. Martin I. Tinio, *Sanctuary Silver*, exh. cat. (The Intramuros Administration, 1982), 8.

48. Margarita Estella Marcos, "Artes aplicadas y marfiles," in *España y el Pacífico: Legazpi*, vol. 2, ed. Leoncio Cabrero Fernández (Sociedad Estatal de Conmemoraciones Culturales, S.A., 2004), 450.

49. Sanz, "Aspectos."

50. See Ramon N. Villegas, *Kayamanan: The Philippine Jewelry Tradition* (Bangko Sentral ng Pilipinas, 1983), 72–73, 108.

51. "Podían lucir en Roma y en Toledo por su valor y por su hechura." Merino, "El Convento," 105.

52. Blair and Robertson, *The Philippine Islands*, 36:202; Francisco de Echave y Assu, *La estrella de Lima convertida en sol sobre sus tres coronas* (Verdussen, 1688), 82; Serafin D. Quaison, *English "Country Trade" With the Philippines, 1644–1765* (University of the Philippines Press, 1966), 47, 73.

53. Aduarte, *Tomo primero*, 422; *Revista de instrucción pública, literatura y ciencias* 5, no. 16 (1860), 251; *Catálogo de documentos del Real Gabinete de Historia Natural (1752-1786)* (C.S.I.C., 1987), 137.

54. Echave y Assu, *La estrella*, 82; Blair and Robertson, *The Philippine Islands*, 36:202; Domingo Fernández Navarrete, *Tratados históricos, políticos, éticos, y religiosos de la monarquía de China* (Imprenta Real, 1676), 57; Aduarte, ibid.

55. Ana Ruiz Gutiérrez, "La ruta comercial del Galeón de Manila: El legado artístico de Francisco de Samaniego," *Goya: Revista de Arte* 318 (2007): 164–66. A more recent essay by Carmen Heredia Moreno calls this attribution into question. See "Una aproximación a los plateros y a la plata labrada en los autos de bienes de difuntos indianos de la época virreinal," in *Las artes suntuarias al servicio del culto divino. Siglos XVI-XVIII*, ed. Laura Illescas et. al. (Universo Barroco Iberoamericano, 2024), 321.

56. APSR, "Libro," f. 1v; illustrated in Regalado Trota Jose and Ramon N. Villegas, eds., *Power + Faith + Image: Philippine Art in Ivory from the 16th to the 19th Century*, exh. cat. (Ayala Foundation, 2004), 218.

57. Will of doña Maria Marquez y Quintos de la Torre, April 12, 1737, quoted in Trota Jose and Villegas, *Power*, 271.

58. Ibid., 162; Pedro Luengo, "Mestizo Musical Iconography: Manila's Santo Niño Cradle," *Cultural and Social History* 16, no. 4 (2019): 13n33.

59. APSR "Libro," f. 2v.

60. APSR, "Libro," f. 56r–58r; AGI Filipinas 652, n. 6, f. 33r–39v. See also Juan Gil, *Los chinos en Manila. Siglos XVI y XVII* (Centro Cientifico e Cultural de Macau, 2011), 168–74.

61. Aduarte, *Tomo primero*, 467.

62. For example, Don Juan Sunco, a sangley silversmith, acted as *celador* in 1686, ensuring the purity of faith of its congregants. Gil, *Los chinos*, 173.

63. APSR, "Libro," 56v.

64. This is anecdotally supported by a donation of silver religious ornaments made to a church in Binondo by the unnamed brother of the sangley Juan de Vera. Aduarte, *Tomo primero*, 100.

65. *Pamanang Pilak: Philippine Domestic Silver*, exh. cat. (Ayala Museum, 1990), 22–23.

66. AGI, Filipinas 28, N. 131, f. 1016r.

A Cabinet of Many Cultures

Clement Onn, Director, Asian Civilisations Museum
and Peranakan Museum

Singapore's Asian Civilisations Museum collection features an unusual small wooden writing cabinet that can be closely associated with some ten other cabinets and chests.[1] The group exhibits an intriguing combination of influences: The form of the fall-front writing cabinet became popular in Europe during the late Renaissance, while the stylistic features of the carving and inlay point to a Chinese source. Moreover, these cabinets are fashioned out of tropical hardwoods found in Southeast Asia. This rich combination suggests that the cabinets were made in a colonial port city in Southeast Asia, almost certainly Manila in the Philippines in the late seventeenth and eighteenth centuries.

The Singapore cabinet in particular adds yet another cultural connection: the Americas, for the inlay decoration on the interior surface of the fall front depicts the founding myth of Tenochtitlan, the capital of the Mexica people (fig. 1). A crowned eagle perches on a nopal cactus, which grows out of the Nahuatl glyph for water (*atl*). The eagle holds a snake in its beak.

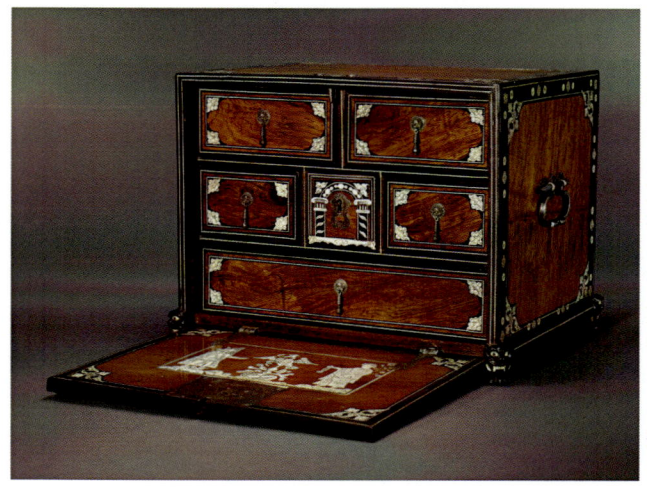

Fig. 1   Unknown artist, Writing cabinet with emblem of Mexico City, Manila, early 1600s. Wood, bone, and silver, 12¾ × 16⅝ × 13¼ in. (32.5 × 42.2 × 33.6 cm). Asian Civilisations Museum, Singapore [2019-00743].

This famous symbol of the Mexica became the emblem of what would become Mexico City. Therefore, the cabinet was probably commissioned by or for a dignitary in New Spain.

Details of the decoration suggest that the patron had a sophisticated knowledge of not just Mexico City but Tenochtitlan. At the left of the composition, a nobleman with a beaded necklace points to the bird (fig. 2). His attire resembles that seen in an

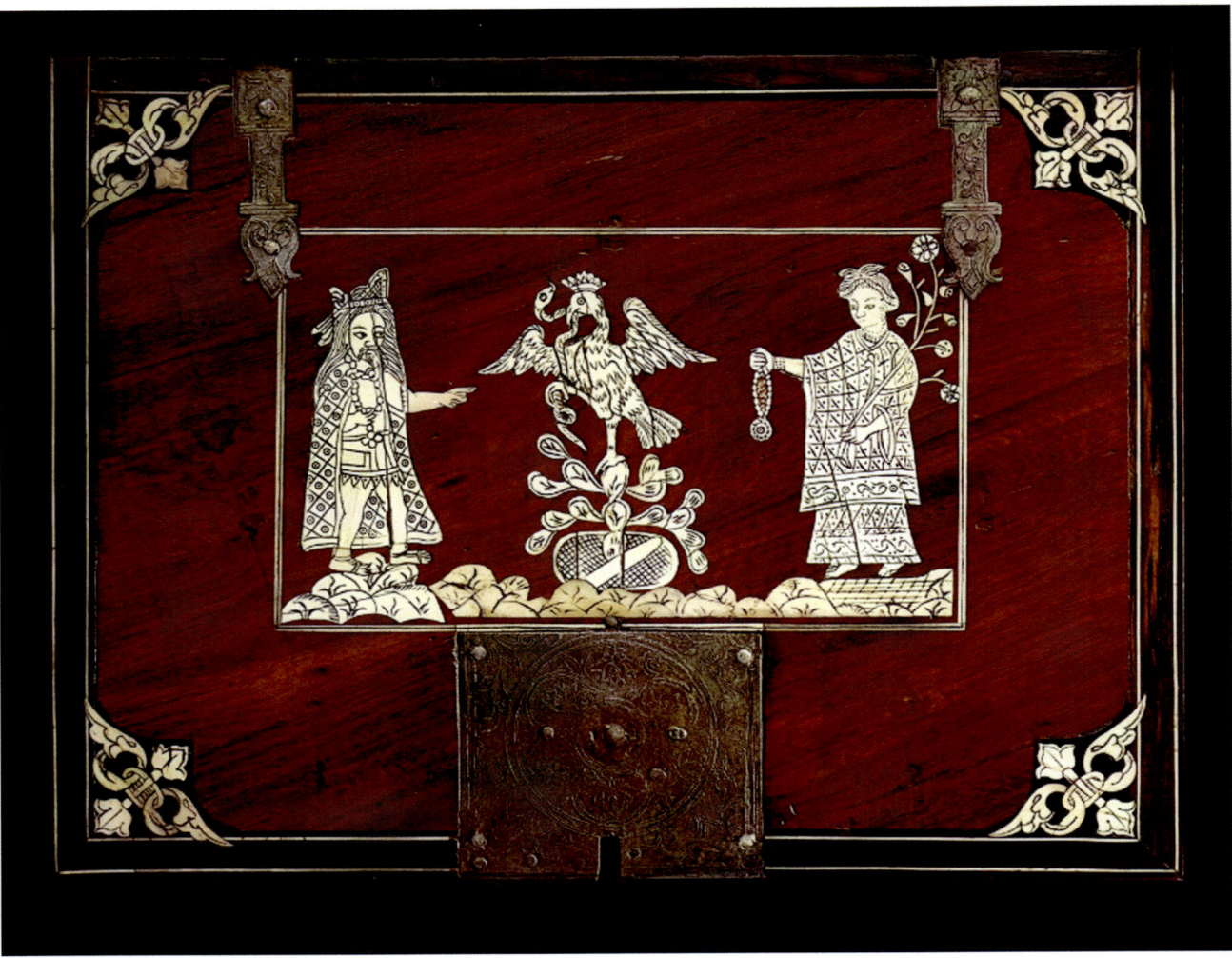

Fig. 2 Detail of fig. 1

illustration of Acamapichtli, the first *tlatoani* (ruler) of the Mexica and founder of the imperial dynasty (fig. 3). On the right, a noblewoman gestures toward the eagle with a necklace in her right hand while holding a flowering branch in her left.

While the basic form of these portable writing cabinets is European, imaginative design variations connect them with Chinese furniture-making in the Philippines. Several features can be found in Chinese furniture, including the beast mask, claw-and-ball feet at the corners, scalloped apron at the lower front, and drawer pulls with lion heads.[2] The inlaid decoration touches on several cultures: In addition to the figures and symbols from Mexica history, the floral bouquets in the four corners are commonly encountered in European art. Although only the Singapore cabinet has a specifically Mexican motif, it seems that other examples from this grouping may also have been made for export to New Spain.

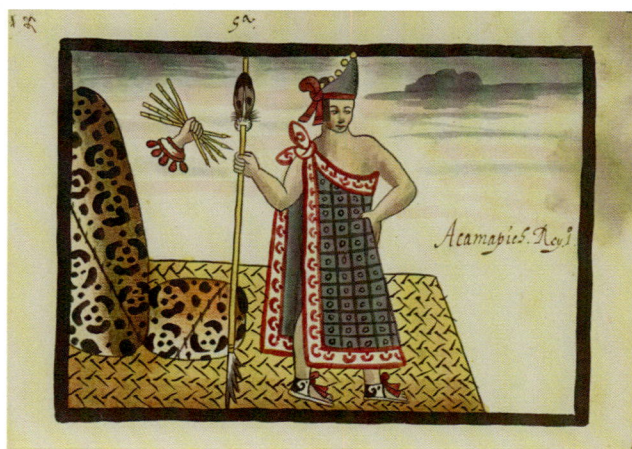

Fig. 3 Unknown artist, *Acamapichtli* from the *Codex Tovar*, fol. 93, Mexico, about 1585. Wikimedia Commons.

The Convergence of Global Goods in Multicultural Emporiums

Beginning in the late fifteenth century, advances in navigation and ship technology opened new routes between Europe and Africa, Asia, and the Americas. Large vessels carrying substantial cargoes could now sail thousands of miles, which allowed for the rapid expansion of trade, military conquest, and the spread of Christianity, often with tragic results for the Indigenous peoples of the world. As this new trading system established outposts in distant lands, people from various cultures gathered and mingled. Indeed, global trade depended on networks of port cities that became vibrant hubs for the exchange of people, goods, technology, and art.[3]

The transpacific galleons that carried goods and people between the Philippines and Mexico were controlled by the Spanish Crown, which regulated ship construction, the nature of the shipments, and their sale in Mexico. The cargoes were sold in Acapulco and transported overland to Mexico City. Some goods continued on to Veracruz, the port in the Caribbean, where they were shipped to Spain or Spanish-controlled cities in the Americas. The Manila–Acapulco Galleon trade lasted from 1565 to 1815, with its heyday in the seventeenth and eighteenth centuries. The ships, which could sail only once a year in each direction, were Spain's only link to Asia, since the route around Africa was mostly controlled by the Portuguese and later by the Dutch and British. The Spanish depended on the safe crossings of the galleons not only for profit but for their political survival in the Philippines.

The galleons made Manila one of the world's most vibrant ports, drawing traders from China, Spain, Mexico, India, and indeed the entire world. In 1662, the Franciscan monk Bartolomé de Letona wrote that "the variety of nations seen in Manila and its surroundings is the greatest in the world; one finds peoples from all the kingdoms and nations, for example, Spain, France, England . . . from the West and East Indies, Turks, Greeks, Persians, Tartars, Chinese, Japanese, Africans, and Asians."[4] Nearly a century later, the Jesuit friar Pedro Murillo Velarde (1696–1753) remained impressed by Manila's diversity: "Not one colony, of all those founded by Europeans in Asia and Africa, equals it in greatness, wealth, abundance, and community. . . . The meeting of various nations—I do not think there is anything like it in the world."[5]

While trade linked Asia and Mexico, it was the interaction of individuals at all levels of society that generated an eclectic material culture. Although the vast majority of surviving Mexican and Philippine colonial art is religious in nature, secular art was also produced for every aspect of colonial society. Elite households in Spain, Portugal, and Mexico often mingled Spanish, Flemish, Italian, German, and Asian furnishings. [6] Contemporary portraits of wealthy individuals display an array of global objects that flaunt their wealth, influence, and sophistication. In Asia, inventories of the multicultural residents of Malacca and Batavia (present-day Jakarta) reveal that individuals accumulated belongings from Europe, China, Japan, Myanmar, Sulawesi, Java, Sri Lanka, and India, among other places. [7] The inhabitants of Manila were no different, and by the late sixteenth century, goods converged there from all over the world. [8]

Philippine Furniture

The Manila galleons primarily carried Chinese goods to Mexico and beyond. For example, the inventories of ships from 1565 to 1576 (*Caja de Filipinas* or *Contaduría*) regularly list porcelain and silk. [9] From the mid-seventeenth century, records of porcelain entering and leaving Cavite, the main port of call in the Philippines, diminish significantly, perhaps because export porcelain was reclassified as private trade and would not have appeared in official records. [10] Moreover, contraband and the falsification of ship registries were common throughout the history of the galleons. [11] Furniture is nearly absent from galleon records: Isolated examples may have escaped the attention of officials and

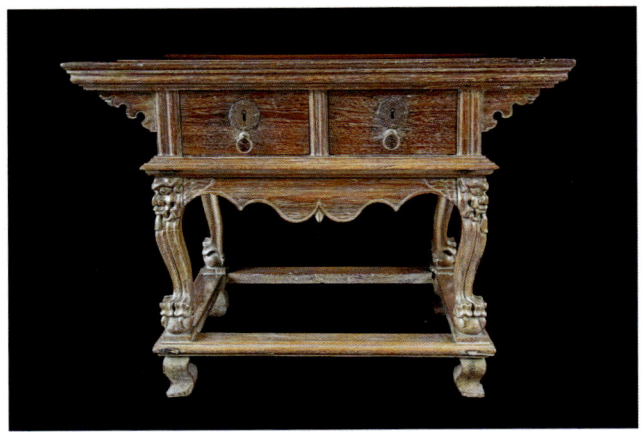

Fig. 4 Altar table, Philippines, 1700s. Wood (balayong) and metal, 27½ × 31½ × 19⅝ in. (70 × 80 × 50 cm). Collection of Paulino and Hetty Que.

in any case were not described in detail. [12] Most cabinets and chests were likely regarded as functional objects meant to transport other commodities, or perhaps they were classified as personal effects to avoid tax.

References to furniture can be found in colonial estate inventories and wills, which sometimes suggest Asian origin. Early Spanish accounts of the Philippines report that there was very little furniture in Filipino residences. [13] Only after a period of Spanish rule did Indigenous life incorporate more European-style furniture in interiors. In fact, most terms used in the Philippines for furniture are derived from Spanish: A chair is a *silya*, from the Spanish *silla*; a table is a *mesa*, and so forth. However, the lack of documentation for most surviving examples of furniture in the Philippines makes it impossible to identify individual furniture makers during the seventeenth and eighteenth centuries, whether Chinese immigrant (*sangley*) or local Filipino artists or collaborations between them.

Chinese styles and techniques were gradually integrated with local motifs to create hybrid forms, with many motifs being shared across Asia and Europe along the trade networks. One distinctive cross-cultural creation of the Philippines is the altar table (fig. 4). This type of table was commonly used in churches and homes for the display of offerings and religious figures. Early examples like the one in figure 4 resemble Chinese tables, with curving legs that end with paws grasping balls. Beast masks with long tongues perch atop each leg. Wide stretchers connect the legs to provide stability, while the short feet protect the furniture from moisture. Aspects of this design can be found in furniture made in China, Europe, and Southeast Asia. The *balayong* tree (cassia) from which the wood comes is native to the Philippines. In the seventeenth century, three regions were known to produce Philippine furniture: Bohol, Baliuag, and Batangas. The latter two regions are noted for such altar tables. Gradually, the demand for these pieces spread to other regions, including Bicol, Mindoro, and Cebu.[14]

Early patrons of Philippine furniture were the clergy and Spanish officials who commissioned Chinese artisans to furnish churches, monasteries, and colonial offices. By the late seventeenth century, Chinese merchants and artists had started marrying into the local community. Despite racial prejudice and legal barriers, individuals of Chinese and Filipino descent came to dominate the production of consumer goods. New groups of affluent patrons moved beyond Chinese-inspired models for domestic secular furniture.[15] Their requirements were naturally quite different from those of churches. By the late eighteenth century, Philippine furniture displayed Chinese and Spanish colonial features, together with local and other European details, all confidently integrated to create a uniquely Philippine aesthetic.

Records indicate that many woodworking shops were found along waterways. Furniture makers would have resided in the major trading towns, acquiring the lumber and distributing their finished products by water. Workshops in the province of Batangas were centered in the towns around Taal Lake: Calaca, Lemery-Taal, San Pascual-Bauan, and Lipa. Manila and central Luzon workshops could be found along the riverine settlements from Tondo-Malabon, Meycauayan-Marilao, Baliuag, Malolos, Calumpit, Apalit, Guagua, and the Pampanga river system all the way up to Nueva Ecija.[16] These workshops flourished over several generations through a system of apprenticeship, while the more popular designs would have persisted over time, often taken up by other furniture workshops.

San Agustin Church, Manila

The collection of the San Agustin Church in Manila, much of which can be documented to the seventeenth century, exemplifies Philippine furniture. For instance, claw-and-ball feet emerging from beast masks and scalloped carving on the apron can be found in numerous pieces. Sometimes thought to have been made in Guangzhou

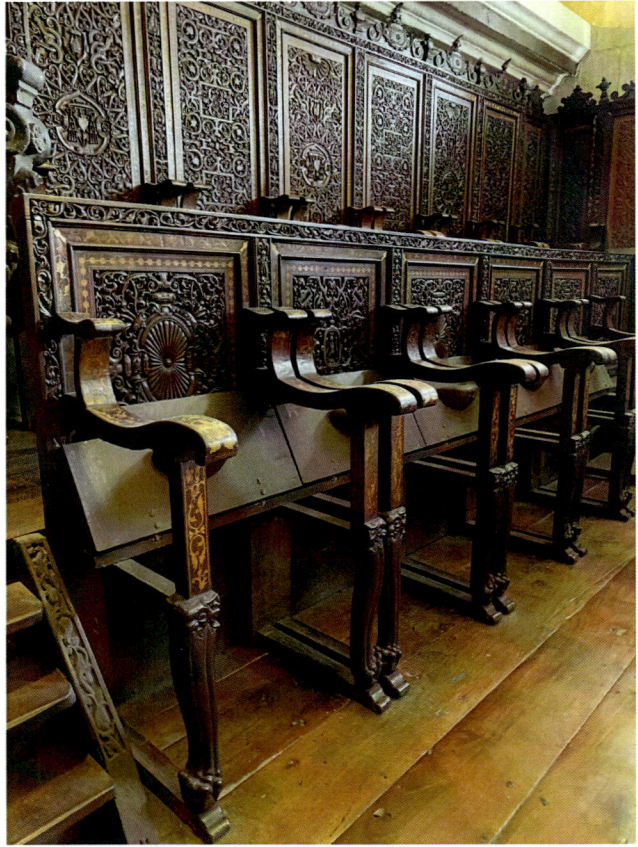

Fig. 5   Choirstalls in the church of San Agustin, Manila, Philippines, about 1608–14. Courtesy the author.

and then exported to the Philippines, many of these pieces are made of tropical hardwoods, which points to an origin in the Philippines. Contemporary observers noted that there was a thriving community of Chinese furniture makers in Manila, who almost certainly collaborated with Indigenous artists.[17]

The church of San Agustin possesses numerous pieces of furniture adorned with Chinese motifs. The most spectacular of these are the sixty-eight intricately carved choirstalls commissioned by Miguel García Serrano between 1608 and 1614 (fig. 5). The strapwork motifs relate to late Renaissance design while the woods are kamagong with inlays of narra, both native to the Philippines.[18] Interspersed among the

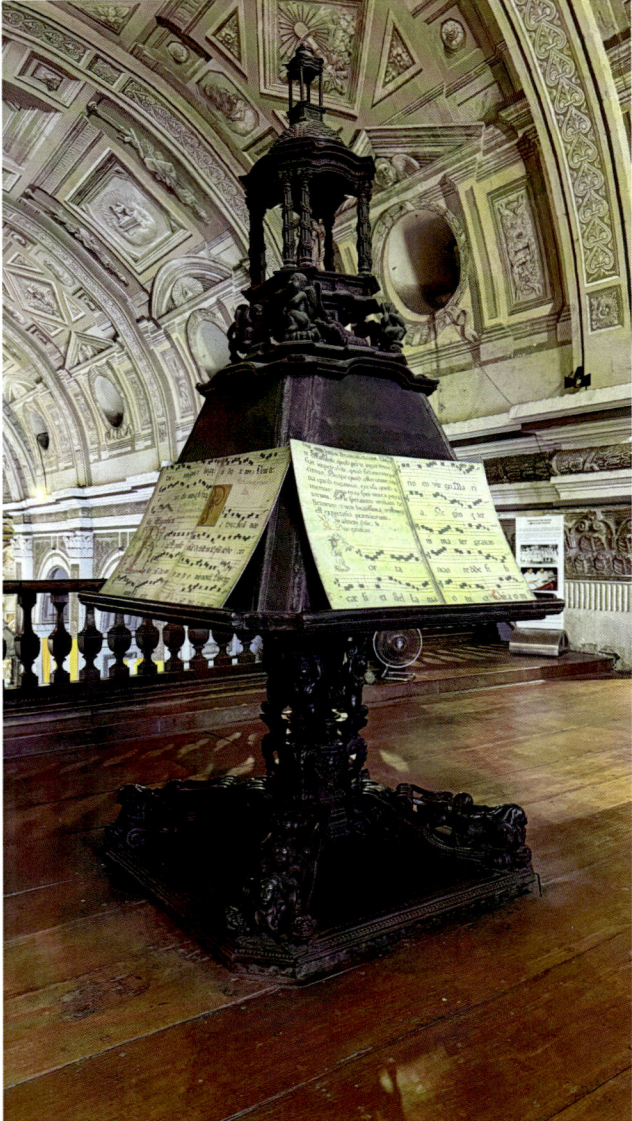

Fig. 6   Choir lectern in the choir loft of San Agustin Church, Manila, Philippines, about 1728–34. Courtesy the author.

decorations are the chrysanthemums common in Chinese and Japanese art, and cabriole legs emerge from beast masks and end in claw-and-ball feet.

The large lectern in the choir loft of the church of San Agustin is said to have been commissioned by Félix Trillo around 1728–34 (fig. 6). The lower part of the choir lectern is a curious mix of motifs, amalgamating Christian figures such as

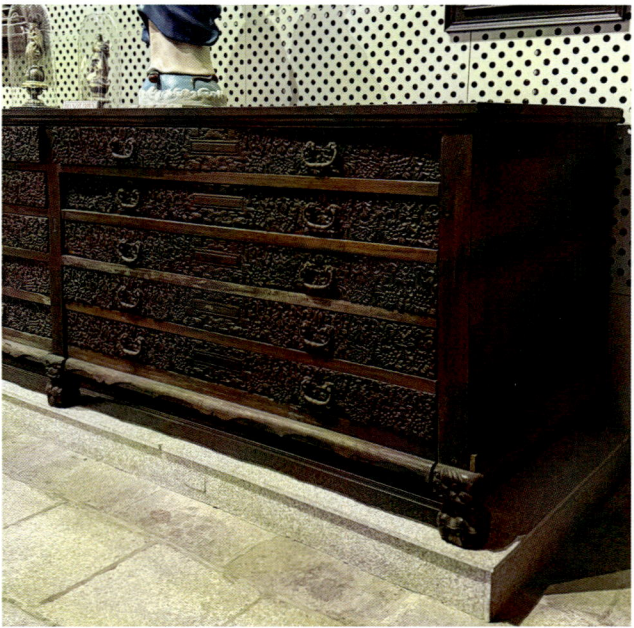

Fig. 7 Cabinets in the sacristy of San Agustin, Manila, Philippines, 1600s or 1700s. Courtesy the author.

cherubs, angel heads, and Augustinian hearts pierced by two arrows with Western female figures, Chinese mythical guardian dogs, and scrolling clouds. Another choir lectern, in Mexico City Cathedral, was carved out of *tindalo*, a Philippine hardwood, and presented in 1762 by the archbishop of Manila, Manuel Rojo del Río y Vieyra.[19] It is likely that these examples were produced by Chinese furniture makers in Manila. Within the sacristy of San Agustin, long cabinets (*cajonerías*) line both sides of the hall (fig. 7). These cabinets store liturgical vestments of the priests. The cabinets rest on beast masks with paw feet; the drawers are carved in rich floral reliefs. The massive furniture in this room was commissioned by Dionisio Suárez between 1653 and 1674.[20] A pair of fall-front cabinets, richly carved in dark hardwood with relief scenes, also bear beast masks and claw-and-ball feet (fig. 8). These

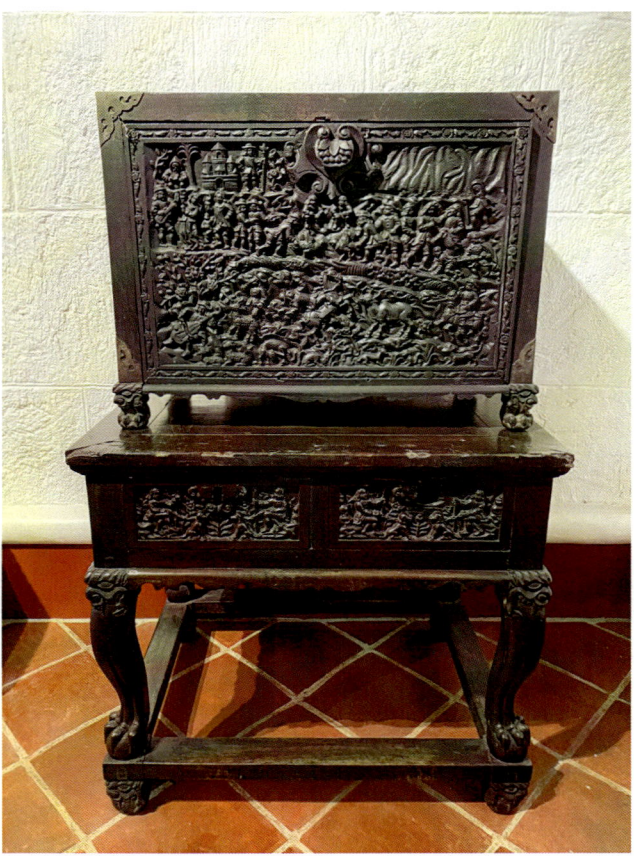

Fig. 8 Fall-front cabinet in San Agustin Church, Manila, Philippines, 1700s. Courtesy the author.

examples help to relate the Singapore cabinet to its larger group.

Writing cabinets enjoyed considerable popularity from the sixteenth to the eighteenth centuries. Essentially a small chest of drawers, they had hinged front panels that could be lowered for use as a writing surface. When the fall front is closed, the cabinet could usually be locked for transport or to secure valuables. These intimate pieces of furniture invite close inspection and are often elaborately decorated. As demonstrated, furniture makers in the Americas and Asia contributed new motifs and materials to the genre, especially through the use of rare hardwoods and exotic materials such as

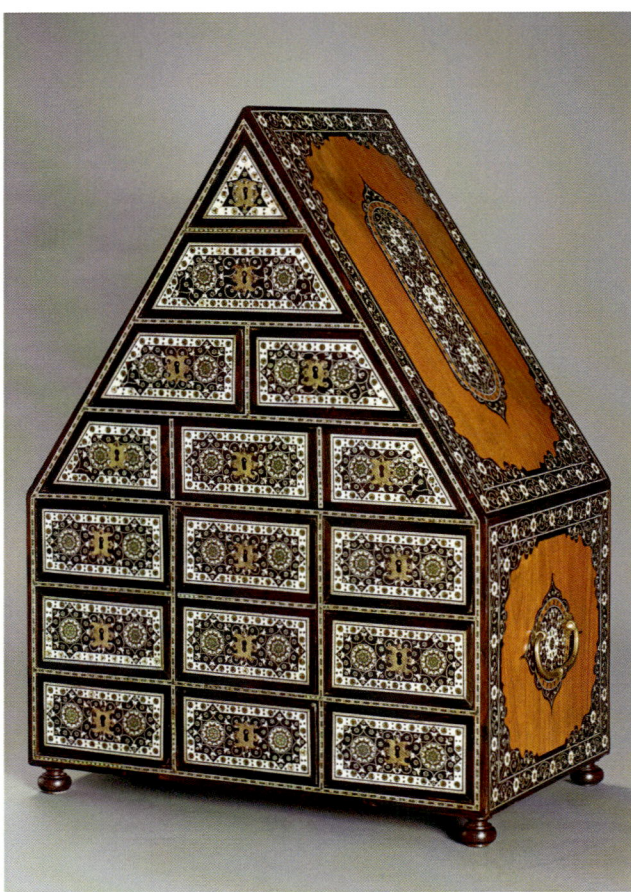

Fig. 9 Cabinet, India, Gujarat, 1600s. Ivory, rosewood, ebony, silver, and metals, 26 × 19¼ × 11¾ in. (66 × 49 × 30 cm). Asian Civilisations Museum, Singapore [2015-00516].

ivory, tortoiseshell, and mother-of-pearl. Lacquered cabinets made in China and Japan were exported to the Americas and Europe, and decorative schemes were borrowed from the symbolic systems of China, Renaissance Europe, and Mexico to delight connoisseurs. Specialized forms of art developed along the trade routes, from China—which for centuries had tailored its products specifically to consumers in other cultures—to the Philippines, Mexico, and the rest of the Americas. Many of these works had multiple connections to European and Indigenous artistic traditions, which changed over time.

A distinguishing feature of these Philippine cabinets is that the inlays are usually bone rather than ivory. Contemporary pieces made in the Indian regions of Gujarat and Sindh for the Portuguese market and in Agra for the Mughal court commonly employed ivory for inlay decoration (fig. 9). Ivory was not especially rare in the Philippines as it was extensively used for religious sculpture, but it may have been regarded as more appropriate for sacred images, which in turn discouraged its use on secular furniture. There may also have been a more pragmatic reason: Bone was cheaper and more widely available. In Spain's Nasrid period (1232–1492), artists in Granada often mixed ivory and bone in their inlaid furniture, and this practice may have also been used in making Spanish colonial possessions.[21] Both ivory and bone were typically shaped, carved, engraved, or pyrographed before being inserted into a wood support. In Baliwag (Bulacan), one of the well-regarded furniture-making towns of the Philippines, were many water buffalo slaughterhouses. The abundant supply of bone might have produced a secondary craft industry of bone inlay to decorate furniture.

An Identifiable Workshop?

Though the work in the Asian Civilisations Museum collection is European in form, the object resembles the fine inlaid furniture produced in India for the Portuguese (fig. 10) or even cabinets made in the Americas. However, this example was made in the Philippines.

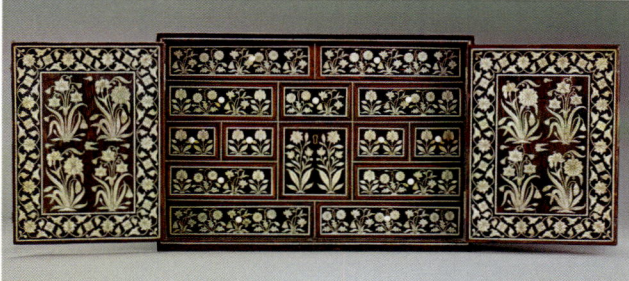

Fig. 10 Cabinet, Mughal India, probably Agra, about 1640. Rosewood, ebony, ivory, and iron, 17¾ × 26 × 17⅜ in. (45 × 66 × 44 cm). Asian Civilisations Museum, Singapore [2013-00164]: Gift of Dr Reshma Merchant and Mr Aziz Merchant, with ACM acquisition funds.

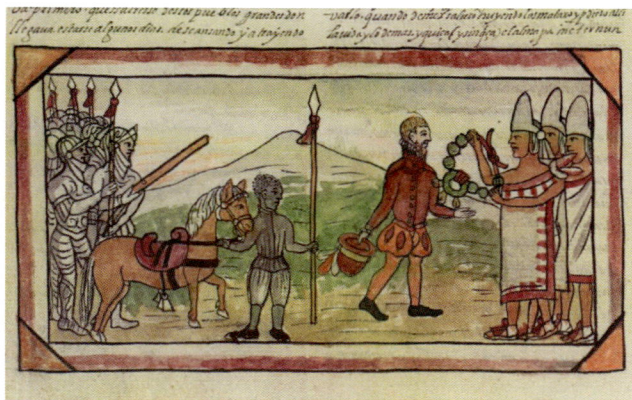

Fig. 11 Unknown artist, Hernán Cortés meeting a local leader on his way to Tlaxcala, from the *Durán Codex*, fol. 214, Mexico, about 1579. Biblioteca Nacional de España, Madrid [Vitr/26/11].

As mentioned, the inlay decoration shows the foundation myth of Tenochtitlan. It is unusual to find such Mexica imagery on a European-style, fall-front cabinet made in the Philippines. The motif of the crowned eagle perched on a flowering cactus is a common one. However, the two flanking figures are more unusual and suggest a specific source in a Mexican codex. The woman on the right stands on a platform, while the man opposite stands on rocky terrain. This alludes to the higher status of the noblewoman. The beaded necklace held by the noblewoman can also be seen in the Durán Codex (1579), where Hernán Cortés meets a local leader on the way to Tlaxcala (fig. 11). A similar beaded necklace was presented, probably as a gift to Cortés by the local chief. In the context of the cabinet, this necklace appears to be a gift of welcome.

The small central drawer is inlaid with an arch supported by serpentine columns, a familiar European motif, although the forms have been somewhat abbreviated. The four supports are carved with beast masks over claw-and-ball feet, a southern

Chinese motif, as already discussed. This suggests that this cabinet was produced by Chinese artists working in the Philippines. Many of these cabinets and chests are decorated with an abstract motif at the corners consisting of two birds joined together—reminiscent of the double-headed Habsburg eagle but with a whimsical flavor since they resemble an abstract flower. The double-headed eagle was a symbol of the Habsburg dynasty, which ruled the Spanish empire between 1516 and 1700. It became extremely common in decorative elements around the world.

The front of the writing cabinet is decorated with a diamond intersected by angled lines that form a swastika-like pattern. This motif, which recalls Chinese patterns, can also be found on other writing cabinets of the group (fig. 12 and those in the collections of the Museo Soumaya and the family of Mr. and Mrs. Lee Kip Lee) but is otherwise absent from furniture of this period, suggesting that these pieces were produced in a single workshop.[22]

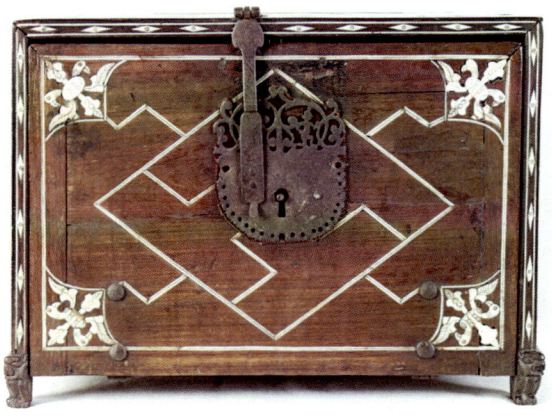

Fig. 12 Writing cabinet, Manila, 1600s. Wood (balayong), bone, and iron, 17⅞ × 12¾ × 13¼ in. (45.5 × 32.5 × 33.5 cm). Fernando and Catherine Zobel de Ayala Collection.

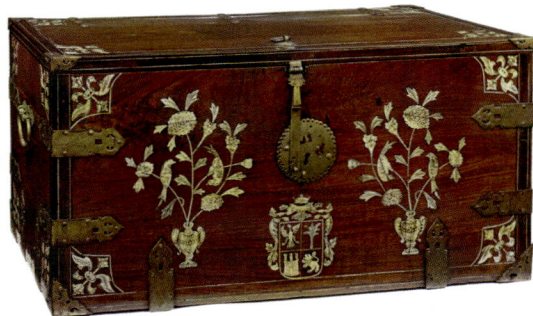

Fig. 13 Chest, Manila, 1700s. Wood (mahogany and dalbergia), bone, and brass, 29⅞ × 47¼ × 22 in. (76 × 120 × 56 cm). Museo Franz Mayer, Mexico City [04929].

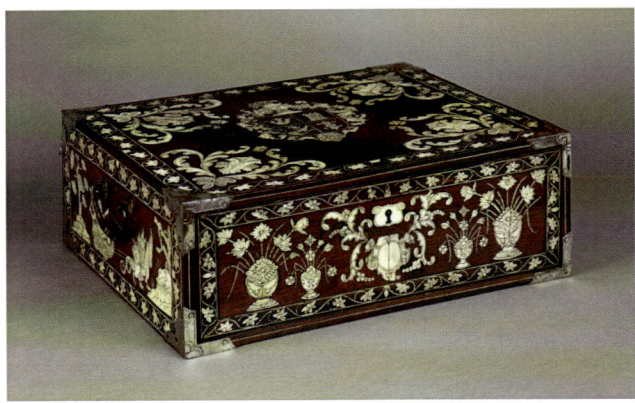

Fig. 14 Box, Philippines, late 1600s. Wood, bone, silver, and iron, 6¼ × 18⅛ × 15 in. (16 × 46 × 38 cm). Museo Franz Mayer, Mexico City [04943].

These closely related cabinets were probably special commissions from important individuals. For example, a chest in the Museo Franz Mayer is decorated with an unidentified coat of arms, surmounted by a three-pointed coronet that identifies the patron as a viscount (fig. 13).[23] The escutcheon is flanked by two vases filled with flowers and pairs of birds resting on the stalks. At the corners are the floral elements from the Singapore cabinet, though here they are even more explicitly birdlike. Another cabinet in the Museo Franz Mayer displays several cross-cultural elements (fig. 14). The sides show chariots drawn by winged dragons, a European Renaissance motif, perhaps transmitted via a print or drawing. The scrolling vine and flower border resembles a design popular on Chinese blue-and-white porcelain and Indian chintz, which also appears in Mexican *talavera* blue-and-white ceramics. On the lid is an unidentified coat of arms, while the corners are decorated with double-headed birds surmounted with a crown and surrounded by stylized acanthus leaves.[24] This version is closer to the double-headed Habsburg eagle than the abstracted motif found on the other cabinets. In the Singapore cabinet, the motif no longer even resembles two birds but appears more like a fleur-de-lis bouquet, a motif also found on Philippine altar tables (fig. 15).

Extravagant Variations

Two impressive cabinets show close affinities with the examples discussed here but are decorated in a more opulent manner (figs. 16 and 17). Complex patterns

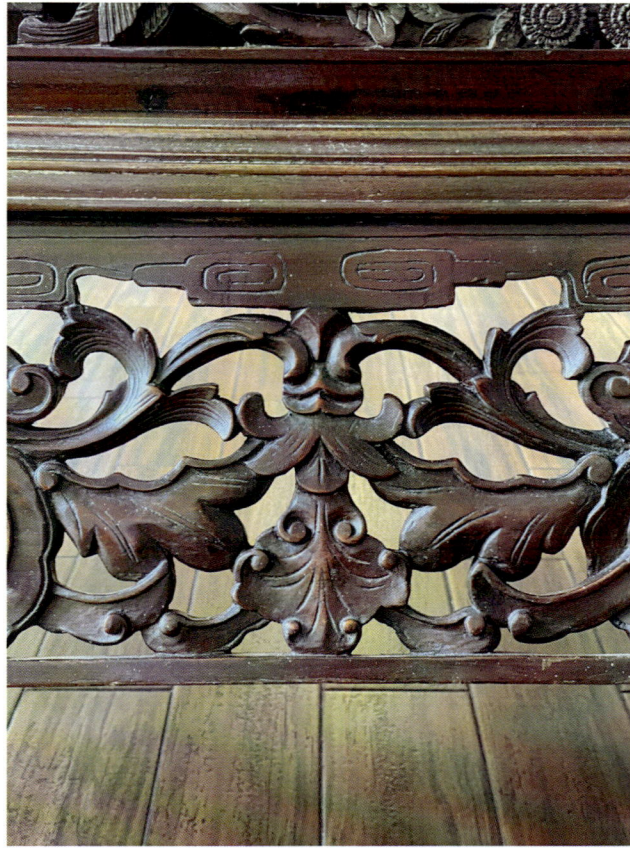

Fig. 15 Altar table (detail), Philippines, 1600s or 1700s. Wood (balayong) and metal. Museo de Intramuros, Manila. Courtesy the author.

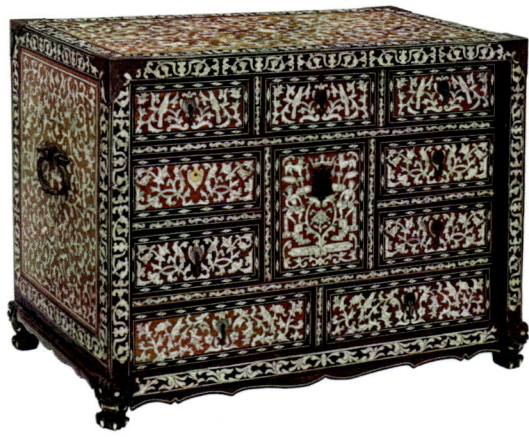

Fig. 16 Cabinet, Philippines, around 1700. Wood, bone, and silver, 23⅝ × 32⅛ × 16⅞ in. (60 × 81.5 × 43 cm). Family of Mr. and Mrs. Lee Kip Lee, Singapore.

of vines, figures, and fantastical animals were created by setting engraved pieces of bone into wooden panels. Both pieces share a characteristic type of segmented vine formed from interlocking C-shaped sections rather than the continuously flowing tendrils often found in European and Chinese designs. This type of decoration is quite different from the presumably earlier inlaid furniture made by Chinese makers in the Philippines, which is sparer in decoration and often has the double-bird motif (see figs. 1, 12–14). Most of these examples have claw-and-ball feet that emerge from beast masks and the scalloped apron. They have certain similarities with furniture made in India for the Portuguese

market, for example, in the fine inlays and combination of European and Asian motifs.[25]

In a cabinet with ten drawers, the center drawer with a lock is decorated as though it were a coat of arms, with a crown above the metal lock plate, flanked by two lions holding fly whisks (fig. 16).[26] Beneath the lock plate, male figures holding palm fronds and baskets flank a lotus flower. The combination of Chinese motifs, such as the lotus and lions, with European Renaissance nudes indicates that this cabinet was produced in a cross-cultural environment like Manila. Additional evidence indicates that the maker was Chinese: Most of the drawers are marked with Chinese characters indicating their positions: 東, 中, 西 (right, middle, and left), with additional indications of above and below, 上, 下.

The top of this cabinet is decorated with vines from which two half-figures emerge. The lower apron of the cabinet may have

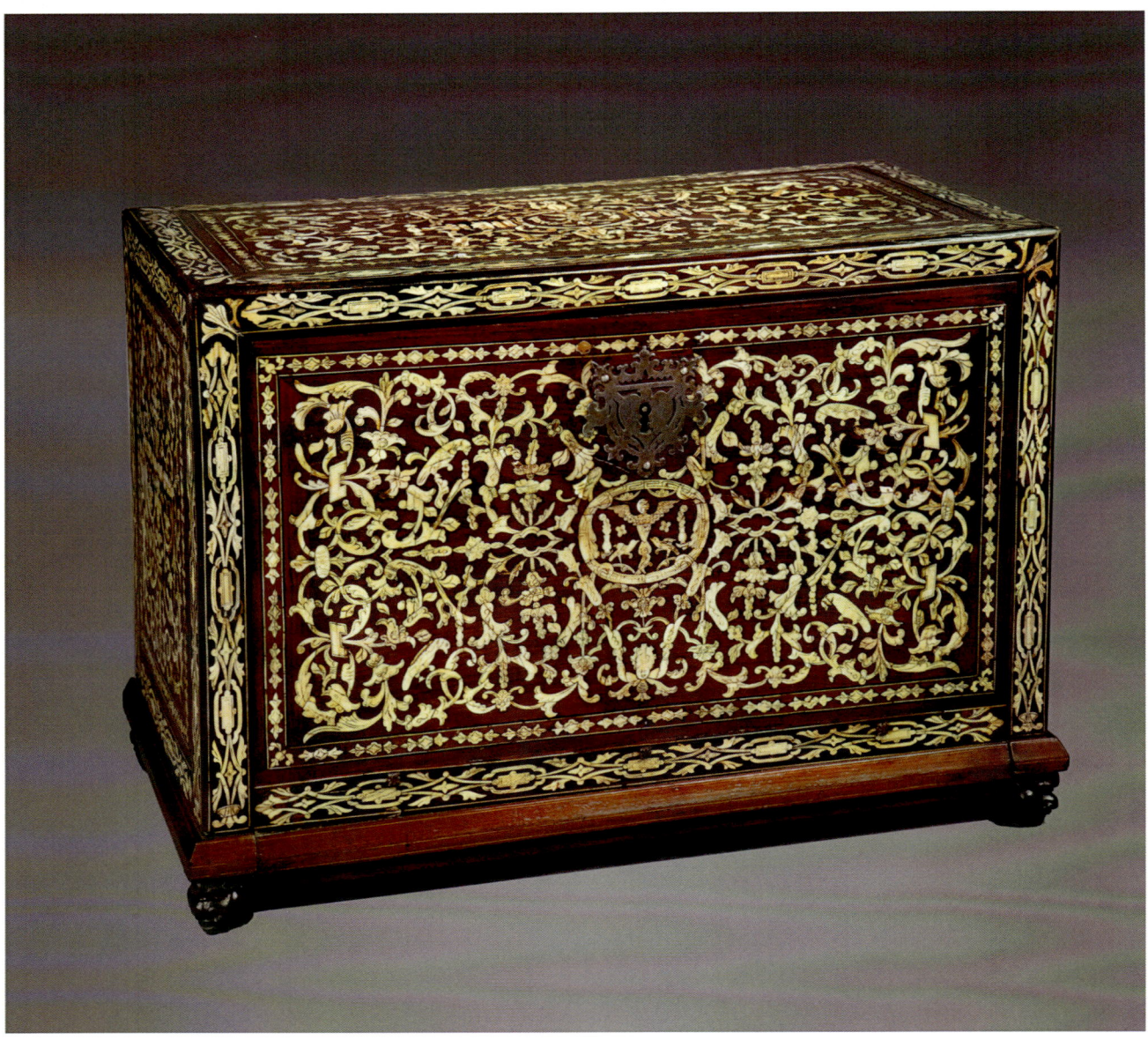

Fig. 17 Cabinet, Philippines, around 1700. Wood, bone, silver, and iron, 23⅝ × 33¼ × 17⅞ in. (60 × 84.5 × 45.5 cm). Museo Franz Mayer, Mexico City [00415].

been reconfigured to support a cover that is now missing. The original probably had neither a fall front nor a cover.

Another writing cabinet with a hinged front is densely inlaid with segmented vines (fig. 17). In the central oval medallion, a large bird spreads its wings, with two smaller birds to either side. This motif closely resembles the Christian symbol of a pelican piercing its breast to feed its young,

representing the sacrifice of Christ. A new base was added to the cabinet, apparently using the original feet.

Given their shared materials and decorative schemes, could these inlaid cabinets, chests, and boxes have been produced by a single Chinese workshop in the Philippines? The variety of sizes, quality of inlay decoration, and the variations in decoration indicate that they did not constitute a single order for a client but multiple orders over a considerable period. It is very likely that some of them were commissioned for Mexico. Until documentary evidence is uncovered, the full histories of these objects remain a fascinating mystery.

Notes

1. In addition to the collections mentioned in the captions for figures 1, 12, 13, 14, 16, and 17, the eleven examples are in the Museo Franz Mayer, Mexico City; Museo Soumaya, Mexico City; the collection of Fernando and Catherine Zobel de Ayala; the collection of the family of Mr, and Mrs, Lee Kip Lee; and Aguiar-Branco Antiques, Paris. See Clement Onn, Alan Chong, and Bejamin Chiesa, eds., *Across the Pacific: Art and the Manila Galleons*, exh. cat. (Asian Civilisations Museum, 2024), 160, 162–67.

2. The mask decoration has been called that of a lion, beast, ogre, or demon. Early collectors and dealers in the Philippines referred to this type of decoration as *demonyo* (Tagalog for demon) or *dinemonyo*. For this paper, the design is called the beast mask.

3. Clement Onn, "Across the Pacific: Artistic Exchanges Around the Globe," in Onn et al., *Across the Pacific*, 14.

4. D. R. M. Irving, *Colonial Counterpoint: Music in Early Modern Manila* (Oxford, 2010), 32; the original text is on 245n29.

5. Pedro Murillo Velarde, *Geographia historia, de las Islas Philipinas, del Africa, y de sus islas adyacentes*, vol. 8 (Madrid, 1752), 52: "Ninguna Colonia, de quantas han fundado los Europeos en el Assia, y Africa, le iguala en grandeza, en riqueza, en abundancia, y vecindario. . . . El concurso de varias Naciones, no creo tiene semejante en el mundo."

6. Jorge F. Rivas Pérez, "Domestic Display in the Spanish Overseas Territories," in *Behind Closed Doors: Art in the Spanish American Home, 1492–1898*, ed. Richard Aste, exh. cat. (Brooklyn Museum in association with The Monacelli Press, 2013), 79.

7. Peter Lee, *Sarong Kebaya: Peranakan Fashion in an Interconnected World, 1500–1950* (Asian Civilisations Museum, 2015), 290–308.

8. Etsuko Miyata Rodríguez, "Early Manila Galleon Trade: Merchants' Networks and Market in Sixteenth- and Seventeenth-Century Mexico," in *At the Crossroads: The Arts of Spanish America and Early Global Trade, 1492–1850*, ed. Donna Pierce and Ronald Otsuka (Mayer Center for Pre-Columbian & Spanish Colonial Art at the Denver Art Museum, 2012), 37–58; Peter Lee and Alan Chong, "Mixing Up Things and People in Asia's Port Cities," in *Port Cities: Multicultural Emporiums of Asia, 1500–1900*, ed. Peter Lee et al., exh. cat. (Asian Civilisations Museum, 2016), 30–41.

9. Ibid., 42–43, citing Archivo General de Indias, Seville, *Caja de Filipinas*, 943–56.

10. William R. Sargent, "Porcelains with the Arms of the Order of Saint Augustine: For New Spain? A Theory," in Pierce and Otsuka, *At the Crossroads*, 57.

11. Arturo Giráldez, *The Age of Trade: The Manila Galleons and the Dawn of the Global Economy* (Bloomsbury, 2015), 178.

12. Jorge Loyzaga, "The Influence of Oriental Trade on Mexican Art, Culture, and Folklore," in *The Manila Galleon: Crossing the Atlantic*, ed. Edgardo J. Angara et al. (READ Foundation, 2014), 94.

13. Ambeth R. Ocampo, *Cabinet of Curiosities: History from Philippine Artifacts* (Anvil Publishing, 2023), 96.

14. Ibid., 96–98.

15. Ramon N. Villegas, "Mueblaje Filipino," in *Filipinos in the Gilded Age*, exh. cat. (León Gallery, 2016), 158.

16. Ibid.

17. Pedro G. Galende and Regalado Trota Jose, *San Agustin: Art and History, 1571–2000* (San Agustin Museum, 2000), 103.

18. Ibid., 136.

19. Ibid., 137.

20. Ibid., 103.

21. María Campos Carlés de Peña, *A Surviving Legacy in Spanish America: Seventeenth- and Eighteenth-Century Furniture from the Viceroyalty of Peru* (Ediciones El Viso, 2013), 90.

22. For figure 12, see Onn et al., *Across the Pacific*, 164. The cabinet with the family of Mr. and Mrs. Lee Kip Lee is also adorned with elaborate decorations, including pierced drawer fronts reminiscent of Kyushu furniture.

23. Onn et al., *Across the Pacific*, 165.

24. Onn et al., *Across the Pacific*, 160.

25. Figure 17 is identified as seventeenth- to eighteenth-century Indo-Portuguese by the Museo Franz Mayer.

26. On figures 16 and 17, see Onn et al., *Across the Pacific*, 166–67.

"Graceful, Rich, and Pleasing to the Eye": Seamless Facture Across the Pacific

Samuel Frédéric Luterbacher, Assistant Professor,
Occidental College

In 1588, Luís Fróis (1532–1597), a Portuguese Jesuit and missionary to Japan, offered striking praise for various lacquered boxes gifted by the warlord Toyotomi Hideyoshi to the viceroy of Portuguese India. On their craft, he declared:

> Undoubtedly, if anyone across Europe sees it, they will marvel at the delicacy and perfection of such a work. For it is entirely covered, inside and out, with a kind of varnish, which in Japan is called urushi, sprinkled with ground gold in the manner of sand... and wrought with flowers and roses made from thin sheets of silver and gold, which are fitted in such a way with said urushi, that in no case can one see any sign of joinery, nor can one understand, if one does not know how such a work is made, by which it becomes very graceful, rich, and pleasing to the eye. [por nenhum cazo se pode ver conjuntura, nem se pode entender de quem o não sabe como se faça tal obra, com que fica mui airoza, rica e aprazivel à vista].[1]

Fróis marveled at the lustrous surface of gold and silver suspended in layers of "varnish," East Asian lacquer known in Japanese as urushi, a natural polymer derived from the sap of the *Toxicodendron vernicifluum* tree. Refined at low temperatures, it can be mixed with pigment to obtain a deep color, most commonly red or black. Once cured in a humidity-controlled environment, it forms a hard, heat- and water-resistant surface. Manipulating urushi is both delicate and dangerous: The raw sap is toxic and can cause severe skin reactions. Artisans prepare a wooden base with a ground foundation before applying several layers of urushi and finishing with meticulous polishing to achieve a smooth, lustrous surface that hides any hint of handiwork. Along with its durability, lacquerware's adhesive properties made it an ideal surface for decoration in East Asian artistic traditions. In Japan, artisans excelled in the decorative technique known as *makie* (sprinkled picture), where silver and gold powder are dusted "in the manner of sand," in Fróis's words, onto wet urushi to create intricate designs.

Fróis's reverence for lacquer's seamless brilliance speaks to its success as an art form within the Iberian world.[2] As the Portuguese and Spanish established a presence in Asia, lacquer workshops across the Pacific rim adapted their techniques to produce chests, writing desks, and religious objects made specifically for export to a Catholic consumer base in the Iberian world. Indeed, Fróis emphasized lacquer's dual function as both a coating and a carrier of sacred Catholic materials, concluding his account by noting that such lacquered boxes "could serve well as chests for relics."[3] Brought to the Spanish Americas by the Manila Galleon trade, surviving export lacquerware bears traces of colonial artistic intervention. Especially prized in New Spain, portable lacquered shrines with hinged doors and removable frames for sacred images were combined with local artistic practices such as painting and feather work.[4]

Fróis's admiration aligns with a broader Iberian missionary discourse that prized such surface effects in the arts newly encountered along Portuguese and Spanish trade routes. But while art historians have tended to emphasize the reflective qualities of these circulating objects, such as their iridescence, Fróis's praise for lacquerwork's surface directs attention not only to the visual but also to the tactile, thereby signaling a further mark of its making: its seamless facture.[5] In the craftsperson's expert hands, "in no case can one see any sign of joinery." Seamless facture was highly prized in preindustrial societies, giving rise to labor-intensive artisanal processes that concealed traces of human handiwork beneath an illusion of effortless creation, evoking objects fashioned by nature, or even by miracle.[6] By blurring the boundaries between nature and artifice, such skill could conjure the *acheiropoieton*: the Christian image ostensibly "not made by human hands" but rather through contact with the divine. Such conceptions of wondrous and miraculous making resonated with Renaissance ideals of authored identity, in which the artist demonstrated the capacity to unify diverse elements into a seamless synthesis of material and form.[7] Fróis's description reveals how Iberian observers recognized the ingenuity and skill of makers outside Europe, an acknowledgment that some scholars argue helped shape an early modern humanistic conception of the arts as a universal phenomenon.[8] I contend, rather, that this discourse on facture discloses a deeper aesthetic tension: The object's surface appearance produces an impression of seamless facture, one that simultaneously showcases artistic virtuosity and obscures the disparate forms of labor that underlie its creation.

Beyond merely imposing European discourse onto foreign artworks, this rhetoric of facture was formed from the very materials and craft cultures that intermingled within the sixteenth- and seventeenth-century transpacific system. Once viewed as peripheral, the Manila Galleon route has emerged in scholarship as a central axis of early modern global trade.[9] It linked far-flung sites of manufacture, enabling the sequential fabrication of art objects as they moved through local workshops within the vast Iberian maritime networks of the Indo-Pacific. Religion and commerce remained inseparable within this system: Mercantile and missionary imperatives did not merely coexist but actively conditioned the creation and movement of objects along these routes. The prizing of seemingly wondrous and miraculous facture extended to circulating artworks, obscuring their underlying imperial systems of production.[10] Through this lens, I argue that the rhetoric of "seamlessness" engaged with the diverse artistic interventions that an object might at once consolidate and conceal. Particularly revealing in this regard are the lacquer shrines made for export, which brought together Christian icons within ornamental housings, attempting to seamlessly integrate radically different forms, materials, and decorative techniques in a single devotional object.

Economies of Conversion

Export lacquerware for the Iberian market emerged from the Christian mission in Japan and its ties to maritime trade. It is now known as Nanban lacquerware, a period term meaning "southern barbarians," applied to Iberian visitors after Portuguese merchants arrived in southern Japan around 1543. Jesuit missionary Francis Xavier established the Catholic mission in Japan in 1549, and by 1580, the Portuguese had made Nagasaki their official port. That same year, the union of the Spanish and Portuguese Crowns informally connected their maritime empires, placing Japan at the crossroads of both the Portuguese State of India (encompassing Goa and Macau) and the Spanish Manila–Acapulco galleon trade. By the late sixteenth century, Franciscan, Augustinian, and Dominican missionaries from Manila had further integrated export lacquerware into the transpacific trade system. This exchange declined when Japan banned Christianity in 1614, and Nanban lacquerware production ceased entirely in 1639 with the termination of commercial and religious ties.

What began within the Jesuit mission expanded into wider Iberian commerce as lacquerware became a common commodity on Portuguese and, later, Spanish ships. Despite their vow of poverty, the Society of Jesus in Japan was heavily involved in the silk trade as a means of gaining favor with local feudal lords (*daimyō*), drawing criticism within the order as well as from competing missionary groups like the Franciscans.[11] Jesuit sources seldom name lacquer artisans, but those mentioned are often identified as Christian converts.[12] Through conversion, missionaries secured access to lacquerware production while

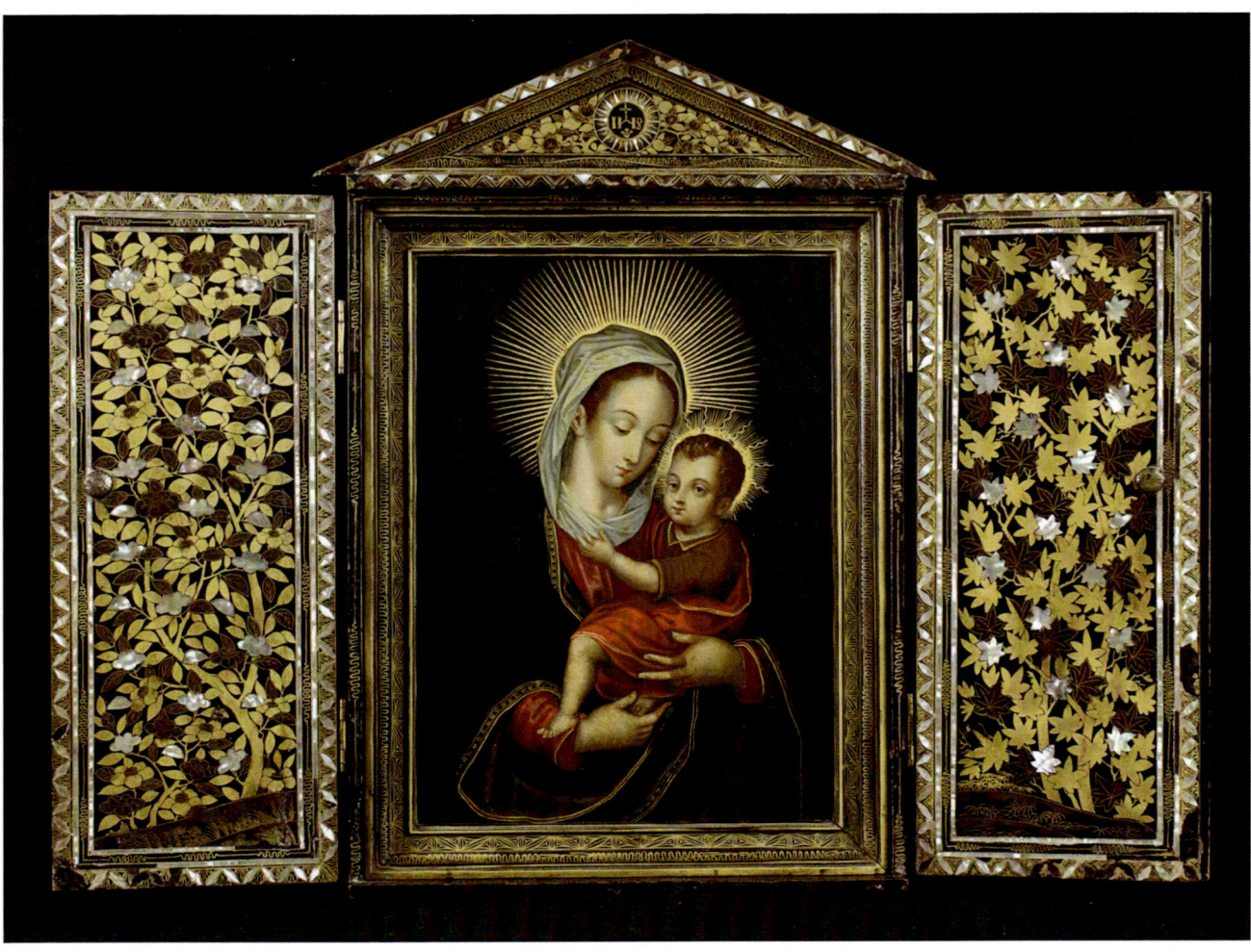

Fig. 1 *Portable shrine with the Virgin and Child*. Shrine: late 16th/early 17th century. Wood base with lacquer (urushi), gold, silver, mother-of-pearl, and copper mounts, 18½ × 13¾ × 2 in. (47.2 × 35 × 5.1 cm). Image: late 16th century. Oil on copper. Santa Casa da Misericórdia, Sardoal, Portugal. © Santa Casa da Misericórdia, Sardoal.

assuring external authorities that genuine Christians crafted their religious items. In Portuguese-controlled Asian territories like Goa, European-style guild regulations were imposed on local craft communities, mirroring practices in the Latin American colonies.[13] In parts of Asia that lay outside direct colonial control—such as Japan— Iberian authorities typically relied on local artisans or formed economic partnerships, leading to more flexible enforcement.

Nanban lacquerware developed alongside Jesuit accommodation strategies during this period of exchange. The early mission benefited from Japan's state of civil war, as Iberian merchants and missionaries sought alliances with rival feudal lords. Missionaries adapted to local customs, adopting Japanese dress and architecture to spread their Christian message among regional elites. Recognizing lacquerware's elite status and sacred role, they promoted it as an evangelical and diplomatic tool. By the late sixteenth century, lacquer workshops already operated on a large scale under a master craftsman who managed orders, designs, and apprentices. These workshops favored *hiramakie* (flat makie), a more expedient technique using metal powder to produce low-relief motifs. This method appealed to Japanese warrior and merchant tastes and allowed quicker production to satisfy growing demand.

These local forms and techniques were adapted to missionary Catholic ends in Nanban lacquer shrines, which developed a distinct decorative aesthetic. Lacquer artisans reconfigured traditional *zushi* (portable shrines) to create versions designed for export to house Christian devotional images.[14] An early example now held at the Santa Casa da Misericórdia in the Portuguese town of Sardoal features hinged doors beneath a roofed gable; enshrined inside is an oil-on-copper painting of the Virgin and Child (fig. 1).[15] The sacrality of the icon is both affirmed and delineated through the use of Japanese techniques and seasonal motifs in an ornamental capacity: The gable and the inner faces of the doors, which surround the image, are densely decorated with camellias and mandarin oranges and maple trees, enclosed within geometric borders. Such seasonal floral motifs were common on Japanese religious shrines, where they carried auspicious associations.[16] The Sardoal shrine's abundant vegetal ornamentation in gold and mother-of-pearl, which carpets the black ground, is characteristic of Nanban export lacquerware. Export pieces often feature *raden,* a mother-of-pearl technique in which thin pieces of shell are affixed to a wooden base, leveled with layers of lacquer, and polished to reveal their iridescence. For export, workshops adopted more expedient and cost-effective methods, adding greater quantities of animal glue, reducing the number of lacquer layers, and blending native urushi with imported *thitsi* lacquer from Southeast Asia.[17] The resulting dense, shimmering decoration catered to Iberian tastes and mirrored other export items that traveled along the Portuguese trade routes, such as Indian furniture and textiles.[18]

Export shrines reflected the increased mobility of sacred images amid the Counter-Reformation's global aims. Iberian expansion and the universal Catholic missionary enterprise facilitated the circulation of religious imagery while intensifying ecclesiastical efforts to control sacred boundaries. In response to Protestant iconoclasm, the Council of Trent (1545–63) reaffirmed the instructional value of religious images yet advocated strict oversight to distinguish sacred from profane content.[19] Believed to be powerful tools for proselytization across linguistic divides, the appearance, display, and use of religious images in rituals remained a constant concern in the overseas missions—especially in East Asia, where Jesuits' accommodative strategies heightened fears that adapting Christian rituals and visual culture to foreign contexts might dilute or alter their content.[20] In Japan, Jesuits imported European prints and paintings, appealing to Japanese concepts of iconicity. The mission later enlisted the Italian Jesuit painter Giovanni Cola (Niccolò) to produce religious artworks as well as to train Japanese novices in a painting seminary to replicate European models, ensuring strict control over form, style, and iconography to prevent semantic slippage.[21] As Alexandra Curvelo has suggested, the Jesuit enterprise likened the copying of religious images to Christian conversion, one that, in their view, proposed a sacred transmission across cultural frontiers, materialized through a seamless process of replication and made manifest in the artworks themselves.[22]

The Icon Reframed

Framing strategies played a key role in seamlessly integrating religious images into the portable ornamental shrines that housed them. Export shrines could function as both physical and metaphorical framing devices for religious images, mediating shifting cultural and geographic mobilities during an era of global Catholicism and post-Tridentine regulation. In this regard, the shrines resonated with contemporaneous European "inset images" (*Einsatzbilder*), sacred images within ornamental frames linked to Counter-Reformation principles of decorum. This seamless integration of the image into its surrounds is evident in Flemish garland paintings, such as the 1608 collaboration between Jan Brueghel and Hendrick van Balen for Cardinal Federico Borromeo (fig. 2). Balen's oil-on-silver Virgin and Child is framed by Brueghel's floral garland,

painted in oil on panel, emphasizing Marian themes of divine beauty and natural abundance. The composite painting employs the "smooth manner," long championed by Netherlandish artists and

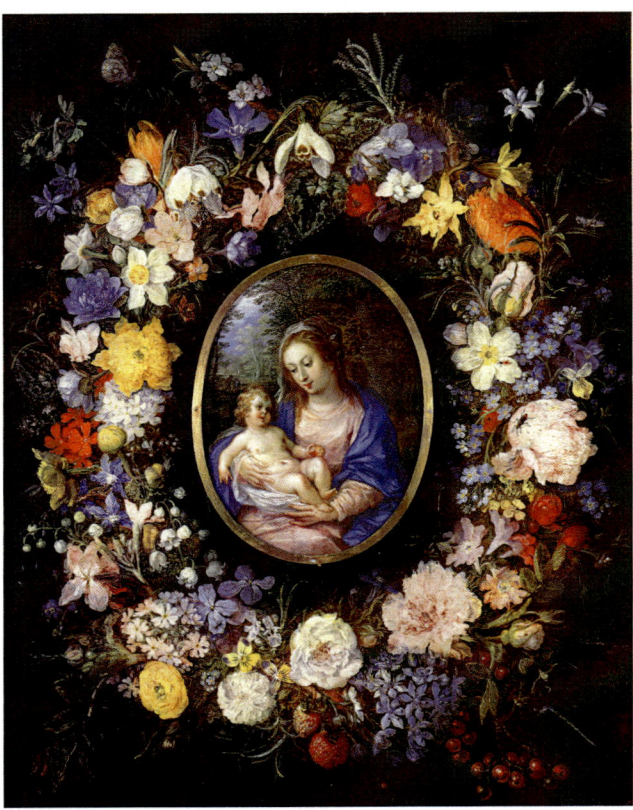

Fig. 2 Hendrick van Balen and Jan Brueghel the Elder, *Madonna and Child in a Flower Garland*, 1607–8. Oil on panel and silver, 10⅝ × 8⅝ in. (27 × 22 cm). Pinacoteca Ambrosiana, Milan. © Veneranda Biblioteca Ambrosiana/ Palolo Manusardi/Mondadori Portfolio.

theorists, a technique that conceals brushwork beneath fine layers of oil paint to evoke the image "not made by human hands."[23] This style elevated the artist's work to the level of the divine by obscuring its manufactured origins. According to Victor Stoichita, the religious icon, set within an illusionistic frame, mediates the escalating tensions between the cult image and the authored artwork, striving to preserve its dual status as both a devotional image and a commodity within a burgeoning art market.[24] Similarly, the Sardoal shrine integrates distinct artistic contributions into a seamlessly fabricated, unified artwork, merging oil-on-copper icon and lacquered ornamental frame. In doing

Jesuit missionaries recognized in Japan the familiar elements of a stratified society with its own artisanal class, the *shokunin*. Not unlike the European guilds, artisanal production in Japan was generally a generational, familial, and male-led enterprise (known as *ie*, "household"), administered by a master craftsman whose knowledge was carefully safeguarded and transmitted only to workshop members.[40] Eiko Ikegami describes the shokunin's skill or mastery (*gei* or *geinō*) as a magical technology or ability "to move or influence nature and to connect this present world with the unseen world beyond."[41] The Japanese lacquerer's ability to not just transform toxic sap into a hard, smooth surface but also to integrate brilliant materials, aligns with the shokunin's near-magical harnessing of natural forces and ties to the spiritual realm. Comparatively, the amanteca's artful use of iridescent feathers was associated with a spiritual essence, known in Nahuatl as *tonalli*, and was later adapted to Christian imagery.[42] Indeed, praised by Catholic missionaries, the invisible handiwork of lacquerers and feather artists was conditioned by a careful balance between revealing and concealing, between the mastery and mystery of their artistry.[43] The missionaries' noted admiration of a non-European technique went beyond neutral aesthetic appreciation; it reflected a desire to access the artisan's secret, even magical knowledge, and repurpose it for global aims. Whether in Fróis's praise of lacquer as a reliquary or Acosta's account of feather work transformed into a Christian icon,

both missionaries attested to the sacred efficacy embedded in these artistic media.

The dynamic interplay of revelation and concealment inherent in the seamless surface persisted through the transpacific circulation of religious art well into the eighteenth century.[44] An export lacquer shrine from the Daniel Liebsohn Collection in Mexico City speaks to the continuation of this phenomenon between the Americas and Asia via the Manila Galleon circuit (fig. 6). The shrine's lacquered doors open to reveal a striking visual palimpsest: a resplendent eighteenth-century oil-on-copper painting of the Virgin of Guadalupe embedded within a seventeenth-century Japanese lacquer shrine, itself imported a century earlier. Affixed to the rear of the shrine is an inscribed piece of paper, an indulgence granted to those who pray before the image, issued by the bishop of Calahorra and La Calzada and dated November 15, 1786, in the Basque town of Mondragón (Gipuzkoa).[45] This Atlantic addition overlays yet another vector of circulation upon the shrine's Pacific trajectories. The gifting of Guadalupe images to Basque-speaking regions was a common colonial practice, reflecting the enduring ties between Basque emigrants to New Spain and their home communities in Northern Spain.[46] The shrine once again merges diverse artistic traditions, while also reflecting the continued preservation and reuse of export lacquerware in the colonial period.

Cherubim wrought in American silver surround the central icon, accompanied by

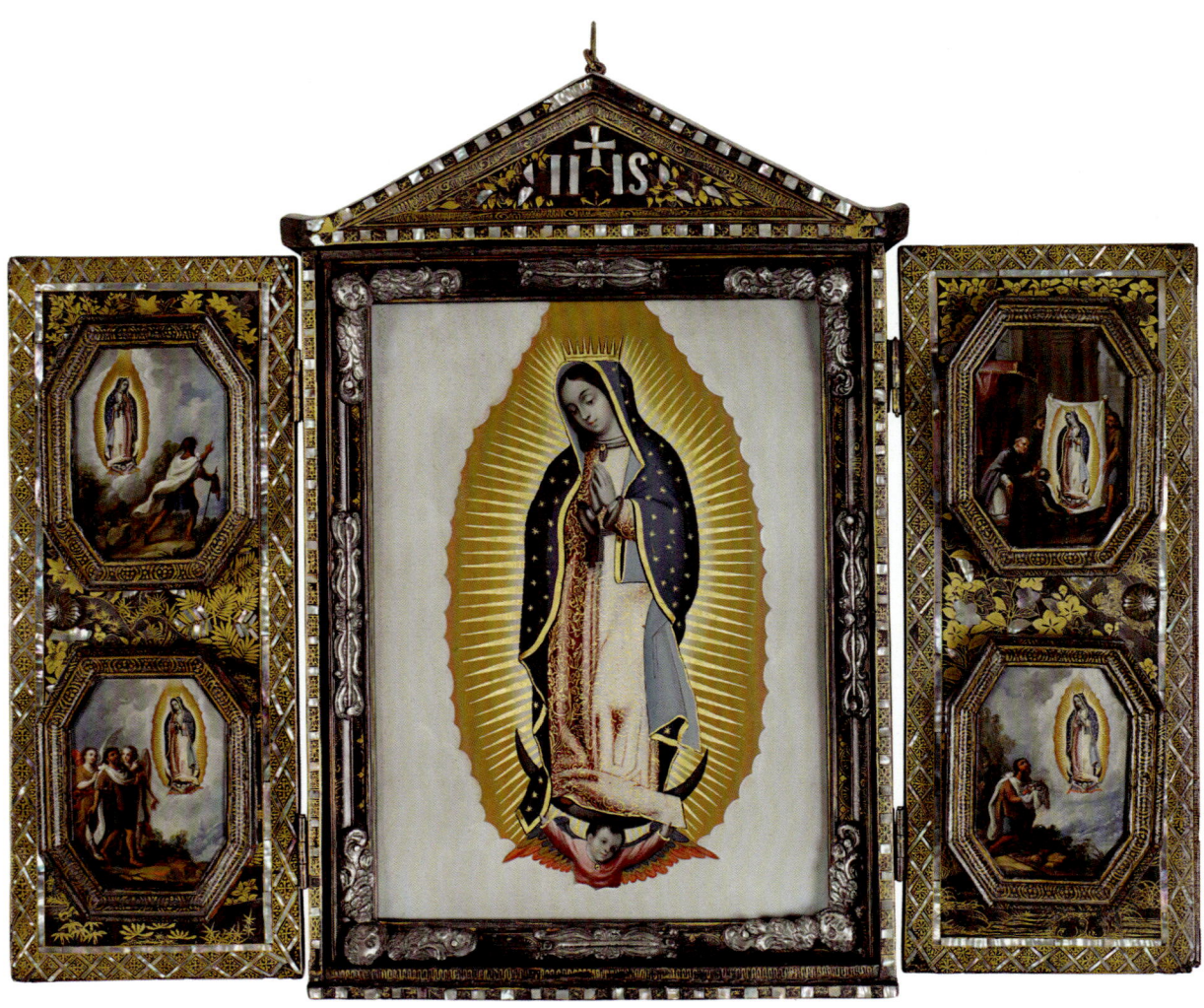

Fig. 6 *Portable Shrine with the Virgin of Guadalupe and the Four Apparitions*. Shrine: late 16th/early 17th century. Wood base with lacquer (urushi), gold, silver, mother-of-pearl, and copper mounts. Images: 18th century. Oil on copper foil with embossed silver applications. Daniel Liebsohn Collection, Mexico City. © Archivo fotográfico F.C.D.L/ Colección Daniel Liebsohn.

four small painted scenes of the Virgin's miraculous apparition, affixed to the lacquer doors. Following period protocols for depicting the Guadalupe, they sequentially capture her apparition to the Indigenous witness Juan Diego and her command to gather roses in his cloak. Appearing before Mexico's first bishop, Diego spills the flowers to reveal the Virgin's image miraculously impressed into the cloth. By the seventeenth century, the apparition narrative had supplanted the account of an Indigenous painter Marcos Cipac de Aquino's authorship, reflecting the imposed layering that shaped artistic production in New Spain: a Catholic icon materialized in an Indigenous substrate—a cloak (*tilma*) of *ayate* (*ayatl*) cloth woven from local maguey or palm fibers. In the Liebsohn shrine, floral decoration and painted scenes engender a missionary myth of seamless overlay.

As recently explored by Derek S. Burdette, viceregal artists served as the prime investigators in determining the

Guadalupe's divine origins.[47] The artists who inspected the image in the seventeenth and eighteenth centuries insisted on the miraculous nature of the surface's painted smoothness, in specific contrast with the "roughness" of the native ayate fabric.[48] For example, the famed New Spanish painter Miguel Cabrera emphasized its miraculous smoothness in his *Maravilla americana*, an examination of the picture published in 1756, drawing deeply on Jesuit discourse that framed the image as a divine imprint beyond human artistry.[49] He writes:

> *What should provoke admiration is the softness* [suavidad] *experienced in this ayate; for all the roughness it presents to the eye, which one would expect from being made of such ordinary material, is converted to the touch into a gentle smoothness very similar to that of fine silk, as I have found on the many occasions I have had the good fortune to touch it; and certainly the other ayates of its kind do not enjoy this privilege.*[50]

Cabrera describes the "ordinary matter" of the cloth as a rough and crude ground transformed into a soft, painted surface. He thus witnesses the miracle through the tactile experience of its conversion from roughness into smoothness. The smooth, seamless surface affirms the image's divine creation while simultaneously concealing the "roughness" of Native craft, and, by extension, its Indigenous authorship.[51]

In closing, it is worth noting that in seeking to describe the tactile effects of the Guadalupe's miraculous materiality, Cabrera opted for a comparison to the handmade commodity of fine silk. Asian export silk, a lifeblood of transpacific commerce, unfurled across colonial society to adorn its interiors and bodies alike. Like lacquer, silk's shining surface captured the Iberian imagination of wonderfully seamless, effortless manufacture. Yet beneath this smoothness lay the entangled histories of transpacific labor and the many skilled hands that shaped such artworks' sheen. The rhetoric of seamlessness enabled these objects to inhabit disparate, yet increasingly interconnected, cultural systems of value.[52] That miraculous facture could be seamlessly converted from the acheiropoieton to the merchandise item announces the object's new commodified status on the eve of the industrial age. Where commerce and religion intersect, the sacred does not so much disappear as become appropriated and generalized within the world of goods, consumption practices, and tastes—surface, in turn, emerges as the primary site for a modern aesthetic judgment sustained by imperceptible labor. In this interplay of revelation and concealment, one glimpses a defining paradox of the early modern world in which artisanal skill was both desired and dissimulated within global imperial economies, outshined by the gleam of an immaculate facade.

I am grateful to Karina Corrigan, Jorge Rivas, and Kathryn Santner for including me in the annual Mayer Center symposium and this publication, and to all participants for their engaging feedback. An earlier version of this essay was presented at the Negotiations of Sacrality and Materiality in the Early Modern Globalized World conference at the Kunsthistorisches Institut in Zurich; my thanks to Raphaèle Preisinger for that opportunity. I also thank Hiroshige Okada for generously sharing materials on the Tokyo shrine, Julia Oswald for her incisive comments and edits, Lisa Regan for her suggestions, and Kathryn Santner and Leslie Murell for their editorial care. Above all, I am most indebted to Sara Frier for her insight, edits, encouragement, and many conversations essential to this paper's development.

Notes

1. Luís Fróis, *História de Japam*, ed. José Wicki, SJ, vol. 5, cap. 50, "Da carta que Quambaco escreveu ao Vice-Rei e do presente que lhe mandou" (Biblioteca Nacional, 1976–84), 378–79. Translations by the author, unless otherwise noted.

2. See Oliver Impey and Christiaan Jörg, *Japanese Export Lacquer: 1580–1850* (Hotei, 2005); Hidaka Kaori, *Ikoku no hyōshō: Kinsei yushutsu shikki no sōzōryoku* (Brücke, 2008); Samuel Luterbacher, "Surfaces for Reflection: Nanban Lacquer in the Iberian World," *Journal of Early Modern History* 23, no. 2–3 (2019): 152–90.

3. Fróis, *História*, 378–79. See also Luterbacher, "Surfaces for Reflection," 152–55.

4. See Kanki Keizō, "Iberia-kei seiga kokunai ihin ni miru chihō yōshiki," *Bijutsushi*, no. 126 (1989): 151–72; Meiko Nagashima, "Japanese Lacquers Exported to Spanish America and Spain," in *Asia and Spanish America: Trans-Pacific Artistic and Cultural Exchange, 1500–1850: Papers from the 2006 Mayer Center Symposium at the Denver Art Museum*, ed. Donna Pierce and Ronald Otsuka (Mayer Center for Ancient and Latin American Art at the Denver Museum of Art, 2009), 107–18; Luterbacher, "Surfaces for Reflection," 152–90; Okada Hiroshige, "Sakuhin to chōsa no gaiyō," in *Kogakuteki kagaku chōsa o jiku to shita shoki yōfūga to Ajia Taiheiyō kaiiki bijutsu kōtsū ni kansuru kibanteki kenkyū hōkokusho*, ed. Okada Hiroshige, vol. 1 Honpen (Osaka Daigaku Jinbun Kagaku Kenkyūkanai Bijutsushigaku, 2025), 8–13.

5. See Brendan C. McMahon, "Contingent Images: Looking Obliquely at Colonial Mexican Featherwork in Early Modern Europe," *The Art Bulletin* 103, no. 2 (2021): 24–49; Charlene Villaseñor Black, "The Iridescent Enconchado," in *Iberian Empires and the Roots of Globalization*, ed. Ivonne del Valle, Anna More, and Rachel Sarah O'Toole (Vanderbilt University Press, 2019), 233–70.

6. Martin Kemp, "'Wrought by No Artist's Hand': The Natural, the Artificial, the Exotic, and the Scientific in Some Artifacts from the Renaissance," in *Reframing the Renaissance: Visual Culture in Europe and Latin America, 1450–1650*, ed. Claire Farago (Yale University Press, 1995), 177–96.

7. See Joseph Leo Koerner, "Factura," *Res: Anthropology and Aesthetics*, no. 36 (1999): 5–19; Alessandra Russo, *A New Antiquity: Art and Humanity as Universal, 1400–1600* (Pennsylvania State University Press, 2024), 128–64.

8. See Russo, *A New Antiquity*.

9. Dennis O. Flynn and Arturo Giráldez, "Born with a 'Silver Spoon': The Origin of World Trade in 1571," *Journal of World History* 6, no. 2 (1995): 201–21.

10. On the occlusion of artistic or labor processes under colonial conditions, see Sara Ryu, "Molded and Modeled: Sculptural Replication in the Early Modern Transatlantic World," in *At the Crossroads: The Arts of Spanish America and Early Global Trade, 1492–1850*, ed. Donna Pierce and Ronald Otsuka (Mayer Center for Ancient and Latin American Art at the Denver Art Museum, 2012), 121–22.

11. On this, see Hélène Vu Thanh, "Poverty, Finances and Evangelization: The Case of the Jesuit Mission in Japan (16th–17th Centuries)," *Bulletin of Portuguese/Japanese Studies*, 2nd ser., vol. 5 (2022): 29–46.

12. Luterbacher, "Surfaces for Reflection," 174–75. See also Kiichi Matsuda, *Kinsei shoki Nihon kankei Nanban shiryō no kenkyū* (Kazama Shobō, 1967), 1022–45; and Rie Arimura, "Escenario de las producciones del arte kirishitan (1549–1639): la contribución de los artífices japoneses a la conformación de un fenómeno intercultural," *Hispania* 55 (2011): 52–54.

13. On the guild system in colonial Goa, see Teotonio R. de Souza, *Medieval Goa: A Socio-Economic History* (Broadway Book Centre, 2009), 123–29.

14. Chu Wa Chan, "The Concept of Zushi: On Enshrinement and Mobility of Buddhist Art in Japan," *Japanese Religions* 43 (2018): 17–37.

15. On this work, see Alexandra Curvelo, "Oratório Namban," in *Discover Baroque Art*, Museum With No Frontiers, 2025, https://baroqueart.museumwnf.org/database_item.php?id=object;BAR;pt;Mus11_A;3;pt.

16. Andrew M. Watsky, "Floral Motifs and Mortality: Restoring Numinous Meaning to a Momoyama Building," *Archives of Asian Art* 50 (1997): 62–92.

17. See Clement Onn, "Circulating Art and Visual Hybridity: Cross-Cultural Exchanges Between Portugal, Japan, and Spain," *Renaissance Studies* 34, no. 4 (2020): 624–49.

18. Hidaka, *Ikoku no hyōshō*, 57–61.

19. See Alfonso Rodríguez G. de Ceballos, "Image and Counter-Reformation in Spain and Spanish America," in *Sacred Spain: Art and Belief in the Spanish World*, ed. Ronda Kasl and Alfonso Rodríguez G. de Ceballos (Yale University Press, 2009), 15–36.

20. On this topic, see Joan-Pau Rubiés, "The Concept of Cultural Dialogue and the Jesuit Method of Accommodation: Between Idolatry and Civilization," *Archivum Historicum Societatis Iesu* 74, no. 147 (2005): 237–80.

21. Alexandra Curvelo, "Copy to Convert: Jesuits' Missionary Practice in Japan," in *The Culture of Copying in Japan: Critical and Historical Perspectives*, ed. Rupert Cox (Routledge, 2008), 111–27.

22. Ibid.

23. Christopher S. Wood, "'Curious Pictures' and the Art of Description," *Word & Image* 11, no. 4 (1995): 332–34; Koerner, "Factura," 5–19.

24. Victor I. Stoichita, *L'Instauration du tableau: Métapeinture à l'aube des temps modernes* (Droz, 1999), 116–20.

25. See Okada, "Sakuhin to chōsa no gaiyō," 8–13.

26. María Olvido Moreno Guzmán, "Mosaico plumario del *Martirio de san Esteban.* Una aproximación a su manufactura," in *Kogakuteki kagaku chōsa*, 52–66.

27. See Allison Caplan, "The Cotinga and the Hummingbird: Material Mobilities in the Early Colonial Featherwork of New Spain," in *The Routledge Companion to Global Renaissance Art*, ed. Stephen J. Campbell and Stephanie Porras (Routledge, 2024), 482–99.

28. The artwork was purchased at an auction in New York in 1980 and entered the Tokyo National Museum's collection two years later. See Okada, "Sakuhin to chōsa no gaiyō," 8–13. See also, Okada Hiroshige, Fukushima Osamu, Miyata Masahiro, "CT sukyan gazō satsuei no kekka to shoken," in *Kogakuteki kagaku chōsa*, 26–30.

29. *Cartas que os padres e irmãos de Companhia de Jesus escreverão dos reynos de Iapão e China...*, book 1, part 2 (Évora, 1598), 168.

30. As Caplan has demonstrated, the use of tropical bird plumage declined in the late sixteenth century, supplanted by more seasonally available species like the hummingbird to meet growing colonial export markets. See Caplan, "The Cotinga and the Hummingbird," 482–99.

31. On this topic, see Barbara Mundy, *The Death of Aztec Tenochtitlan, the Life of Mexico City* (University of Texas Press, 2015),105–7.

32. Luisa Elena Alcalá, "Reinventing the Devotional Image: Seventeenth-Century Feather Paintings," in *Images Take Flight: Feather Art in Mexico and Europe, 1400–1700*, ed. Alessandra Russo, Gerhard Wolf, and Diana Fane (Hirmer, 2015), 386–405.

33. Ibid.

34. The CT scan reveals that the picture was inserted with a slight tilt to fit the shrine, which is visible in the unstraight bands of paper at the top and bottom. See Okada et al., "CT sukyan," 26–30.

35. José de Acosta, *Historia natural y moral de las Indias*, vol. 4 (Juan de León, 1590), 284–85.

36. Rensselaer W. Lee, *Ut Pictura Poesis: The Humanistic Theory of Painting* (W. W. Norton, 1967), 9–22.

37. See Marc Fumaroli, "De l'icône en négatif à l'image rhétorique: Les autoportraits du Christ," in *L'immagine di Cristo: Dall'acheropita alla mano d'artista; Dal tardo medioevo all'età barocca*, ed. Christoph L. Frommel and Gerhard Wolf (Biblioteca Apostolica Vaticana, 2006), 413–48. On these missionary interminglings of devotion and natural history, see Lea Debernardi, "Finding Christ in Roots and Seeds: Crucifixes Produced by Nature in Quaresmio's *Terrae Sanctae Elucidatio*," *Mediterranean Historical Review* 38, no. 2 (2023): 251–71.

38. Acosta, *Historia natural*, 285.

39. Kemp, "'Wrought by No Artist's Hand,'" 177–96.

40. See Christine M. E. Guth, *Craft Culture in Early Modern Japan: Materials, Makers, and Mastery* (University of California Press, 2021).

41. Eiko Ikegami, *Aesthetic Networks and the Political Origins of Japanese Culture*, Structural Analysis in the Social Sciences (Cambridge University Press, 2005), 82.

42. Alessandra Russo, "Plumes of Sacrifice: Transformations in Sixteenth-Century Mexican

Feather Art," *Res: Anthropology and Aesthetics* 42 (2002): 226–50.

43. Glenn Adamson, *The Invention of Craft* (Bloomsbury, 2013), 53–126.

44. Another trajectory related to seamless facture is the ivory carvings of Chinese migrants in Manila, such as a crucifix from the Dominican monastery of San Esteban in Salamanca with an ivory Christ on a Nanban lacquer cross.

45. María Isabel Astiazarain, "La iconografía de la Virgen de Guadalupe. Dos cuadros de Miguel Cabrera en Guipúzcoa," *Cuadernos de Arte Colonial*, no. 7 (1991): 139–49.

46. On this topic, see Juan Javier Pescador, *The New World Inside a Basque Village: The Oiartzun Valley and Its Atlantic Emigrants, 1550–1800* (University of Nevada Press, 2003).

47. Derek S. Burdette, "The Power of Expertise: Artists as Arbiters of the Miraculous in New Spain," in *Collective Creativity and Artistic Agency in Colonial Latin America*, ed. Maya Stanfield-Mazzi and Margarita Vargas-Betancourt (University Press of Florida, 2023), 107–36.

48. Ibid., 120.

49. Jaime Cuadriello, "Zodiaco mariano, una alegoría de Miguel Cabrera," in *Zodiaco Mariano, 250 años de la declaración pontificia de María de Guadalupe como patrona de México*, ed. Jaime Cuadriello (Museo de la Basílica de Guadalupe/Museo Soumaya, 2004), 9–129.

50. Miguel Cabrera, *Maravilla americana* (Imprenta Real, 1756), 4.

51. See Luisa Elena Alcalá, "The Image and Its Maker: The Problem of Authorship in Relation to Miraculous Images in Spanish America," in *Sacred Spain: Art and Belief in the Spanish World*, ed. Ronda Kasl (Yale University Press, 2009), 56.

52. I draw here on William Pietz's discourse of the fetish, rooted in early modern encounters between the Portuguese and West African societies. See William Pietz, *The Problem of the Fetish*, ed. Francesco Pellizzi, Stefanos Geroulanos, and Ben Kafka (The University of Chicago Press, 2022).

Biombos in Modern Mexican Interiors

Aldo Solano Rojas, Professor, School of Architecture,
UNAM

With the consolidation of the maritime commercial route of the Manila Galleon in 1565, innovative artistic forms were introduced to New Spain. These objects—including porcelain, lacquer, and silks—quickly had an impact on local taste. Among these novel objects were *biombos*, or folding screens, Japanese imports that were soon adapted by local artists to New Spanish tastes. In the seventeenth and eighteenth centuries, the folding screen became a symbol of refinement and an almost ubiquitous feature of colonial interiors.

Folding screens were then reinvented in the twentieth century by Mexican modern interior designers and architects. Some drew on the biombo's links to the colonial past, while other designers saw them as modernist pieces of furniture, stripped down to their barest elements. In Mexico, both of these ways of understanding the biombo were influenced by history, reinforced by famed and prominent

screens that were being collected or displayed in museums as national treasures.

This essay identifies three ways in which to explore the biombo in modern interiors. First, antique screens appeared in modern interiors as status objects that reaffirmed their owners' links to the colonial past. Second, biombos were used as supports for artistic expressions that sought to vindicate Mexican folk arts and traditions: In this case, the format of the screen itself may have contributed to the perceived Mexicanness of the object (in other words, these artists may have seen the biombo as a traditionally Mexican support). Finally, modern screens were stripped of their most obvious references to the past or tradition: Lacking iconography, they became vehicles for different architectural and material discourses. At the same time, their function changed, and they were sometimes transformed into a fixed architectural element, becoming an extension of the building and abandoning the portability that had originally contributed to their popularity.

Origins

The word "biombo" is a corruption of the Japanese *byōbu* (wind wall), and it remains the only term used in Mexico today, demonstrating its enduring link to Asia.[1] Folding screens were first introduced to the Iberian world as diplomatic gifts from Japanese envoys in the sixteenth and early seventeenth centuries and were soon shipped across the Pacific via the Manila Galleon to eager consumers in New Spain.[2] The first screens to arrive were made of layered paper stretched over a wooden frame and adorned with ink washes and gold ornamentation, trimmed by lacquer and silk edging. Almost immediately on arriving in the Mexican capital, local artists began to reinvent the Japanese screen according to local tastes using readily available materials like cotton canvas and oil paints.[3] In the hands of New Spain's painters, biombos became important supports for secular subjects in the seventeenth and eighteenth centuries, in contrast to the religious themes that otherwise predominated. They often featured historical scenes like the Conquest of Mexico, literary characters, mythological allegories, landscapes, and scenes of leisurely life (*fêtes galantes*), but they could also be covered with decorative patterns, especially on the reverse face. Because they were typically painted with complex iconographic programs, biombos were

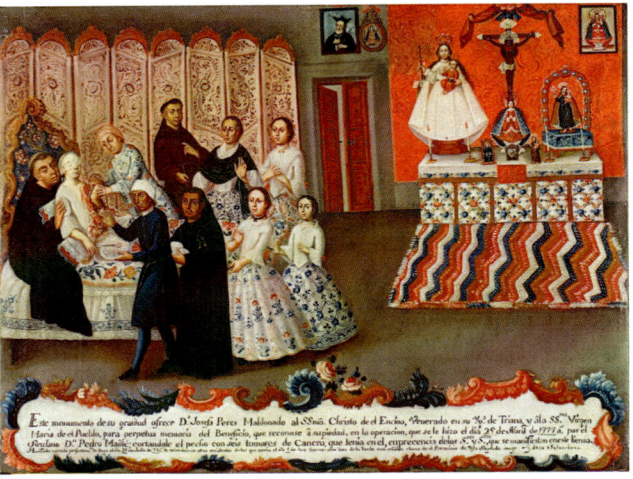

Fig. 1 Unknown artist, *Peres Maldonado Ex-voto*, Mexico, 1770. Oil on canvas, 27¼ × 36½ in. (69.2 × 92.7 cm). Davis Museum at Wellesley College: Museum purchase with funds provided by Wellesley College Friends of Art, 2004.10.

considered art objects rather than furniture in the colonial period.[4]

Whether made locally or imported, the screens' association with not only the luxury and fantasy of Asia but also elevated rank and courtly power made them attractive to the newly enriched nobility of New Spain, and their popularity radiated outward to the rest of colonial society. They were hallmarks of the remarkable cosmopolitanism of New Spanish consumers, and to own one was an explicit statement of that sophistication. Within the colonial home, biombos were typically placed around the *estrado*, a women's sitting room that often displayed a family's most luxurious objects. Biombos became such an important part of interior design that they were portrayed in several *ex-votos* and *casta* paintings. One such example can be seen in an eighteenth-century ex-voto where the biombo serves to protect a patient undergoing surgery (fig. 1). The pictured eight-leaf lacquered screen tells us how established the use of this object was by the eighteenth century, as well as its position and scale within the home.

While the biombo never lost its link to Asia—in 1726, the *Diccionario de Autoridades* still noted: "It is a treasure that came to us from China or Japan" (*Es alhaja que nos vino modernamente de la China o Japón*)—its reinterpretation by local artists transformed it into a fundamentally New Spanish object.[5] With the end of the galleon trade, the fashion for Asian goods diminished, and over the course of the nineteenth century, the production of biombos rapidly declined. Biombos ceased to be decorated with sophisticated programs drawn from mythology or landscape painting, instead becoming folk objects featuring phytomorphic or abstract decorations.

Repurposing Antique Screens

Until rather recently, historians of Mexican furniture—few though they were—paid less attention to the biombo than to furnishings like chests, chairs, or tables. Abelardo Carrillo y Gariel's *Evolución del mueble en México* (1957) was one of the first studies to trace a continuous and convincing history of furniture in Mexico, including prehispanic versions. He focused on chairs and other seating and relegated the screen to the end of the book, including only three examples. One of them is a famous eighteenth-century biombo depicting a *sarao* (a type of courtly dance) in a garden by Miguel Gerónimo Zendejas (1724–1815),

now in the National Museum of History in Mexico City. While undoubtedly an important artwork, Gariel ignores other examples of great historical importance and omits references to the evolution of the biombo, which he includes for chairs and tables.[6] This is common in publications dedicated to the history of Mexican furniture at mid-century: The biombo is acknowledged as an important historic object, but without information on its development, it appears immutable. Only later would designers and historians acknowledge the evolution of screens and their links to contemporary production.

This early history reminds us that one way the painted biombo was incorporated into modern Mexican interior design was as an antique. Considered both a work of art and a relic of the past, the screen lost its function of demarcating space within the home. Instead, these objects were displayed as symbols of high social status, protagonists in the construction of interiors that sought to project tradition and aristocratic ancestry. For those not lucky or wellborn enough to inherit one, biombos were readily available from Mexico City's antique dealers. An alternative was to install a neocolonial screen of contemporary manufacture. In either case, these screens shared the same purpose: explicitly claiming the prestige associated with colonial institutions of power such as the Church or the Crown, in direct opposition to the post-revolutionary discourses that privileged the prehispanic past and the Indigenous origins of Mexico as the foundation of a national identity.[7]

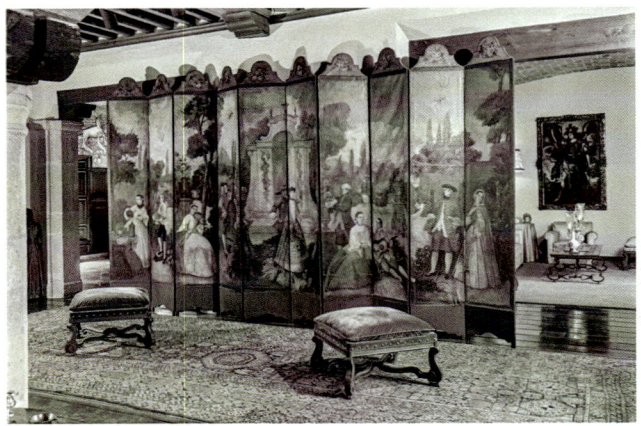

Fig. 2 Unknown artist, Copy of mid-eighteenth-century biombo showing a fête-galante in the house of Manuel and Teresa Barbachano Ponce, Mexico City, 1978. Oil on panel. © Bob Schalkwijk.

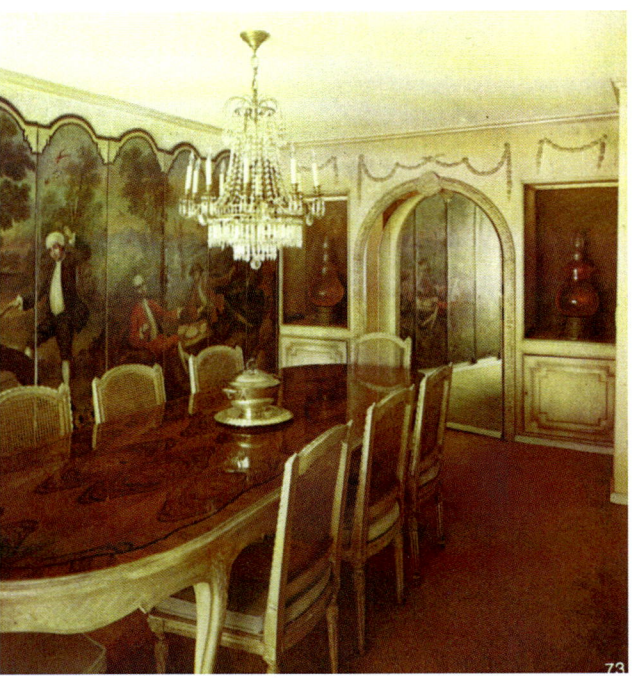

Fig. 3 Biombo Showing Fête Galante, Mexico, 1700s. Corcuera House. Image from *Diseño. Sugerencias para Vivir Mejor,* May 1973.

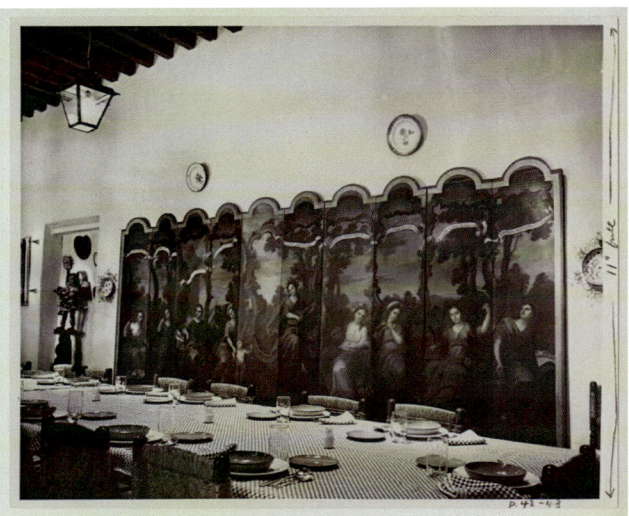

Fig. 4 Attributed to Miguel Cabrera (1695–1768), Biombo with the Muses, Mexico, mid-1700s. Verna Cook Shipway Papers, Special Collections & Archives, UC San Diego.

A good example of the use of the biombo as a legitimizing element of class and social status can be found in the house of Manuel Barbachano, a famous film producer and director. Located in San Ángel, a colonial village in the southern part of Mexico City, it was decorated in 1957 by the noted interior designer Arturo Pani (1915–1981). He often drew inspiration from eighteenth-century rococo and nineteenth-century Beaux Arts traditions, streamlining them rather than copying them slavishly.[8] For the Barbachano house, he continued to reference the past, using a reproduction of the Zendejas sarao biombo to anchor a large interior space (fig. 2). The screen took a leading role at the center of the main room of the house, where its visible position reaffirmed elegance and tradition, referencing a specific antique displayed in a museum dedicated to Mexican history.

While designers like Pani left the biombo as a freestanding element, other designers chose to wall-mount biombos, simultaneously reaffirming the screens' position as artworks while removing their function as partitions. This mode of display emphasizes their iconographic and symbolic messages but also conceals one side of these often dual-faced objects. It was in this manner that interior design books

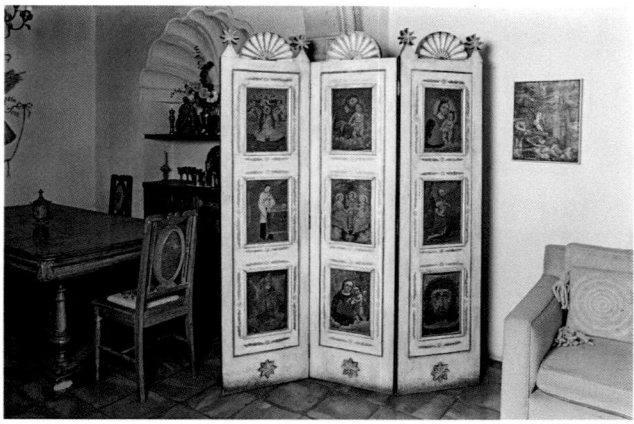

Fig. 5 Unknown artist, Wood Biombo with Retablos in the House of David and Anne Wilson, San Miguel de Allende, Guanajuato, Mexico, 1979. © Bob Schalkwijk.

and magazines from mid-century promoted the use of folding screens: displayed flat and transformed into paintings. One magazine stated that once wall-mounted, a biombo could function as "a sort of mural."[9] In designing the house of the elite Corcuera family, José Gómez de Parada installed a ten-panel biombo featuring a scene of a fête galante in Tlalpan and attributed to Miguel Cabrera, against a wall in the dining room alongside a collection of New Spanish masterworks (fig. 3). Other interior designers followed this new way of displaying antiques (fig. 4).

Images of mid-century interiors featuring colonial biombos were popularized in a series of books dedicated to Mexican interiors edited by the American architect Verna Cook Shipway and her husband, Warren Shipway, between 1960 and 1970. As Catherine Ettinger has discussed, the Shipways were pioneers, and their books document not only interiors but furniture design, gardens and topiary, and architectural elements in towns like Cuernavaca, Taxco, Guanajuato, and

Mexico City, where many American expatriates lived. They promoted a "Mexican" language of interior design in which antiques and religious art coexisted with modern furniture, usually in neocolonial residences, although more modern interiors were sometimes included.[10] These books are useful not only to see how antiques were being deployed but to know how taste was being shaped for a broad audience and coalescing around a standardized "Mexican interior."

One book in the series, *Mexican Interiors* (1962), included sections dedicated to architectural typologies, decoration, crafts, and furniture such as biombos, where colonial and revival examples are shown indistinctly.[11] Sometimes the two were mixed, creating pastiches where neocolonial wooden screens incorporated retablos or paintings of saints on tin (fig. 5). This is proof of the popularity of the screens and their perceived Mexican quality, which was being exploited by designers and collectors to forge an interior design style that bridged the modern and colonial periods.

In the 1970s, antique biombos also appeared in the country's leading design magazine: *Diseño. Sugerencias para Vivir Mejor* (Design: Ideas for better living) (1969–75), the first Mexican publication dedicated to interior design. While short-lived, the magazine was a beacon for freedom of speech amid the official repression against students and political dissidents in this period: It portrayed interiors of all social classes but frequently

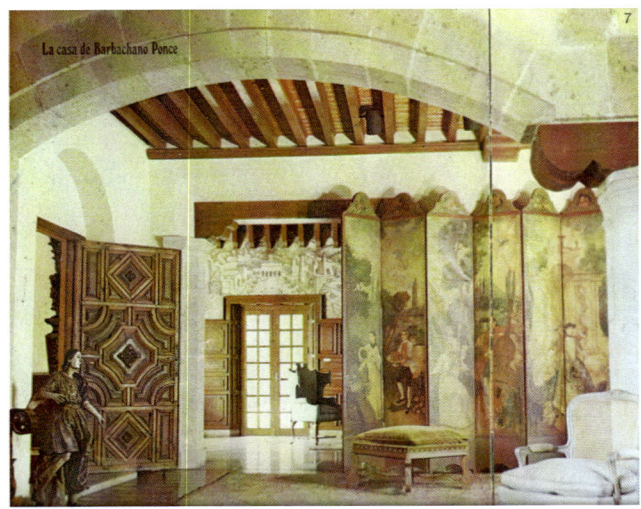

Fig. 6 Interior design by Arturo Pani (1915–1981), House of Barbachano Ponce, Mexico, 1957. Image from *Diseño. Sugerencias para Vivir Mejor*, January 1970, 72–73.

highlighted the homes of members of Mexico's art world.[12] *Diseño* showed folding screens in several issues, including a photo essay featuring the Barbachano home, proof of the continued relevancy of both Pani's interior design and biombos to a wide audience (fig. 6).

The biombo was promoted as a useful element in interior decoration, as well as an example of what to collect. It was so ubiquitous that the editors even published instructions for how to make one's own folding screen, noting its long history as a type of furniture.[13] In another essay focused on biombos, published in August 1970, the magazine explained the two roles of these screens, both traditional and current:

> *In classic interiors the biombo is, generally, antique and in the case of being a work of art, it gives more relevancy to its surroundings... The concept of the biombo itself and its usefulness have changed a lot in recent times, it is no longer just a means of protecting something from prying eyes. At present, it is an element of decoration with a life of its own that is used in different ways.*[14]

The Biombo as Support

Although *japonisme* had been an important part of colonial Mexican visual culture, the renewed fervor for Japan that struck the West in the nineteenth century did not find fertile ground in Mexico. By the beginning of the twentieth century, only a few of its intellectuals had visited Japan, and the influence of the Asian nation on design and architecture was negligible. The multi-hyphenate José Juan Tablada (poet, art critic, diplomat, and journalist) was a rare exception, and while his enthusiasm for Japanese art and culture was great, it was not part of a larger wave.[15] The relevance of the biombo in this period resulted from its position as an icon of Mexican material culture rather than as a Japanese export.

Early-twentieth-century artists used the format of the biombo as a support for more nationalist artistic expressions. One of the earliest examples of this impulse is a 1929 screen by Roberto Montenegro (1885–1968), one of the pioneers of the muralist movement in the early 1920s and a close collaborator of José Vasconcelos, Secretary of Public Education and intellectual architect of the new Mexican art.[16] Across six panels, Montenegro depicted a map of the Mexican Republic in which images of popular arts, flora and fauna, and typical dances are placed across the landscape, as if they were part of the Mexican geography

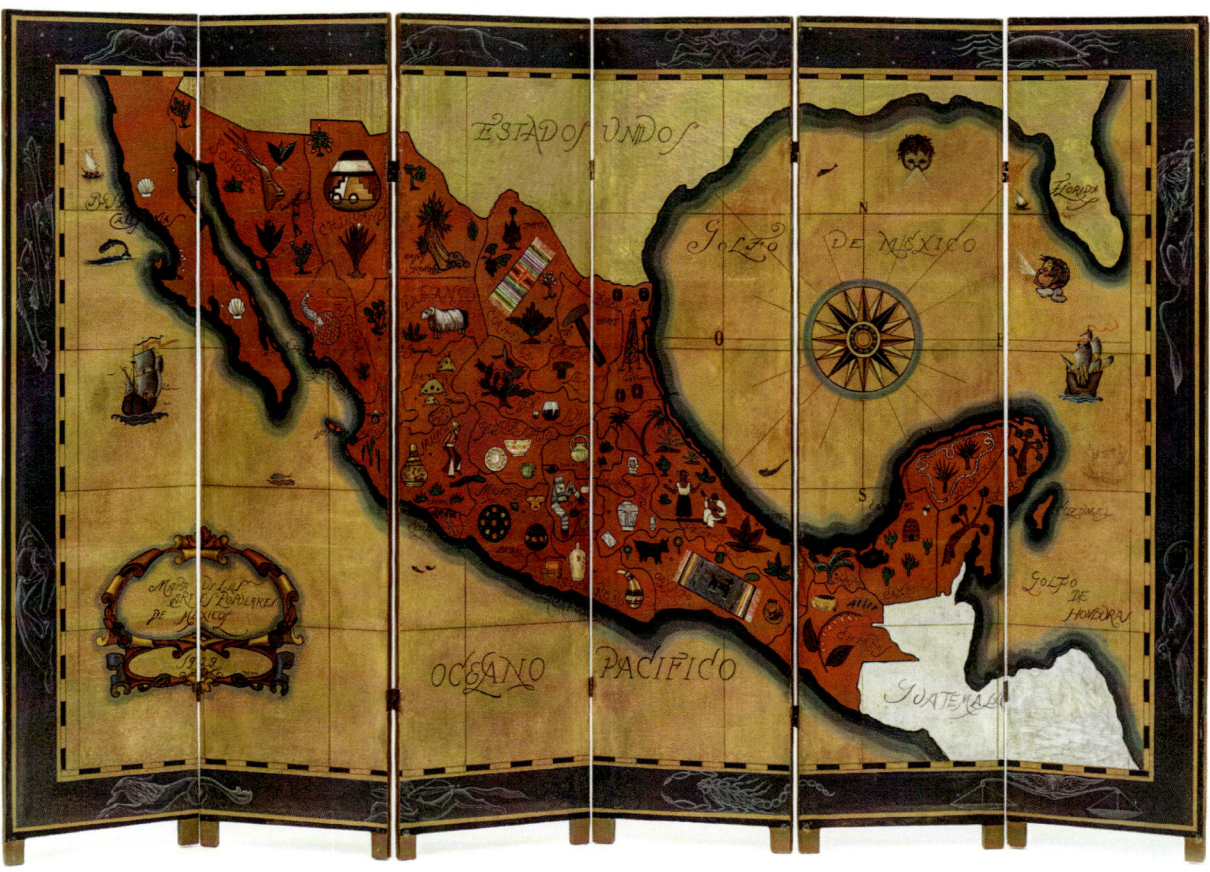

Fig. 7 Roberto Montenegro (1885–1968), *Biombo (Map of the Popular Arts of Mexico)*, Mexico, 1929. Oil on canvas, 78¾ × 118⅛ × ¾ in. (200 × 300 × 2 cm). © The Phoebus Foundation, Antwerp

(fig. 7). A direct prototype was the work of nineteenth-century cartographer Antonio García Cubas, who used this strategy to depict Mexico's resources and encourage economic development, partly for foreign audiences.[17] As Delia Cosentino and Adriana Zavala have shown, the use of a screen was a way of elevating the popular arts (illustrated on the map) to the field of fine arts, a crucial part of the post-revolutionary discourse that shaped the early years of Mexican muralism.[18] This biombo was painted the same year that Montenegro, together with diplomat Moisés Sáenz, founded the Museum of Popular Arts in Mexico City. This work would affirm the status of the biombo as a Mexican folk art object divorced from its Japanese origins.[19]

Montenegro repeated this formula in 1951: Across four panels, he reproduced a lithograph of the bay of Acapulco from 1628, a work by Dutch artist Adrian Boot. Montenegro even copied the cartouche—an element present in colonial biombos that narrated battles or showed local fiestas—that held a legend to the map. In doing so, Montenegro referenced the tradition of mestizo and Indigenous artists in New Spain who reproduced European designs entirely, including cartouches and other editorial details like engravers' signatures.[20]

Another of these pictorial screens was painted by the Austrian American artist, curator, and collector René d'Harnoncourt. D'Harnoncourt arrived in Mexico in 1925, where he met the antiquarian and dealer Frederick Davis, with whom he traveled the country buying and studying antiques and popular arts.[21] Painted in 1931, *View of Miacatlán* measures about five feet tall and shows the bucolic and idealized Indigenous village of Miacatlán, located in the state of Morelos, south of Mexico City. D'Harnoncourt emphasized the traditional houses and local residents, ignoring the seventeenth-century church and nineteenth-century buildings in the town. An inscription at the bottom of the biombo recalls less the cartouches on colonial screens than those on popular ex-votos that detail miraculous events. D'Harnoncourt was certainly familiar with the ex-voto tradition, since he included several examples in the exhibition *Mexican Arts* that he curated for The Metropolitan Museum of Art in 1930. He included no biombos in that show but surely knew of them through Davis's shop.[22] It recalls colonial biombos showing Indigenous life, like the famous seventeenth-century screen at the Los Angeles County Museum of Art showing festivities, including *voladores*, at an Indigenous wedding. In *View of Miacatlán*, however, d'Harnoncourt mixed colonial and folk art to create something new.

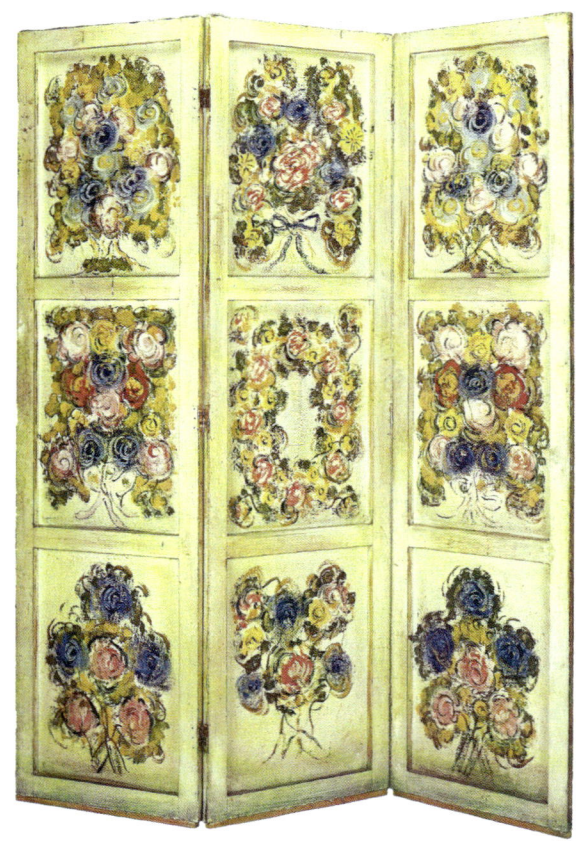

Fig. 8 Jesús "Chucho" Reyes Ferreira (1882–1977), *Biombo*, Mexico, ca. 1960. Oil on wood. Courtesy Chucho Reyes.

In subsequent decades, other artists revisited the biombo as a support full of symbolic and historical meaning. The antique dealer and collector Jesús Reyes Ferreira (1880–1977), known as Chucho Reyes—a leading figure in Mexico City's art scene at mid-century—created a series of wooden biombos in the 1950s.[23] Reyes decorated them with his characteristic thick and quickly applied brushstrokes, depicting vases and baskets of flowers along with birds in a semiabstract garden (fig. 8). They resemble the works on paper he was creating at the same time (originally designed as wrapping paper for the fragile antiques he sold), which, as in this example,

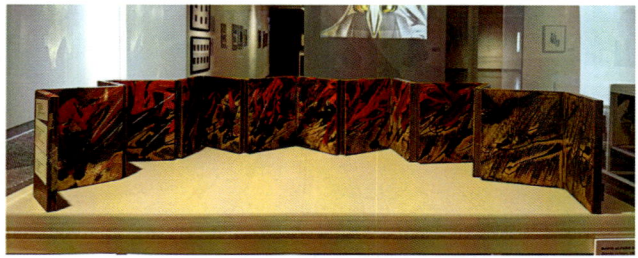

Fig. 9 David Alfaro Siqueiros (1896–1974), *Miniature Biombo with Fourteen Panels*, Mexico, 1965. Pyroxylin on wood. Sala de Arte Público Siqueiros/ Instituto Nacional de Bellas Artes y Literatura. Photograph by the author.

referenced vernacular painting and folk decorations, such as those found on ceramic tiles used in eighteenth-century religious architecture.

Around the same time, other prominent artists such as David Alfaro Siqueiros (1896–1974) were experimenting with the folding screen format. In 1960, Siqueiros was apprehended and imprisoned by the government for his support of union leaders and the Communist Party in a political climate marked by repression and official paranoia. While in prison, he painted several biombos as backdrops for plays staged by the inmates, using them as vehicles for social criticism.[24] Lacking references to popular arts, Siqueiros relied on the familiarity of the typology in the Mexican collective imagination but also used screens because of their mobile quality, an especially useful feature when applied to set design. In a maquette from 1965, one year after he was released from prison, Siqueiros produced a series of miniature biombos covered with abstract gestural brushwork with thick layers of paint (fig. 9). In these experimental works, the folds of the screens and their freestanding quality served the artist as starting points for spatial exploration, playing with perspective and light.

The fact that Siqueiros used the biombo format not only proves the relentless experimental drive of the artist but also the uninterrupted presence of the folding screen in Mexican life. Siqueiros created several of these maquettes, probably as experiments that later influenced major works of architecture like the Polyforum in Mexico City or his studio "La Tallera" in Cuernavaca, where leaning walls with corners at acute angles were intensified by the painter's abstract compositions. Thus, biombos remained a typology associated with art, constantly being revisited as a support for painting, even for abstract and experimental works of art, only in this case, completely disengaged from domestic interiors.

The Architectural Screen

At mid-century, several interior and furniture designers, including Arturo Pani—whose use of antiques has been discussed—and Luis Barragán (1902–1988), whose plain biombos are perhaps the most well-known, brought the screen into the modern home. In the process, they were drained of iconography, and materiality became more important. In their mid-century revival, biombos were considered part of the architectural space, especially their impact on spatial movement and light.

Almost every modern Mexican designer and architect designed at least one biombo; the format proved useful in displaying a versatile vocabulary. Pani, for example, created screens using diverse styles, sometimes looking back to classical Renaissance motifs, while also showing strong influence from the streamlined forms of Scandinavian design. Other designers more explicitly referenced the Asian origins of biombos. The US-born designer Frank Kyle, who moved to Mexico in the early 1950s, drew on his interest in Japanese forms and typologies to create several biombos, some featuring hidden joints in unexpected places, brass ornaments, and Japanese imagery. The decorator and designer Eugenio Escudero, a favorite of Mexico's jet set, was also fond of transforming screens into abstract, transparent, and architectural sculptures.[25]

Of all of these modernists, however, it was Barragán who really redefined the screen, making it a key element in his innovative, spare interiors, using it to divide spaces and shift our perception of light. Barragán reinvented antique furniture typologies throughout his career, as in the case of the lectern, which he streamlined in cedar wood while leaving its medieval origins obvious. He also reformulated low chairs of wood and woven palm, Talavera vessels, and even *petates* (woven bedrolls), making slight changes in proportions and materials but preserving ancestral techniques and functions and displaying them in avant-garde interiors, creating a modern and international language that simultaneously referenced Mexican sources. Barragán abstracted Mexican vernacular furniture with a surprising level of synthesis and sobriety, similar to what Anni Albers did

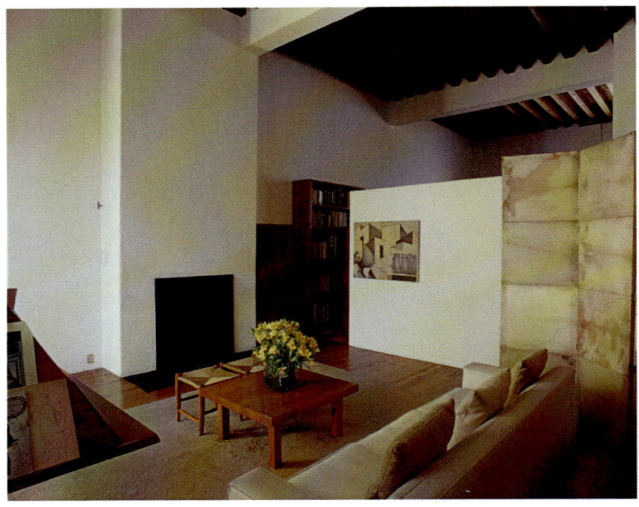

Fig. 10 House of Luis Barragán, Tacabuya, Mexico City, 1948. Photograph by Alberto Moreno Guzmán.

with Mexican textiles or what Clara Porset (1895–1981) did with the traditional *butaque* seat.[26]

In fact, screens play an important role in Barragán's interiors, where he used them as an articulated extension of the low walls that divide rooms and spaces without interrupting the flow of light reflected across the double-height ceilings. Often considered mere background elements, these screens are crucial to understanding the architect's interior design, not least because they remain largely *in situ*, unlike the other screens that have been discussed so far (fig. 10). Indeed, screens were already sited in Barragán's original floor plan (indicated by zig-zag lines), proving that the architect thought of them as an architectural feature, not to be moved and as important as any wall (fig. 11).

Perhaps the first of these screens to be made was the one in the living room in his house-studio in Tacubaya, a historic neighborhood near Chapultepec Park,

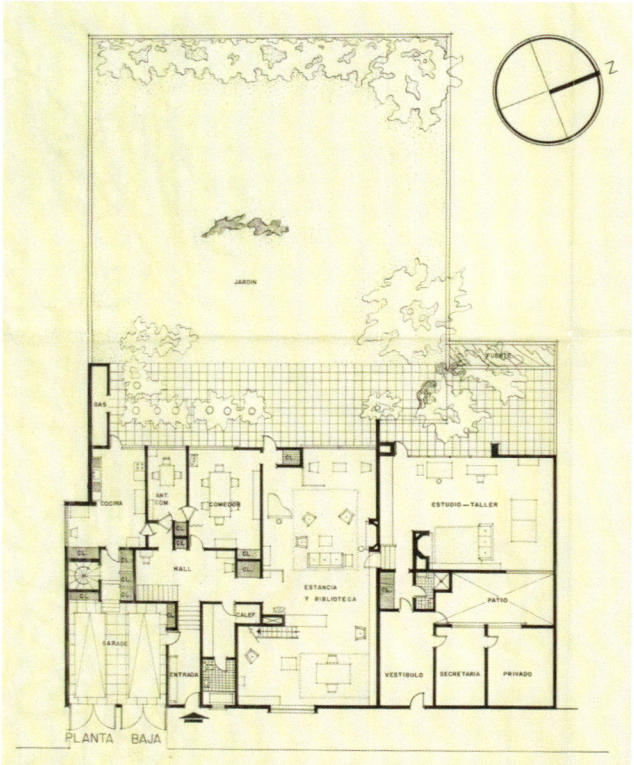

Fig. 11 Luis Barragán (1902–1988), Original Floor Plan Drawing with Furniture Layout for Barragán's House, Mexico City, 1948. Courtesy Barragán Foundaiton. © 2025 Barragán Foundation, Switzerland / Artists Rights Society (ARS), New York.

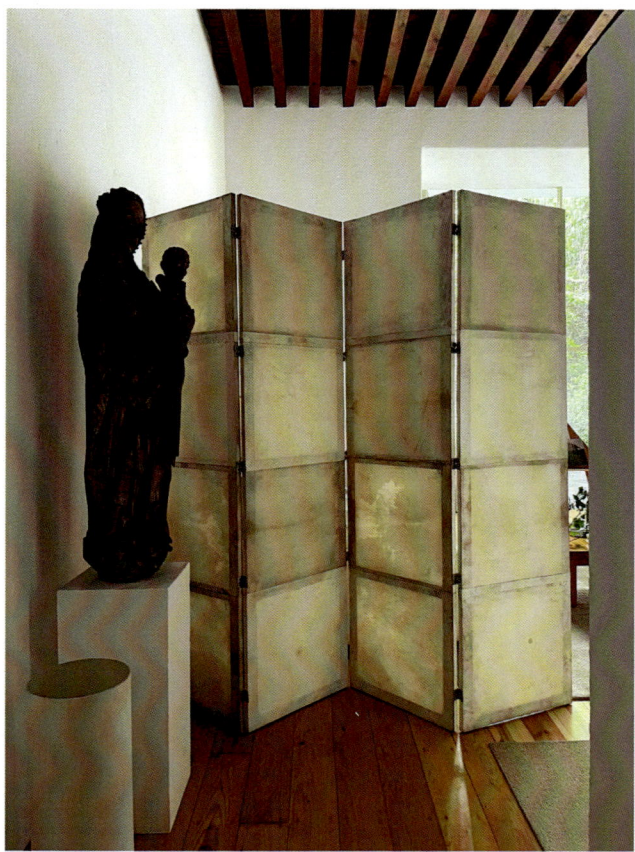

Fig. 12 View of Parchment Biombo, house of Luis Barragán, Tacabuya, Mexico City, 2024. Courtesy the author.

completed in 1948 (fig. 12).[27] It consists of four panels, each just over eight feet high and just over two feet wide (almost ten feet wide if fully extended). The height of the screen is almost the same as the wall that divides the living room from the entry hall, creating a space reduced in width although without a ceiling, providing intimacy without sacrificing luminosity or the monumentality that the double-height ceiling gives the space. The panels are made of wooden frames covered by sheets of parchment, an old-fashioned translucent material (common in medieval manuscripts) that makes the screen both a reflective surface and a protective wall. Barragán paid close attention to the

meaning and history of materials, using them to create a cohesive atmosphere, from the exterior of the unpainted facade to the smallest detail inside. He thus frequently used parchment in his designs, including for lamp shades: Its ivory white color is similar to the raw cotton textiles (*manta de cielo*) and undecorated white Talavera ceramics that Barragán also favored.

In the library, Barragán placed another, more modest three-panel screen in which the wooden supports are covered by white "manta." It measures six-and-a-half feet tall, exactly the same as the wooden wall that projects from the adjacent monumental bookshelf. Here the screen extends the wall and divides the bookshelf, creating a more intimate reading room, equipped with couches, a table, and chairs. The screen also reflects the natural light that enters through a large square window with frosted glass. These elements combined provide the space with an intense but soft light, without shadows or colors that might inhibit reading or distract one from concentration. Two other screens were installed in the more intimate spaces in the upper floor, both made of wood and white manta. Those screens are a bit lower, just under six-and-a-half feet, scaled, perhaps, to the architect, who was just over six feet tall.

Barragán also designed biombos for houses he built for private clients, where they play the same role as in his own home. The Casa Prieto López, the first he built in the elite housing project known as the Jardines del Pedregal de San Ángel, also completed in 1948, included a six-panel screen covered in fabric, with the same dimensions as the one in his library.[28]

By the mid-1950s, Barragán had mastered the use of biombos as a defining architectural element strategically placed to change light, give privacy, extend walls, and create dialogues with the furniture. In 1955, for the Casa Gálvez, he designed three fabric-covered screens that remain in situ today. We see a standardization of materials, measurements, and function— but not of color. In the main living areas, he used raw white manta, but for a biombo in a reading space, more private and less well-lit, he selected an intense fuchsia fabric. Cristina Gálvez recalls that both the

architect and her father (the client) referred to the hedge in the garden as a biombo of jasmines, marking the path to discover the mysterious garden and linking the interiors with the exterior.[29]

For Barragán, the materiality of these screens was of the utmost importance; their materials and handmade facture connected them to folk art and the colonial past, allowing him to modernize tradition. Almost at the same time Barragán was furnishing his house in Tacubaya, Charles (1907–1978) and Ray (1912–1988) Eames were designing their own folding screen but moving in an opposite direction, creating an industrially produced object with uniform and smooth modular plywood sheets joined with hidden hinges. Although the biombo typology was widespread and contemporary designers were using it in different parts of the world, its symbolic charge was different in Mexico, where even in the most abstract examples it was linked to New Spain.

Barragán's use of screens and their incursion into modernist architectural spaces had a powerful impact on his circle of friends and collaborators. A fuchsia biombo was placed in the renovated house of Chucho Reyes, a project not officially recognized as Barragán's work but on which both collaborated. Architect Juan Sordo Madaleno (1916–1985), with whom Barragán worked on many projects, also incorporated screens in his interiors, where they guide the flow of users and light. In his office, a heavy folding wooden door partially divided the room (fig. 13). This

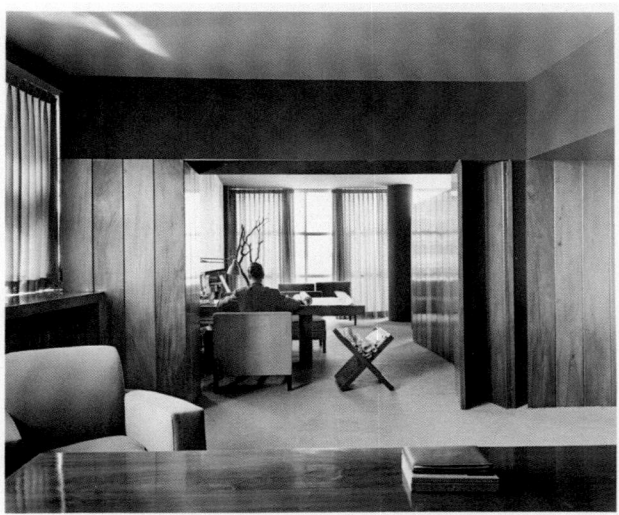

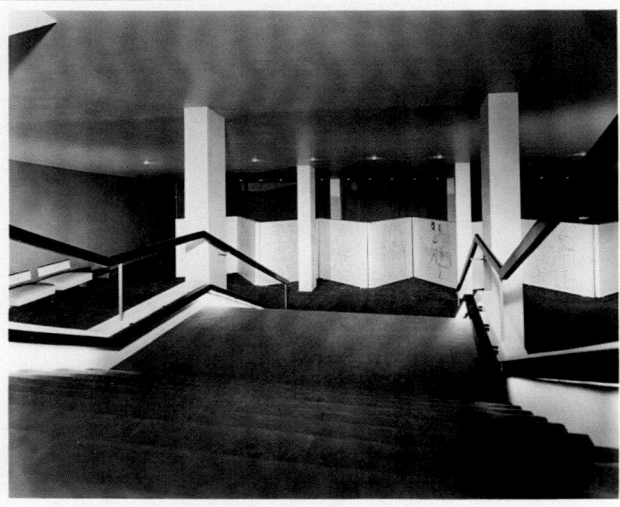

Fig. 13 Juan Sordo Madaleno (1916–1985), *Architect's Studio*, Mexico City, 1948. Photo by Guillermo Zamora, courtesy of Fundación Sordo Madaleno.

Fig. 14 Juan Sordo Madaleno (1916–1985), furniture by Clara Porset (1895–1981), Interiors of the Cine París, Mexico City, 1954. Photo by Guillermo Zamora, courtesy of Fundación Sordo Madaleno.

might be thought of as a sort of biombo, now permanently fixed to the wall and continuing the use of natural wood.[30]

This research has also identified the use of biombos in commercial spaces, like the Cine París, built in 1954 by Sordo Madaleno. It was one of the most modern movie theaters at the time, located on the Paseo de la Reforma (it has since been torn down).[31] A monumental screen divided the bar, which was furnished by Clara Porset, from access to the theater (fig. 14). Unlike those in Barragán's houses, here the biombo is used as an opaque barrier whose white, square panels serve as a support for reproductions of etchings or drawings by Picasso.

The monumental openwork steel screen on the main entrance of the Camino Real Hotel, built in 1968 by architect Ricardo Legorreta (1931–2011) for the Mexico City Olympics, might also be understood in the context of this history of the modern biombo (fig. 15). Legorreta commissioned

Mathias Goeritz (1915–1990) to design this feature, which has long been understood in terms of plastic or visual integration, the interrelationship of sculpture and architecture that largely defined mid-century architecture in Mexico. Goeritz created a monumental lattice; although originally black, it later acquired its characteristic bright pink—recalling the fuschia biombos in Barragan's houses—that mediates between the street and a courtyard that leads to the hotel lobby. Its position is fixed, yet it gives the impression that it is an articulated object that could well move or change position.[32]

Biombos continued to be part of Mexican art history long after the last galleon docked in the port of Acapulco in 1815. Consistently revised and reinvented, the Japanese byōbu quickly became a part of New Spanish identity and therefore of the new Mexican pantheon of objects and supports after the Mexican Revolution,

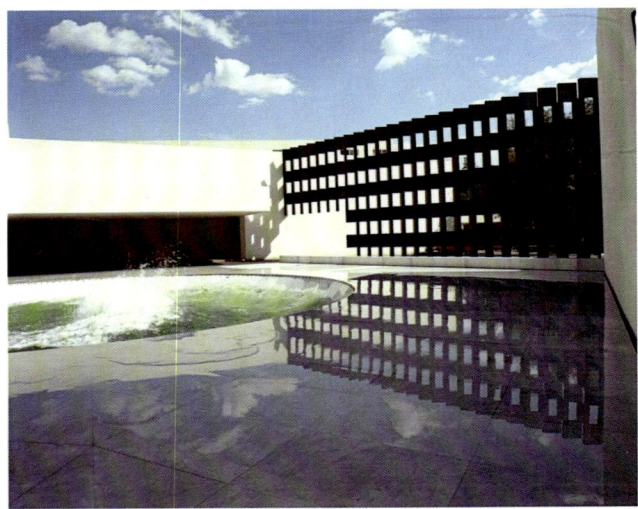

Fig. 15 Mathias Goeritz (1915–1990), Lattice for the Entryway of Ricardo Legorreta's Hotel Camino Real, Mexico City, 1968. Photograph by Armando Salas Portugal.

later to be exploited to its limits and finally becoming an abstract and even architectural object thanks to the experimentation of the modern movement in Mexico. Biombos are one of the few testimonies of the intense transpacific trade that is still a part of the Mexican vernacular, a long and ongoing travel with unexpected results.

Notes

1. Teresa Castelló Yturbide, *Biombos mexicanos* (Instituto Nacional de Antropología e Historia, 1970), 11.

2. Sofia Sanabrais, "The *Biombo* or Folding Screen in Colonial Mexico," in *Asia & Spanish America: Trans-Pacific Artistic & Cultural Exchange, 1500–1850*, ed. Donna Pierce and Ronald Otsuka (Mayer Center for Pre-Columbian and Spanish Colonial Art at the Denver Art Museum, 2009), 71; Sanabrais, "From *Byōbu* to *Biombo*: The Transformation of the Japanese Folding Screen in Colonial Mexico," *Art History* 38, no. 4 (2015): 783–84.

3. Sanabrais, "From *Byōbu*," 785.

4. Sanabrais, "The *Biombo*," 83.

5. Sanabrais, "From *Byōbu*," 790. Original found in *Diccionario de la lengua castellana...*, vol. 1 (Francisco del Hierro, 1726), 609.

6. Abelardo Carrillo y Gariel, *Evolución del mueble en México* (Dirección de Monumentos Coloniales, Instituto Nacional de Antropología e Historia y Secretaría de Educación Pública, 1957), 165–67.

7. This discussion raged for years among architects and historians. Some found in colonial architecture and furniture design a mixture of European and Indigenous features, making it "a true Mexican style." As time went on, only the most conservative sectors of society were still building and furnishing homes and office buildings in this fashion, as opposed to the functionalism associated with socialist ideas or, later, following the trend for folk art popular among the jet set. See Jorge Alberto Manrique, "México se quiere otra vez barroco," in *Arquitectura neocolonial: América Latina, Caribe, Estados Unidos*, ed. Aracy Amaral (Fondo de Cultura Económica, 1994), 39.

8. "Así vive Barbachano Ponce," *Diseño. Sugerencias para Vivir Mejor* 2, no. 10 (1970): 68–73.

9. *Diseño. Sugerencias para Vivir Mejor* 2, no. 16 (1970): 23.

10. The titles are *The Mexican House Old and New* (1960); *Mexican Interiors: Mexican Homes of Today* (1964); *Decorative Design in Mexican Homes* (1970); and *Houses of Mexico: Origins and Traditions* (1970). See Catherine Ettinger, "Un discurso de modernidad y tradición,

Verna Cook Shipway y la representación de la casa mexicana,"*Academia XXII* 5, no. 8 (2015): 75–93.

11. Verna Cook Shipway and Warren Shipway, *Mexican Interiors* (Architectural Book Publishing Co., 1962), 71–74.

12. Aldo Solano Rojas, "Arte, coleccionismo y decoración: la revista *Diseño. Sugerencias para Vivir Mejor* (1969-1975)," *Bibliographica* 4, no. 1 (2021): 168–92.

13. Álvaro de Regil, "La belleza funcional del mueble moderno. El biombo, clave de separar sin dividir," *Diseño. Sugerencias para Vivir Mejor* 4, no. 45 (1973): 46–49.

14. "Bienvenidos a los dobleces," *Diseño. Sugerencias para Vivir Mejor* (August 1970): 30–32. Translated by the author.

15. Amaury A. García Rodríguez, "El Japón quimérico y maravilloso de José Juan Tablada. Una evaluación desde las artes visuales," in *Pasajero 21. El Japón de Tablada*, ed. Miguel Fernández Félix (INBAL, 2019), 67.

16. Claude Fell, *José Vasconcelos: los años del águila (1920-1925): educación, cultura e iberoamericanismo en el México postrevolucionario* (UNAM, 1989), 384.

17. On the key role of cartographers in the construction of Mexican identity in late nineteenth century, see Amaya Larrucea Garritz, *País y paisaje. Dos invenciones del siglo XIX mexicano* (UNAM, Facultad de Arquitectura, 2016), 92.

18. Adriana Zavala and Delia Cosentino, *Resurrecting Tenochtitlan: Imagining the Aztec Capital in Modern Mexico City* (University of Texas Press, 2023), 85.

19. Rick A. López, *Crafting Mexico: Intellectuals, Artisans, and the State After the Revolution* (Duke University Press, 2010), 157.

20. My thanks to Kathryn Santner for pointing this out.

21. López, *Crafting Mexico*, 111.

22. Richard Townsend, *Indian Art of the Americas at the Art Institute of Chicago* (Art Institute of Chicago, 2016), 17. D'Harnoncourt's biombo is now part of the Philadelphia Museum of Art (2022-72-151).

23. See Lily Kassner, *Chucho Reyes* (Editorial RM, 2002).

24. Elena Poniatowska, *Siqueiros en Lecumberri: una lección de dignidad, 1960-1964* (CONACULTA, INBAL, 1999), 19–24.

25. Both Kyle and Escudero still remain under-researched. Some bits of information can be found in catalogs of the period, but monographs on each are still necessary.

26. See Ana Elena Mallet, *Clara Porset: Butaque* (Museum of Modern Art, 2024); and Anni Albers, Brenda Danilowitz, and Juan Tovar, *Anni Albers: Del Diseño* (Alias, 2019).

27. Louise Noelle, *Luis Barragán. Búsqueda y creatividad* (UNAM, 1996), 26.

28. Sadly this screen was sold, and its whereabouts are now unknown. Noelle, *Luis Barragán*, 141.

29. Interview with Cristina Gálvez by the author, Chimalistac, Mexico City, November 1, 2024.

30. Louise Noelle, *Arquitectos contemporáneos de México* (Trillas, 1999), 142.

31. Noelle, *Arquitectos contemporáneos,* 146.

32. Jennifer Josten, *Mathias Goeritz: Modernist Art and Architecture in Cold War Mexico* (Yale University Press, 2018), 238.